H.J. Eysenck

Psychology Is About People

A Library Press Book
Open Court
La Salle, Illinois

Psychology
Is About People

There is nothing more fearful than ignorance in action.

It is wrong, always, everywhere, and for everyone, to believe anything upon insufficient evidence.

People who believe absurdities will commit atrocities.

Contents

INTroduction

THIS BOOK was written in England, by a German-born author who received some of his education in France, and has taught at various American universities. What it has to say is not tied to any particular part of the world, nor are the facts on which it relies derived exclusively from one country. Psychologists in the United States have perhaps contributed more to modern scientific psychology than those of other countries; this is certainly true when we look at the period following Hitler's accession to leadership in Germany, and the consequent dismemberment of German psychology. It is curious how incompatible psychology and dictatorship really are. Long before he got entangled with genetics (in the infamous Lysenko affair) Stalin, too, decided that he had to put a ban on psychological research, for fear that its findings might go counter to his dictates and teachings. Only democracy has provided a fruitful ground for psychology (and the other social sciences) to flourish; and one reason why this particular refugee from Hitler's terror decided to write this book was to try and indicate that, in return, psychology might be able to repay part of its debt by throwing light on a variety of problems which are puzzling us, and about which open democratic discussion has been going on for a very long time.

Many people are incredulous when such a claim is made. They feel that psychologists have little that is worth-while to contribute to that fund of wisdom on which we have to draw whenever we make decisions of social importance. I point out the reasons for this incredulity in the book; they are unfortunately not easily dismissed, although I do not feel that they are insuperable. Psychologists have often done and said very silly and stupid things. They have often claimed to know far more than they did in fact know. They have often indulged in meaningless and purely formal scientism, instead of truly advancing our genuine knowledge of nature. True, psychologists are human, and have their share of human infirmity. But they have also put forward theories of great social importance and relevance; they have carried out researches the results of which may yet transform our lives— for the better, one hopes!

I may, of course, be wrong in thinking that all this is as important as I believe it to be; nevertheless I do feel that the facts should be made widely available, so that readers can form their own judgment. Like it or not, these recent advances in psychiatry, in education, in criminology will affect our lives. It does not seem unreasonable to suggest that the man in the street should have an opportunity to learn what is going on, what sort of ethical problems are likely to arise, and how he himself is likely to be affected. This is what this book is all about, and although it does not deal specifically with the present-day American scene, yet this scene is not all that different, in important aspects, from the English scene, or the European scene. We all share the really important problems, even though these may assume slightly different forms in different countries. If psychology can make any contribution to their solution, even he who runs may be willing to hear!

—*H. J. Eysenck*

January, 1972
Institute of Psychiatry,
Maudsley Hospital,
London

①

THe RAt or THe Couch?

I HAVE ALWAYS been fascinated by humor; jokes, cartoons, satire—these I have found irresistible, and a much more interesting guide to the national consciousness than more weighty tomes and analyses. Perhaps the reason is that my father was a famous comedian—a kind of highbrow Bob Hope; he used to make puns in Latin and get away with it. In any case, I think that the principle could be defended that we can learn a lot about the "image" of a person, or a country, or a group (such as policemen, or prostitutes, or psychologists) by looking at the types of jokes which are told about them, or the cartoons which they inspire.

Look at psychology in this light, and what do you find? There are clearly two sets or classes of jokes current about psychology and psychologists. (I include under this heading psychiatrists and psychoanalysts: not because they know much about psychology—it does not form any major part of their teaching, contrary to common belief, or even to common sense—but because the man in the street does not make this differentiation; after all, he is the person for whom the joke is intended!) These two classes of jokes refer, respectively, to experiments with rats and to psychoanalytic patients on the couch. Readers will no doubt be familiar with many of these jokes and cartoons, many of the best of which have appeared in the *New Yorker* (no doubt because Americans are more familiar with psychology, and its pretensions). Nevertheless a small sample may set the stage for the subsequent discussion, which will take us into the much wider field of the nature and purpose of psychology, and its place in the modern world. Let me begin with the rat joke, and then go on to the couch.

Beachcomber, the London journalist, used to introduce some of his very funny pre-War columns by saying: "Experiments with rats have proved . . ."

He would then go on to mention something far removed from anything that could conceivably be proved by experiments with rats—such as that Northumberland miners have a low opinion of Mr. Chamberlain, or that women with large feet seldom win dancing championships. The implication was clear. How foolish these psychologists are, working away in the laboratories with rats, thinking that their results can be of any relevance to the very real problems of our society. The same thought is contained in the famous cartoon showing a rat entering an imposing university building, turning round and asking: "Which way to the psychology department?"—implying that only psychologists are foolish enough to bother with rats, whereas sociologists and other sensible academicians work with people. And last, the equally famous cartoon of a rat in a box, pressing a lever and saying to another rat: "I sure got my human well conditioned— whenever I press this lever, he drops a food pellet into the chute!" These jokes and cartoons are legion, and they all make the same point—psychologists believe that they are scientists, but they have only taken over the empty formalism of science. The real essence escapes them, and they play around with pseudo-problems, using rats as an excuse for their failure to work out a proper human psychology which could be of some use to us in our problems. This criticism is, of course, not confined to jokes. It is often made by more serious writers, and even by psychologists themselves. But of that, more anon.

Couch and analyst jokes typically base themselves on the glaring incongruity between claim and performance, fact and fiction. The classic is the cartoon showing two analysts, one young and looking exhausted, the other old but spruce and fresh, emerging from a hospital building. "How do you manage to listen to them for all these hours, and yet remain so calm?" asks the young man. "Who listens?" replies the older one. Equally well known is the story of the rich mother who calls in the analyst every time her little boy misbehaves, being unable to deal with his problems herself. One day he refuses to get off his rocking horse, in spite of her entreaties; in despair she calls the analyst. He comes, goes over to the child and whispers a few words in his ear. It works like magic. Obediently he gets off the horse, and behaves like an angel all day long. Mother cannot imagine what the analyst said to the boy; father comes home, is told the story, and can't think of an answer either. Finally they ask little Johnny, who bursts out crying and says: "He told me he'd cut off my tiddler if I didn't behave!" *Sic transit gloria mundi.* Where the rat joke, therefore, attacks the psychologist for doing careful, scientific research, but on unimportant, irrelevant topics, the couch joke recognizes that the psychologist may deal with important and relevant matters, but does so in an unscientific manner, behaving ultimately in a very common-sensical way, and hiding his ignorance behind a cloak of verbiage and pretense. Apparently you can't win—either you are a remote pedant painstakingly doing ivory tower research that doesn't impinge on life in any way, doesn't lead to any important or interesting discoveries, and is merely "busy-work-type" scientism—or you meddle with real problems in your rash exuberance, confuse everybody with pretentious and endless jargon, and finally fail to deliver the goods which you have so rashly promised. Which of these you do depends on whether you are an extrovert or an introvert—rat men are introverts, couch men are extroverts, with rare exceptions. But in either case, psychology is a useless, confused and unimportant game played according to arbitrary rules by strange and somewhat ridiculous people. Whether this is a true picture (parts of it are too accurate for comfort, as we shall see) or not does not matter at the moment. This is how the cartoonist sees the matter with his acute grasp of what the public thinks.

Jokes, cartoons, wit and humor in general require interpretation, according to Freud. Can we interpret these results? It has often been said by philosophers and writers generally that there are two elements in humor, the formal and the emotional. On the formal side humor depends on incongruity, and the bringing together in some punch line of the incongruous elements in some surprising form of synthesis, while on the emotional side the joke may either serve to discharge hostile, aggressive or sexual feelings, or else may simply express good humor, happiness and contentment. The rat and couch jokes certainly express criticism and aggression. The question arises as to whether this aggression and hostility is conscious or unconscious. Freud has no doubt, of course. Aggression is repressed because of fear of the consequences of expressing it, and humor (like dreams and "accidental" error in speech) allows it to escape from this repression, producing laughter and amusement as a consequence of this escape. But is it true that these feelings about psychology are in any sense "unconscious"? I have talked to many lay audiences, and with many people who would not claim to be psychologists, and there is no doubt that most, if not all, harbored views of the kind so well portrayed by the cartoonists—the reader can of course do the experiment on himself and ask himself whether these ideas express the general tenor of his thinking about psychology, or whether they are a repressed background to his consciously quite different thinking, brought to light by cartoons and jokes like the ones mentioned.

MY OWN THEORY OF HUMOR is quite the opposite of Freud's. It might be called a trait theory, or even a "state and trait" theory. According to this view, people are ranged along a continuum of "aggressiveness," or "sexuality"—going from the very aggressive, or very actively sexual, through average to very non-aggressive and timid, or little concerned with sexual matters. According to Freud, the apparently non-aggressive, non-sexual people have repressed their aggressive and sexual tendencies, and appreciate hostile and sexual jokes because these release their "unconscious" feelings. Aggressive and sexually active people do not need such release and do not appreciate these jokes particularly. The evidence, of which there is quite a lot, clearly disagrees with the Freudian interpretation. Work reported by several psychoanalytically oriented experimenters, and my own as well, shows that extroverted people are more overtly aggressive and sexually active, and also prefer hostile and sexual jokes. In other words, people express their habitual traits of aggressiveness or sexual arousal in many different ways, of which appreciation of congruent jokes is one. The same result is found when you take a group of people and make them angry through some form of manipulation, or arouse them sexually. When so aroused they like hostile and sexual humor better than they did before. Thus both the "trait" approach and the "state" approach (i.e. determination of the habitual level of aggressiveness, or experimental manipulation of the present level of aggressiveness) confound Freud's views; as people are in general, so do they react to jokes. This suggests that most people have attitudes towards psychology which are not the opposite (consciously) of some deeply unconscious hostility and irreverence. Rather, people genuinely feel that something is wrong with psychology, and that psychologists on the whole are not to be trusted; that psychology, like the Roman god Janus, presents two entirely different faces, and that this in turn must make any claims of it to be a "science" rather doubtful.

These feelings are not confined to laymen. The famous psychologist Koffka recounts in one of his books how disappointed he was when, as a young student, he presented himself in the psychology department to learn about emotions and personality, about insanity and social attitudes, and was told to get to work on the mechanism of color perception! Many students have experienced this conflict, and it haunts even older and more experienced members of the profession. In my book on *Sense and Nonsense in Psychology*, I have pointed out the prevalence of this schizophrenic attitude, which divides psychology into an experimental and a social section—two sections which are hardly on speaking terms, which publish in different journals, and hardly ever read the other side's books! This schism is well documented. We have turned our scientific attitude inwards and learned the facts about what articles members of each side read, where they publish their papers, and whom they quote. The facts are not in dispute. Popular opinion has certainly hit the nail on the head as far as this guilty secret is concerned. But the rot goes much farther than this.

The failure of the two sides of psychology to come together has precluded it from achieving that essential unity which characterizes a genuine science. Most students of psychology, on opening and reading their first textbook, are struck with the fact that there are no connections or relations between chapters. Each chapter—on perception, on conditioning, on memory, on intelligence, on learning, on attitudes, on mental abnormality—is a separate unit of its own. The chapters can be read in almost any order, and frequently are presented by different instructors in quite different orders. The facts and theories of one chapter do not lead on logically to those of another. You finish one chapter, and the next one does not take up the thread, but starts along quite a different and novel route. Hence different textbooks adopt quite different methods of ordering their material. None is naturally marked out, or superior to any other. Some start with a biological introduction (to give the student a general background in physiology, neurology and anatomy), go on to solid experimental work in conditioning and learning, perception and memory, then end up with the "soft" options of social psychology, abnormal psychology and personality. Others reverse the process, hoping to interest the student by starting with "interesting" topics, and finally make him appreciate the scientific attitude by ending up with the more experimental matters. But it is all quite arbitrary. There is no compelling reason for preferring one method to another, and other alternatives have been successfully tried out.

Allied to this is the problem of the fundamental concepts which underlie a science. Chemistry came of age with the enunciation of the atomic theory by Dalton; what would chemistry be without the atom? Biology is founded securely on the concept of the cell. Genetics is based on the notion of the gene. Examples could be multiplied, but there is no need. It is obvious that a scientific discipline stands in need of such fundamental, underlying concepts. Where is psychology's to be found? Some have suggested the reflex, or the conditioned reflex. But this can hardly be considered seriously—perception, or social psychology, or even verbal learning are not obviously based on the laws of conditioning, although these may serve to explain certain phenomena and facts in all these fields. Other suggestions have been made, even less confidently; but in no case has there been much enthusiasm, and the proposal has usually been quietly buried, without benefit of clergy. It is the purpose of this chapter to suggest such a fundamental unit; to show how it can be used to unite the various separate fields of psychology; and to demonstrate how we can harness the power of experimental psychology to the solution of social problems. It is not of course claimed that such a suggestion can, as if by magic, solve all the problems which I have indicated in the preceding pages. What it can do, provided it is judged to be on the right lines, is direct the scientific vigor and enthusiasm of students of the subject into more rewarding and worthwhile channels, and act as a possible catalyst in the unification of psychology.

BRIEFLY—to be expanded presently—my proposal is that *personality* is the fundamental unit in psychology; that this concept, in order to be scientifically acceptable, requires to be anchored firmly to both antecedent and consequent conditions which are capable of being accurately observed, precisely measured, and meaningfully quantified; and that neither an adequate experimental psychology nor a scientifically acceptable social psychology is possible without the inclusion, at the most fundamental level, of this concept of personality.

These are strong words, and they clearly require some discussion before their actual meaning and import can be properly understood. The general idea, which I have faithfully propagated since the publication of my first book (*Dimensions of Personality*) in 1947, is not one which has recommended itself to most psychologists. I simply managed to fall between two stools, as it were. The experimentalists refuse to consider the possibility that personality might be a useful scientific concept, or that it might have any relevance to their work; and the social psychologists refuse to work with a concept of personality which insists on being rigorously based on biological and experimental findings. Nevertheless, I hope to be able to demonstrate that a causal chain can be constructed all the way from a consideration of anatomical and physiological structures in the basal ganglia and the cortex, through neurological concepts like "arousal" and the "visceral brain,"* to individual differences in learning,

---

*"Arousal" is a property of the cortex which ranges along a continuum from sleepiness and drowsiness, at one extreme, to marked mental excitation, at the other. This is usually measured by means of the electroencephalograph (EEG), which records a person's "brain waves," *i.e.* the electrical activity of his cortex, picked up from his scalp. There is some evidence that this arousal is essential for mental activity, and is in turn

conditioning, perceiving, sensory thresholds and other topics in experimental psychology. These are the "antecedent" conditions to which the concept of personality may be linked. On the "consequent" side we then have a variety of social phenomena, like neurosis, criminality and anti-social behavior generally, educability, sexual behavior and attitudes, social attitudes in general, and even more specific types of behavior, such as the acquisition of V.D., the production of out-of-wedlock children, proneness to accidents, or excellence at sports. Figure 1 shows in rough outline this causal chain, beginning and ending in observable facts, and containing in the center the all-important but not directly observable concept of personality.

It will be obvious that the concept of "personality," while crucial to this model, requires careful definition. The term is used in so many different senses, even by psychologists, that any particular definition must to some extent be arbitrary, and can only be defended on heuristic grounds. Fundamentally, there are three conceptions of personality current in modern psychology. It would not be difficult to unearth many more, but additional ones would be either variants on those to be discussed presently or used by so few people that detailed consideration of them would be mere pedantry.

Two of these conceptions would neatly remove the term

---

determined by a brain-stem structure called the reticular formation. EEG patterns characteristic of high arousal are significantly more frequently found in introverted persons. Emotional behavior is largely controlled by a system somewhat independent of the central nervous system and the cortex, namely the so-called sympathetic and parasympathetic system, often called the "autonomic system" because of this degree of independence. This system is governed by another brain-stem structure, the so-called "visceral brain." Evidence suggests that this is over-active in emotional and neurotic persons. The emotional activation system and the cortical arousal system are independent for much of the time; but when a person experiences strong emotion this spills over into the arousal system.

inherited differences
in anatomical and
physiological structure:

observed differences
in experimental
studies:

personality:

social
phenomena:

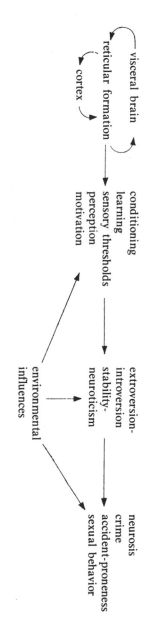

visceral brain

reticular formation

cortex

conditioning
learning
sensory thresholds
perception
motivation

extroversion-
introversion
stability-
neuroticism

neurosis
crime
accident-proneness
sexual behavior

environmental
influences

Figure 1. An example, grossly simplified, may serve to illustrate (not prove!) the existence of such a chain. Take a person who is endowed with a visceral brain which predisposes him to have strong, long-lasting emotions, particularly of fear and anxiety and who also possesses a reticular formation which keeps his cortex in a constant state of high arousal. Such arousal facilitates the production of strong conditioned responses. Thus in the laboratory we will find this person giving rise to strong physiological fear reactions when exposed, say, to the threat of an electric shock. He will also be found to produce conditioned responses quickly and strongly. Such a person will tend to develop personality traits characteristic of the introvert and of the potential neurotic; and if circumstances are at all unfavorable he is likely to have a neurotic breakdown, with symptoms of anxiety, phobic fears, obsessive-compulsive symptoms, reactive depression, and so forth. Conversely, the absence of strong cortical arousal leads to poor conditioning, an impulsive personality likely to indulge in anti-social activities.

The evidence for such statements as these is reviewed in my book on *The Biological Basis of Personality*; here these assertions are made very dogmatically merely in order to illustrate the meaning of the diagram.

from scientific usage altogether, although along quite different lines of argument. Let us first of all take the view adopted by German *geisteswissenschaftliche* (philosophical) psychologists. This is often labeled "idiographic," and contends essentially that all individuals are unique; this uniqueness constitutes their personality; science cannot encompass uniqueness in terms of general laws, and—hey presto—the scientific study of personality is impossible! This argument is based on a true premise. As Spinoza pointed out, everything that exists is unique—there is nothing in the world exactly like my old slipper. This has not prevented the sciences of physics and chemistry from making a modest success of their attempts to construct a series of universally valid statements, and the existence of cars, television sets, atomic bombs, penicillin and other goodies (each one unique and never exactly like any other car, or television set, or bomb, or chemical extract) seems to show that there is a flaw in the argument. You may doubt that one car, say, is not exactly like any other; but consider such variables as the exact number of molecules of air in each tire, the precise thickness of the paint (in Ångström units) at every point, the exact number of drops of petrol in the tank, or even simply the spatio-temporal coordinates of the car at successive moments—clearly identity cannot be assumed, and is in fact unattainable. All we can say is that two "things" can be sufficiently similar to be treated as identical in our formulae for a given purpose. In other words, the remaining differences may prevent two "things" from being identical but they are irrelevant to the particular scientific purpose under consideration. The truth of the doctrine of uniqueness is only paralleled by its irrelevance to scientific purposes. The scientist looks for invariances, and in so far as he succeeds in finding them, scientific study of the phenomena in question is possible. Whether he does or does not find such invariances is an empirical question. We cannot on *a priori* grounds tell him that he is on a fool's errand—

although of course he very well might be! There are now sufficient facts to demonstrate beyond question that certain invariances in the behavior of human beings can be detected. Whether in due course this generalization can be extended to all human behavior is a matter for speculation which cannot at the moment be decided on empirical grounds.

The outcome of this discussion is that although the fundamental fact of uniqueness of personality remains undoubted, it does not necessarily preclude the use of the concept in a scientific framework—provided we use it in a restricted sense, with a precise understanding of the invariances in conduct to which we wish to apply it. Vague generalizations are out; we have been warned, and the warning is well taken. We must justify our usage of the term, and demonstrate at each step that we are, in fact, in order in treating certain groups of people as equivalent, *i.e.* that those characteristics in which they differ are irrelevant to our particular purpose.

The idiographic point of view lies at one extreme of a continuum at the other extreme of which lies what might be called a neo-behavioristic point of view, represented explicitly by B.F. Skinner and his followers, but implicitly accepted by most experimentalists. According to this point of view, behavior is a function of certain contingencies which we can manipulate. If pressing a lever in a box is followed by food, the rat will learn to press the lever. By varying the timing of the rewards (regularly after every hundredth press, or randomly, or according to some other system) I can gain complete control over the rat's performance. Similarly, experimental psychology is concerned with the general problem of discovering laws of the form: $a=(f)b$, *i.e.* behavior a is a function (the precise nature of which is to be discovered) of stimulus (or set of stimuli) b. A complete and satisfactory psychology can be built up on the basis of a set of general laws of this kind. In our example, a (lever pressing) is a function of *b* (reinforcement by food), and all the experimentalist has to do is to discover the precise function involved by experimenting with different schedules of reinforcement.

Where does personality enter into this picture? Nowhere. It has become superfluous. All organisms behave according to the laws laid down (or rather, discovered) by the psychologist, for all the world as if they were uniovular twins. There might be slightly troublesome differences in the "reinforcement history" of different people (we do not have to worry about this in rats, as their history is closely controlled). But these slight differences can be ironed out if necessary, and on the whole we can disregard the organism which is performing its functions according to our laws. This is the doctrine of the "empty organism." Where to the idiographic psychologist individuality was so precious as to be all-important and unanalyzable, for the neo-behaviorist it ceases to exist at all, or at least to be of any interest or consequence.

This idea is not always made explicit. It is implicit in the very ways the experimentalist sets up his experiment. Suppose he is interested in discovering to what degree rote learning, say, is determined by the level of difficulty of the material learned. He will take a few students (who are required by regulations to take part in psychological experiments as subjects for so many hours per term), administer to them a series of nonsense syllables, or of paired associates (such as *xir—puw*, in which you have to learn to say *"puw"* on being presented with *"xir"*), taking care in the construction of these materials to have some series easy to learn and others difficult. A series might be easy because the association value of the syllables is high (*"nod"* is easier than *"puw"*), or the association between two nonsense syllables might be difficult because the first had previously been paired with a different one. In any case, the experimenter would average the time taken by his subjects over the learning of the different lists, demonstrate that the differences could not have arisen by chance, and conclude that difficult lists are learned more slowly than easy ones.* The experimenter would also find that there are very large individual differences in the time taken to learn either list, even among such highly selected subjects as university students, and he might even find that some of these in fact succeeded in learning the difficult list more quickly. These facts he would quickly and shamefacedly bury in that convenient rag-bag of unconsidered trifles provided by statisticians for that express purpose, the so-called "error term"—originally introduced to take care of that part of the variation in experimental results which could be ascribed to chance errors, and assumed to be kept very small by adequate experimental control over relevant variables.

Now the odd thing about most psychological experiments is that the error term, far from being respectably small in comparison with the effects produced by the variables the experimenter has manipulated (such as difficulty level in our example), is in fact enormous—often far greater than the "main effects" which the experimenter is really interested in. You can get over this difficulty statistically by increasing the number of subjects, or repeating the experiment. In this way you get results which convention enables you to describe as "statistically significant." But this legerdemain does not remove the fundamental weakness of all this work—the fact that different people have reacted differently to identical sets of stimuli! Your uniovular twins have turned out to be separate individuals, and the shock of this traumatic event has been so severe that experimental psychologists have completely repressed it into their unconscious. Some have suggested that the paradigm of the stimulus-response (S-R) sequence of events should be expanded to read stimulus-organism-response (S-O-R). But few experimentalists have

---

*Readers who do not believe that results of such crushing banality form the staple diet of many psychological journals are invited to look at a few.

taken heed, and the recommendation has been honored more in the breach than in the observance.

Skinner and his followers do not even accept this verbal compromise. As I have said, they treat the organism as "empty" (non-existent—or at least unimportant and irrelevant). This cavalier treatment is sometimes excused on one of two grounds.

(*1*) It is suggested that science is interested in laws which are universally applicable. The differences between individuals are not lawful, and hence are properly relegated to the error term.

(*2*) Individual differences arise solely because relevant variables have not been properly controlled. When they are so controlled, then they will vanish.

Neither point is accurate. As we shall see, individual variations are lawful, and hence must form part of scientific psychology. And it has never been shown, except in trivial instances, that better control rules out individual differences. Often, improving the controls increases them!

Perhaps an example will serve to make this discussion more real. Suppose we ask a question which to the experimentalist will appear quite meaningful. In nonsense syllable learning, will it make any difference to the number of errors committed before learning is perfect whether the syllables are presented at a rate of two seconds or four seconds? A typical experiment would sort out subjects into two groups. One would be given the task with the one rate of presentation first, then with the other rate of presentation. The other groups would have the rates of presentation in reverse order. The outcome would be that the two-second rate of presentation is productive of many more errors. This sounds perfectly sensible, and agrees with what one might have expected. The pressure exerted on the subject when he has to learn the material quickly makes him less able to learn it properly—or else the need of having to reproduce learned material very quickly acts as a brake.

However, let us take this argument a little farther. People obviously differ in the degree to which they are liable to be flustered by speeding up. Emotional people, with a tendency to neurosis, might be particularly liable to this "flustering." Suppose we administer a personality questionnaire to our subjects, asking them questions about their worries and anxieties, their headaches and their sleeplessness; and we then look at the results produced by those who have many "emotional" or "neurotic" answers, and those who have few. The outcome is instructive. For the stable individuals it makes no difference whether we have a two-second or a four-second rate of stimulus presentation. They make an average number of 65 errors either way. But the "neurotic" subjects (the adjective is put in quotes to indicate that these are not clinically neurotic patients, but perfectly normal students whose questionnaire responses show a slight tendency in the direction of emotional upset) make twice as many errors under the fast rate as under the slow—90 as against 45. In other words, we find that changing conditions affects some people, but not others—thus no general conclusion is possible. We find that these individual differences are not chance effects, but perfectly meaningful, and indeed predictable—the experiment was in fact set up to test precisely this hypothesis. We find that the effect of a high degree of "neuroticism" cannot be said to be favorable or unfavorable. This depends on the conditions. "Neurotics" are better than stable subjects when working under conditions which do not produce anxiety to any marked extent, i.e. when they are not pressed for time. They are worse than normally stable subjects when conditions are made difficult. All these important findings would have been swept under the carpet by our experimentalist, relegated to the error term, and forgotten. All that we would be told in his final write-up would be the allegedly universal truth that fast rates of presentation are disadvantageous as compared with slow rates—a statement at best partially true, and one which grossly misrepresents the complexity of the situation.

ATTENTION TO PERSONALITY as an intervening variable enables us to discover several further facts about the experiment. It enables us to reduce the size of the error term dramatically; and it enables us to make predictions about the behavior of individuals with much greater precision. Thus we might extrapolate (with all due caution, of course!) that school children high on N (emotionality) would perhaps do better in routine tests (mechanical arithmetic) and fall down on tests requiring original working out of problems; or that children high on N would do better in "trial" examinations, but might fail in serious ones. (Both these predictions have received some experimental support.) Finally, this extension of the experiment to include personality variables enables us to test theories about the nature of learning, or of anxiety; and it also makes it possible for us to answer those who maintain that questionnaire measures of personality are useless because they can be faked so easily, and because children (or adults for that matter!) don't know themselves. Clearly they know themselves well enough to make experimental verification of predictions possible, and they have not falsified their results sufficiently to interfere with the experiment.

Even rats have their individuality. It is by no means true that what can be said about one rat will hold of another. In one experiment the question was raised of the effect of alcoholic fumes on the activity rate of rats. This seems a perfectly simple and straightforward problem. However, the investigator tested six different strains of rats. He found that for two the fumes increased activity, for two they decreased activity, and for two they produced no observable effect! What price now the "uniovular twin" theory—clearly, it is possible to obtain any outcome desired in many experiments by suitable choice of subjects, whether human or animal. (And remember that subjects of psychological experiments are in the vast majority of cases highly selected; random samples of the population are practically never tested. Instead we have a complete reliance on very bright, sophisticated university students, highly motivated and full of ideas as to the purpose of the experiment they are asked to participate in—how can we generalize any findings from such extremely unusual populations?)

It has even been suggested that some of the ferocious theoretical struggles between opposing camps in learning theory were due not to any genuine differences, but simply to the fact that one group worked with rats bred specially to form an "emotional" strain, while the other group worked with "unemotional" rats! Thus does the neglect of individual differences and "personality" variables avenge itself, even when we are dealing with the humble rat.

If experimental psychologists are guilty, however, so are social psychologists. They commit exactly the same error. The questions asked, and the problems stated, are nearly always phrased in universal terms. The sociologist asks: Do broken homes produce crime? The educationalist asks: Is praise better than blame in motivating children? The psychiatrist asks: Is psychotherapy better than sociodrama? But these are not meaningful questions, and these are not problems which have a unique answer. For some types of people the effects may go one way, for others another. Experiments have suggested that introverted children thrive better when only given praise. Extroverted children are more highly motivated by blame. Similarly, anxious children respond differently from non-anxious children. Psychiatric patients react differently to different types of treatment. There is some evidence that phobics with very strong anxieties respond better to so-called implosion therapy, while phobics with weaker anxieties respond better to desensitization.* Broken homes have

---

*Implosion and desensitization therapy are two different varieties of extinction treatment for conditioned emotional fear reactions, such as phobias. In the former, the patient is exposed to the feared object or situation for a long time, and great fear and anxiety are produced. A cure is produced because in the end the patient (or rather his autonomic system!)

different effects on different children; no universal generalization is possible. Social psychologists often pay lip service to these considerations, but their work does not bear witness to any thoroughgoing conversion.

In spite of all I have said so far, there is of course a basic remainder of good sense in the behavioristic argument. Certain experimental effects are so broad and universal that individual differences do not make very much difference. Here general laws based on "averaging" may be useful and sensible. Hungry people (and rats!) will seek food; thirst will lead to drinking behavior. But such fairly universal generalizations are few and far between, and they are hardly world-shaking discoveries. Some real and important discoveries have been made, and I would be the last person to disparage genuine experimental work. However, the fact remains that in the great majority of cases individual differences play an important role, and are neglected at the investigator's peril.

But if we want to introduce "personality" into both the experimental and the social fields as an intervening variable, how can we discover the important and invariant variables which we are seeking? The term "personality" is obviously too broad and general to stand for anything but a program of research; it has to be analyzed in considerable detail before we can make use of it. The usage suggested lies about half-way between the two extremes we have just criticized. Personality

---

realizes that nothing fatal or even dangerous is happening to him, in spite of this exposure. Or possibly there is simple habituation; you cannot keep up a state of strong fear for ever.

Desensitization gradually exposes the patient to the thing or situation he fears, taking care that he is relaxed. All strong emotional reactions are avoided, and he is trained gradually to encounter the feared object or situation in a more and more threatening form.

Both forms of therapy have been shown to work reasonably well; but there is still argument as to when one is to be preferred to the other, and why the one works better in one case, the other on other occasions.

is neither as unique as the idiographic psychologists suggest, nor is it as universal as the behaviorists would have it. Instead, it is suggested that there are certain dimensions of personality which are important and relevant to the kinds of questions and problems which we are concerned with; dimensions along which people can be ordered from high to low, and which give rise to typologies like that of extroversion-introversion. Thus, we break up the total population into groups which are relatively homogeneous with respect to certain attributes which theory suggests are important, relevant, and relatively invariant. Whether the theories according to which we select our dimensions and our groupings are in fact borne out by experiment is of course an empirical matter. It is useless to insist, as many psychologists have done, that such a program of research does violence to human individuality, or that it introduces pointless complexity into the field. Facts alone must decide whether such a program does or does not work, and makes a genuine contribution to psychology. *A priori* reasoning in science is anathema. We have come a long way from the time when the philosopher Hegel laid it down as obvious that there could never be more than seven planets, this being a magic number—only to have an eighth planet discovered shortly after. It may of course not be easy to discover the most useful divisions, or to measure them accurately, or to integrate them into a general theory which also includes experimental and social psychology. Nevertheless, the rewards of success may make the venture worth the sweat.

THE THEORY WHICH SEEMS BEST to fit the case is one which reaches back to respectable antiquity, although admittedly it has needed some repainting and refurbishing generally. The four temperaments—choleric, sanguinic, phlegmatic, melancholic—go back to the Greek physician Galen, in the second century A.D., and even beyond. Immanuel Kant made them common coin in every educated drawing-room in Europe when he based the discussion of personality in his *Anthropologie* on them. Wilhelm Wundt, sometimes called the father of modern psychology, carried out the major repair job needed. He dismissed one fundamental tenet of the ancients when he pointed out that it was absurd to consider these four "types" as mutually exclusive, and to categorize people in terms of one or the other. Instead he insisted that melancholics and cholerics were both emotional types, phlegmatics and sanguinics unemotional; thus people

Figure 2

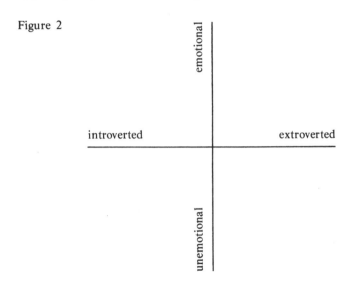

could be graded along a dimension of emotionality. Cholerics and sanguinics were both changeable (extroverted we would now say), while phlegmatics and melancholics were unchangeable (introverted). Thus people could also be graded along a second dimension of extroversion-introversion, at right angles to the first. In this way we have two continuous dimensions rather than four independent categories. The original four "types" are now found in the four quadrants generated by this pair of right-angled dimensions, forming as it were a cross, with extremely emotional and unemotional people at the ends of the one dimension, and particularly extroverted or introverted people at the ends of the other, as shown in Figure 2. Cholerics are thus emotional extroverts, melancholics are emotional introverts. This scheme, with minor emendations, has stood the test of time. There are few well conceived investigations of personality, using sufficiently broadly based tests or questionnaires, which do not emerge with these two dimensions prominently displayed. I have reviewed all this voluminous literature in *The Structure of Human Personality*; here let me just state the fact, without elaborating it.*

Galen's, Kant's, and even Wundt's theories were based upon observation; they are none the worse for that. But unaided observation is rightly distrusted by science; we look for objectivity, accuracy, measurement. What in fact does the theory say? It suggests that certain traits, such as sociability, impulsiveness, carefreeness, talkativeness, liveliness, activity, and so on, are usually found together. This alleged empirical fact requires us to postulate some supraordinate concept like "extroversion." "Types" are thus based on the observed intercorrelations between traits. It is not implied that everyone must be either a raving extrovert or a withdrawn introvert, but merely that everyone can find a place on this particular continuum or dimension. Indeed, it has been shown that most people are in fact between the extremes, giving rise to a curve of distribution of scores very much like that found with respect to height, or weight, or intelligence. The same is true of emotionality or neuroticism. Do the facts bear out the theory? The answer is that hundreds of investigations, not only in

*Many investigators have of course used different names for these two factors or dimensions. R.B. Cattell calls extroversion-introversion "exvia" and "invia," and emotionality or neuroticism, "anxiety." Others use still other names. This is of course not important; names are arbitrary, although the multiplication of terms can be misleading.

European countries, or in the U.S.A., but also in Japan, India and other non-white cultures, have brought forward convincing evidence that these concepts possess very wide applicability. It would be too much to say that they were universally applicable, because there are many groups which have not been tested (from Eskimos to Bushmen); but such exceptions as there might be can only be relatively unimportant. The dimensions described are, therefore, fairly characteristic of humankind; and their historical derivation suggests that they are equally applicable to the Greeks and Romans of 2,000 years ago.

MOST INVESTIGATIONS use ratings, *i.e.* scores given to the subjects of the study by observers on the basis of their behavior, either in life generally, or else in experimentally arranged special situations. Thus, if you were interested in persistence, you could ask teachers, parents and school friends of a given set of boys or girls about their persistence in everyday life, at school, in sport, etc., or you could rig up special tests which, unbeknown to the children, measured their persistence. For instance, you could give them an intelligence test and measure the time taken over each item. If now you introduce an item which is too difficult for the children to do, the length of time taken until they finally gave up would be such a measure. Or else you might measure their muscular strength with a dynamometer; then ask them to pull the dynamometer at one-half maximum strength for as long as they could. Having thus equated them for strength, their endurance is a measure of persistence. Such "miniature life situations" correlate quite well with each other, and also with outside ratings. Together, these measures provide a reasonably accurate picture of certain human traits. Such ratings also agree quite well with questionnaires, *i.e.* self-ratings made by the subjects of their own personality. These are of course subject to faking, and such faking is usually observed when the person involved is motivated to put himself in a particularly good light—for instance, when he is applying for a job, and incidentally asked to fill in a questionnaire. (The book *The Organization Man* contains some rules which help the applicant to beat the inventory; most people don't seem to need these rules, and do quite well without. Questionnaires are of very doubtful value for the purpose of occupational selection.) But when there is no such motivation, people are astonishingly truthful—and insightful. I used to be very skeptical of results obtained by questionnaire, but the evidence is pretty convincing. Such inventories are reasonably valid provided they are well constructed, properly validated, and administered under suitable conditions. These qualifications are of course vital. The absurd questionnaires which one occasionally finds in Sunday newspapers, under headings like: "Are you a good husband?" or "How is your sex life?" are quite valueless.

Results of such studies are sometimes said to have no scientific value because they lead to a circular argument. Indeed, the whole notion of "trait" psychology is declared to be no improvement on the ancient doctrine of instincts. It used to be said that when men behave in a sociable manner, that is due to an "instinct" of gregariousness; when they are hostile, that is due to an "instinct" of aggressiveness. And what was the evidence for these convenient instincts—why, simply the fact that people were sociable, or aggressive! Clearly, this does not get us much farther. Are traits equally useless? We certainly derive the notion of a trait of sociability from observation of certain instances in which a person preferred going to a party to staying at home reading, or enjoys talking to people, or is unhappy when left to himself. Admittedly this does not enable us to explain his sociable behavior in terms of this trait. We still do not know anything about the causal elements in the situation, *i.e.* we cannot tell why some people are behaving in this manner, while others are not. But this, of course, is not the aim of trait psychology.

Description precedes causal analysis. We must know first of all just what it is that we have to account for before we can hope to give a proper developmental or causal account of it.

Take sociability. Detailed study has shown that there is not one single trait of sociability, but at least three—all quite independent of each other. Introverts are unsociable because they don't particularly care about other people, but they can function perfectly well in a social situation when they feel so inclined. Neurotics are so inclined, but they are afraid of other people, or of making fools of themselves. People with psychotic tendencies are inclined to hate other people, and hence keep away from them. These findings clarify the descriptive situation, and make it possible to now go and state causal hypotheses. Vague notions of "gregariousness" would not give us this necessary springboard for further advance. As long as we do not overestimate the success we have achieved in our statistical analyses of personality into "traits," we may claim with some justification that we have gone beyond common sense, and have achieved some success in the first, descriptive phase of our investigation.

DESCRIPTIVELY, THEN, we arrive at what might be described as a two-dimensional picture of man, locating his infinite complexity at some point of intersection of the two dimensions of extroversion-introversion and emotionality-stability. Most people, including many psychologists, find this picture an almost ridiculous over-simplification, and heap derision on anyone so simple-minded as to think that such a flat and monochromatic picture could do justice to human nature "in the round." But, of course, this is not the intention. The psychologist does not try to rival the artist in portraying life. His aim is analysis, however much that may be anathema to the artist. Analysis means to grasp one strand out of an infinitely varied twist and follow it all the way. Analysis means to translate the beauty and mystery of the rainbow into the simple light-ray-shining-through-prism experiment of

Newton. (Remember the fury of Goethe, and his vain attempts to overthrow Newton's work on color and light, motivated by a poetic lack of understanding and sympathy for the task of the scientist.) Analysis means Mendel reducing the infinite variety and complexity of hereditary mechanisms to a simple counting of the number of smooth and wrinkled peas in the offspring of the parental generation of the two kinds of plants. To be sure, he was laughed out of court, and nobody took him seriously even among his fellow scientists who were much more concerned with the totality of inheritance—trying to account not for just one trait, but for a large and almost infinite number. Yet as it happened Newton and Mendel were right, and Goethe and the others who scoffed were wrong. Science has its own rules and procedures, and should not be judged in terms alien to itself. If you want poetry, go to Shakespeare, or Goethe; psychology does not pose as a rival. But if you want a *scientific* understanding of why people act the way they do, then psychology, poor as it is, is your only guide.

Most people of course, whatever they may say, do not in fact want a scientific account of human nature and personality at all—indeed, this is the last thing they really wish for. Hence they much prefer the great story-teller, S. Freud, or the brilliant myth-creator, C. G. Jung, to those who, like Cattell or Guilford, expect them to learn matrix algebra, study physiological details of the nervous system, and actually carry out experiments, rather than rely on interesting anecdotes, sex-ridden case histories, and ingenious speculation. After all, after-dinner conversation can easily encompass the Oedipus complex, or penis envy; it would be much more difficult to talk about a non-Gramian matrix, or the reticular formation! Poets and dramatists, too, are duly thankful for ideas which they recognize as being similar in nature to those which form the warp and woof of their art. As long as their audience is also familiar with these notions, they are happy enough to play the game of interpretation and symbolism, regardless of whether there is any factual truth behind it or not. One might almost say that the test of whether a theory of human nature is scientific or not is whether it claims to encompass all of life or not. If it does, it isn't. (The reverse of course is not true; a theory may have limited claims, and still be rubbish.)

A two-dimensional theory like that here developed does not of course do all one would like it to do. However, as we shall see, it does a few things, quite important ones at that, and it may improve and do even better in due course. We do not blame Newton for the fact that his theory of gravitation does not explain the facts of electricity. A given theory covers only a small portion of a very large territory. Provided that the theory is in line with the known facts, can predict previously unknown facts, and suggests manipulations of the environment which ultimately turn out to be helpful in controlling it, we may say that the theory has done all that can be expected of it, and may be allowed to flourish until displaced by a better, truer, more inclusive one. But just wishing will not give us such a better theory; it has to be worked for. All scientific theories had to go through stages where their accomplishments were very modest. Chemistry in its early days had the alchemists to contend with, and they made tremendous claims for their art. In the same way astronomers had to fight off the inflated claims of the astrologers. What alchemists and astrologers were to chemists and astronomers, psychoanalysts are to psychologists; every science has to pass through its ordeal by quackery.

THIS IS strong language. Is it justified? I have discussed the evidence for such a belief so often that I hesitate to devote much space to it for fear of wearying the reader who may have looked at one or other of my Pelican books, or who has dipped into my more serious writings. However, a brief résumé of the main criticisms of Freudian beliefs may be interpolated here, for those not familiar with the argument; others may with advantage skip the next few pages.

Let me note first of all that psychoanalysis was originally introduced as a method of treatment of neurotic disorders, and as a theory to explain the causation of such disorders. The theory has undergone many subtle changes, and I shall assume it to be too well known to require restatement except in the very briefest outline. To the psychoanalyst, neurotic symptoms are merely the observable signs of underlying complexes, repressed well into the unconscious but too strong to remain completely suppressed. These complexes date back to childhood years and are associated with the Oedipus complex which is their *fons et origo*. Treatment consists in *uncovering* the original infantile experience which laid the basis for the later neurosis.

This type of treatment has now been going on for some sixty years, and many thousands of psychiatrists and psycho-analysts have been practicing it in practically all civil-ized countries of the world. One would imagine that after all this time some definite knowledge would have accumulated about the effectiveness of psychotherapy as so practiced. This, it is interesting to report, is not so. Psychoanalysts have always been eager to hide their light under a bushel as far as evidence of the success or otherwise of their treatment is concerned. This contrasts rather sharply with the impression, given wittingly or unwittingly by psychoanalysts, that their method is the only one which gives positive and lasting results in this field. What psychoanalysts have usually done has been to publish individual cases, almost invariably cases in which the patient got better, and to argue from these illustrative examples to the general case. The argument may be formally stated in a way that exposes it as one of the classical examples of the *post hoc ergo propter hoc* fallacy. The fact that a patient, John Doe, who is suffering from a phobia, gets better four years after psychoanalytic treatment has been initiated, is not proof that John Doe has got better *because* of such psychoanalytic treatment; and to reason thus, even by implication, is so obviously absurd that I will not waste space by arguing the case. There is no method of treatment—from prayer to giving neurotics cold baths, and from hypnosis to extracting their teeth in order to eliminate septic foci—which has not given rise to similar claims to those of psychoanalysis, and which has not published clamorous and lengthy accounts of "cures" so accomplished. Clearly the assessment of therapeutic claims in this field is complex and difficult and requires a certain degree of sophistication.

The most obvious difficulty that arises is the problem of what is sometimes called *spontaneous remission*. It is well known that neurotic disorders often clear up without formal treatment of any kind. Indeed this is true of the majority of cases. They also clear up after types of treatment which are completely nonspecific and which, according to the psychoanalysts, should have no effect at all. A particularly good example is the famous study of Denker in which he studied five hundred severe neurotics who had complete disability pensions because of their neuroses. Not only did these five hundred fail to receive any kind of psychoanalytic treatment; they were also, because of their pensions, highly motivated to retain their illness. Nevertheless, some two out of three completely recovered within two years, having had no other treatment than the usual pink pills and pep talks of their family doctors. After five years the percentage of recoveries rose to some 90 per cent. There are many other studies giving rise to similar conclusions, to wit, that neurotic disorders are generally of a self-terminating kind and, however severe, are not likely to last for more than two or three years even when left untreated, or when treated by people with no training in psychiatry or psychoanalysis.

To prove its efficacy, psychoanalysis would clearly have to do better than this. If people treated by psychoanalysis did not recover more quickly or in greater numbers than when left untreated, then clearly the claims of psychoanalysis, as far as curative powers are concerned, would have to be rejected. Actually one might anticipate a positive showing for psychoanalysis even though the method was not in fact efficacious. The reasons for this are as follows. Psychoanalysts, by and large, only treat the better-off and more intelligent types of patient, and furthermore they tend to select their patients very stringently in terms of their likelihood to benefit from treatment. On these grounds their patients should have a better recovery rate than the more unselected groups on which the spontaneous recovery base line was established. In actual fact the data suggest very strongly that, if anything, patients treated by psychoanalysis *take longer to recover* and *recover to a lesser extent* than do patients left untreated. This conclusion is arrived at by averaging the claims made by various psychoanalysts and psychoanalytic institutions with respect to their patients. These claims are taken at face value, although there is the ever-present danger that each analyst would be prejudiced in favor of his own successes, thus giving a more optimistic view than would be warranted had an independent examination been made of the patients.

Such an actuarial comparison is, of course, defective from many points of view. It is difficult to be certain that the persons in the various groups are in fact suffering from equally serious disorders. And it is difficult to be sure that the criteria of "cure" and "recovery" used by different people are in fact identical. Much could be said in relation to both these points; but however much we might be willing to favor the psychoanalytic side, and however much our assumptions might strain probabilities, yet on no account can the figures be interpreted to give any support whatsoever for psychoanalytic claims. This verdict is borne out by several studies, much better controlled experimentally, where patients have been divided into various groups, submitted respectively to treatments of various kinds or no treatment at all. The results of these studies bear out the findings that psychoanalysis has no apparent effect as compared with other treatments or no treatment at all. Again, therefore, psychoanalytic treatment receives no support from the outcome of the experiment.

One might have thought that, with respect to children, psychoanalysis might be more positively placed, as these might be considered to be more impressionable and more easily cured. Here also, however, an extensive review of the literature shows a picture almost identical in every detail with that found in adults. There is no evidence that psychoanalysis of children produces any kind of effect on the neurotic symptoms of these children.

In 1952 I published a short paper listing the evidence and describing what I thought was the only possible conclusion to which it could lead, to wit, that the null hypothesis had not been disproved, i.e. that psychoanalysts had failed to show that their methods produced any ameliorating effects on people suffering from neurotic disorders. This brief, factual and innocuous paper produced a whole shower of replies, critiques, refutations, arguments and discussions. It did not, however, produce a single mention of an experiment or clinical trial which had demonstrated a positive effect for psychoanalytic treatment. Indeed, in recent years the more official and better informed psychoanalysts have become rather more chary of making any claims of therapeutic effectiveness for psychoanalysis. Glover, to take but one example, has explicitly rejected such claims in his latest book; the Chairman of the Fact Finding Committee of the American Psychoanalytic Association has explicitly stated that his Association had no positive evidence on the point, and did not make any kind of claim of therapeutic usefulness; Schmiedeberg and many other practicing analysts have come to a similar conclusion in print. It has been left to the large herd of faithful believers, who have no direct knowledge of psychoanalytic practices and are ignorant of the very existence of a large experimental literature, to continue to make claims which are not, in any way, supported by the evidence.

Why is it, the reader may ask, that in spite of its apparent uselessness, psychotherapy is so widely praised by people who have undergone it, and who claim they have been cured by it? The answer, I think, lies in a famous experiment, reported by the American psychologist, B. F. Skinner. He left a group of pigeons alone in their cage for twelve hours but arranged for an automatic hopper to throw out a few grains of corn at intervals to the hungry animals. When Skinner returned in the morning, he found that the animals were behaving in a very odd manner. Some were jumping up and down on one leg, some were pirouetting about with one wing in the air; others again were stretching the neck as high as it would go. What had happened? The animals, in the course of their explorations, had happened to make that particular movement when the hopper had released some corn. The pigeon, not being a slouch at the *post hoc ergo propter hoc* argument, imagined that the movement *preceding* the corn had, in fact, *produced* the corn, and immediately began to repeat the same movement again and again. When, finally, another reward came tumbling out of the hopper, the pigeon became more firmly convinced of the causal consequences, so throughout the twelve hours the pigeon performed the movement—and the hopper, at irregular intervals, dispensed the corn. To leave out the anthropomorphic terminology, and to put it in slightly more respectable language, we may say that the pigeon became conditioned to make a particular response in order to receive a particular reward. There is nothing mysterious about the experiment, which Skinner entitled "A Study in the Growth of Superstition." We can directly relate it to the growth of the belief in the efficacy of psychoanalytic treatment, both among patients and among psychoanalysts themselves.

Neurotics get better regardless of treatment; this improvement constitutes the reinforcement, and is equivalent to the corn received by the pigeon. The actions of the psychotherapist are as irrelevant as is the behavior of the pigeon in the experimental situation. Neither is instrumental in producing the reinforcement, but both become connected with it through processes of conditioning. Thus a superstition is created, both in the pigeon and in the patient, linking the one with the other. Much the same is true of the therapist himself. For him, too, the reinforcement is the improvement reported by the patient. This is independent of his actions; but because it follows them in time, the conditioned response is established. There is nothing in the published evidence to contradict this hypothesis, and much to support it.

It has often been said that psychoanalysis is more than a curative technique, and that a failure to prove the efficacy of psychotherapy would not necessarily invalidate the truth of the psychoanalytic doctrine in other respects. (Conversely, it might be said that even if psychoanalysis were found to be a successful method of therapy, this would not necessarily prove the truth of the psychoanalytic doctrine.) Up to a point this may be true; but I think it should be accepted only with grave reservations. In the first place, the whole doctrine of psychoanalysis was based on information obtained during the treatment of neurotic patients and in the course of trying to effect an amelioration of their symptoms. To admit that the primary purpose of psychoanalysis had resulted in complete failure, but that nevertheless the doctrine was correct and scientifically valuable, seems, on the face of it, an unlikely contingency ("By their fruits shall ye know them").

But this, of course, is not all. If the theory of psychoanalysis is correct, then *spontaneous remission* and the various non-analytic methods of treatment should not be effective and should leave the individual, if anything, worse off rather than better. Thus we have a quite specific deduction from the hypothesis which the facts disprove very thoroughly indeed. While it thus remains a theoretical possibility that parts, at least, of psychoanalysis might conceivably be correct, although its therapeutic methods were shown to be useless, nevertheless we would require very strong evidence indeed before accepting such a conclusion. A great deal of experimental work has, of course, been done in attempts to verify or disprove parts of the psychoanalytic structure. This is not the place to review this very large body of work. It must suffice to say that, on the whole, it has been very detrimental to the psychoanalytic claims. In saying this I must make one important distinction. Most laymen completely misunderstand the Freudian doctrine, and, therefore, mistake as confirmatory evidence, facts which in reality are quite neutral. Freud used certain well-known facts in a rather peculiar manner; the facts themselves may be true, but their verification does not imply that his use of these facts was correct. As an example of this, let me take the concept of *symbolism*.

The facts of the matter are clearly consistent with the notion that we frequently use symbols in our discourse, in our writings, and possibly also in our dreams. These facts have been known for thousands of years; the reader may like to recall the biblical dream of the Seven Lean Kine and the Seven Fat Kine. Modern apologists of the psychoanalytic movement sometimes write as if Freud had discovered symbolism (as well as sex and a great number of other important factors). His actual contribution, however, has been quite different. He has suggested ways of deciphering the symbolic language of the dream. I do not know of any evidence to indicate that these contributions have a factual basis, and I know many reasons why they should be considered highly unlikely.

Let us take only one or two considerations into account. In the first place, one and the same dream is often interpreted along entirely different lines by different analysts; frequently these accounts are contradictory. It would seem, therefore, that if any one account is "correct," all the others must be false. We are not, however, given any means of deciding which is the "correct" account; nor is the possibility ruled out that all of these accounts are in fact erroneous and have no reference to reality. Analysts often suggest that the proof of the correctness of the interpretation can be found either in the fact that the patient accepts the interpretation, or else in the fact that the patient gets better after the interpretation has been made. Arguments of this kind are too illogical to deserve an extended reply. A patient's "acceptance" of the analyst's interpretation can hardly be regarded as scientific evidence. And as I have stated previously, the patients are likely to get better anyway, dream interpretation or no dream interpretation. Consequently the improvement is irrelevant to the truth or falsity of the theory.

It may be said altogether that for Freud there was a distinct failure to comprehend a distinction between a fact and the interpretation of that fact. This failure is rendered less obvious than it would otherwise be by Freud's excellent command of language and by his admirable skill in presenting his case to its best advantage. But woe betide the reader who tries to separate the facts from the interpretations, in order to discover whether or not the former can in truth be said to give rise in any unequivocal manner to the latter! He will find his task made almost impossible by the skillful way in which Freud has hidden and glossed over important facts, and the brilliant way in which he has highlighted his interpretive account of what may, should, or ought to have happened, but which, as far as one can discover, probably never did happen.

As a supreme example of this, the reader is urged to go back to Freud's original writings and reread his "Analysis of a Phobia in a Five-year-old Boy"—the famous case of little Hans.* This has achieved considerable historical importance

---

*Collected Papers of S. Freud. Vol. III, Basic Books, 1959.

and has been universally praised by psychoanalysts as the inauguration of all child analyses. Let us have a look at little Hans, who developed a fear of horses after having seen a horse, which was pulling a bus along the street, fall down in front of his eyes. It is noteworthy that Freud only had one short interview with little Hans. All the rest of the material was provided by the father of little Hans, who, we are told, was an ardent follower of Freud. The father, as will be seen by anyone reading through the account, is constantly telling little Hans what he wants him to say, and usually continues until little Hans (who after all was only five years old) gave some kind of consent. When even this produced no results, the father had no doubt that Hans really meant exactly the opposite of what he actually said, then treating this, in itself, as an established fact. Freud seems to have realized this to some extent, and he says:

It is true that during the analysis Hans had to be told many things which he could not say himself, that he had to be presented with thoughts which he had so far shown no signs of possessing and that his attention had to be turned in the direction from which his father was expecting something to come. This detracts from the evidential value of the analysis but the procedure is the same in every case. For a psychoanalysis is not an impartial scientific investigation but a therapeutic measure.

Freud, himself, followed exactly the same procedure as the father because in his interview with the boy he told him "that he was afraid of his father because he himself nourished jealous and hostile wishes against him." The boy, his introspections, his sayings and his thoughts, are never really in the picture. What we always get is what either his father or Freud told him he should think or feel on the basis of their particular hypothesis. And whether the child could finally be made to agree or not, the result was always interpreted as being a vindication of the theory. No one who has a scientist's almost instinctive veneration for facts can regard this psychoanalytic classic as anything but a straightforward attempt to fit the child's testimony into the limits of a cut-and-dried theory, previously determined upon. It is difficult to imagine anything little Hans could have said or done that could not in this manner have been transfused into support of the theory. Even so, however, there are glaring cases of inconsistency in the account. Thus little Hans was afraid of the "black things on the horses' mouths and the things in front of their eyes." Freud claimed that this fear was based on moustaches and eyeglasses, and had been "directly transposed from his father on to the horses." In actual fact the child was thinking of the muzzle and the blinkers which had been worn by the horse that fell. Again Freud interpreted the agoraphobic element of Hans's neurosis "as a means of allowing him to stay at home with his beloved mother." Nevertheless, both the horse phobia and the general agoraphobia were present even when little Hans went out with his mother!

There is, of course, a very simple explanation of little Hans and his phobia—his fear of horses is a conditioned fear response acquired on the occasion when he saw the horse fall. Just as in Pavlov's experiments the bell, when paired a number of times with the saliva-producing food, finally gives rise to salivation when presented by itself, so the pairing of the horse with a situation producing fear caused a conditioned connection which persisted—particularly as little Hans had already had two fear-producing experiences with horses. This explanation is parsimonious; it is based on mechanisms of learning well established in the laboratory; it does not require the suppression and even inversion of little Hans's testimony, as does Freud's own account. Nevertheless, most people seem to prefer Freud's story—perhaps because it has all the attraction of one of the tales from Scheherazade. In comparison with such inventive, almost poetic genius, science seems prosaic, boring, simple. The fact that these prosaic, boring and simple theories actually produce methods of therapy that work (as we shall see later), whereas Freud's fairy tales do not, does not seem to influence many people. The charm of Freud the story-teller has convinced many people of the truth of the doctrines advanced by Freud the theorist. It hardly needs pointing out that this is a *non sequitur*, but will doing so persuade artists of the falsity of the message of a fellow artist?

LET ME NOW TURN to the promised attempt to link personality so defined and described to its antecedents, *i.e.* the biological, innate aspects of temperament. I will not here argue at great length about the inheritance of individual differences in personality. I have reviewed the evidence in detail in *The Biological Basis of Personality*, and the outcome of the many dozens of investigations which have been done in this field, notably with identical and fraternal twins, brought up together or in isolation from each other, has been quite unanimously that heredity plays a very important, indeed central, part in making each of us occupy his particular position on the two dimensions of extroversion-introversion and emotionality-stability. Numerically, the contribution of heredity to these two type-constructs is about the same as that which has been found to characterize intelligence, *i.e.* about ¾. This leaves ¼ of the total variance to be accounted for by environmental differences. This generalization of course must be restricted to our own time, to our own type of culture, and it must also be understood to be an average applying to a whole population. The proportion just quoted may not apply to any particular individual. Estimates of the contribution of the *genotype* to the *phenotype* always and invariably suffer from these restrictions. It is never meaningful to think of heredity in the abstract, and apart from a particular type of environment. But given these restrictions, there is no doubt that here and now heredity plays an immensely important part in making us what we are. This does not imply any neglect of, or discourtesy to, environmental influences. These have been so over-emphasized in the past 50 years that a slight swing of the pendulum seems only reasonable and just. There is no intention on my part of making this swing go too far in the opposite direction. Neglect of environmental determinants is as unscientific and as foolish as neglect of heredity.

What, then, are the structures in our nervous system which underlie the individual differences in extroversion and stability which we observe? Again, I will only briefly mention theories developed in great detail in *The Biological Basis of Personality*. Emotionality-stability seems indissolubly linked with the *autonomic* nervous system, which regulates the expression of the emotions, and which in turn is organized and governed by the "visceral brain." It is well known, from animal and human studies, that differences in these structures, and in their functioning, are largely determined by heredity, and indeed animal experiments have shown that we can breed rats selectively for high or low emotionality. There seems to be little doubt that we could do the same for humans, if there were no ethical objections. We might characterize that which is inherited as individual differences in the strength of emotional arousal, and the duration of that arousal, consequent upon certain types of stimulation which either genetically or through learning and conditioning produce autonomic reactions. A person who is high on "emotionality" is not of course necessarily a neurotic, but there is a certain predisposition to neurosis. In the same way a person with brittle bones is not a fracture case, but he is more likely to break his leg, or his arm, than a person with thick, strong bones—provided both encounter the same environmental hazards. Hence the term "neuroticism." It refers to the predisposition, and does not imply an actual neurotic breakdown.

The physiological distinction between introverts and extroverts seems to be related to a particular property of the cerebral cortex often referred to as *arousal.* This term came into use first of all when it was discovered that brain waves, as they appear on the electroencephalograph, are more synchronized when the person is drowsy. Alert states of mind are characterized by desynchronization. Experimental work soon disclosed that, in general, persons in an alert state of mind had alpha waves (*i.e.* waves from 8 to 13 cycles per second) which were relatively fast (high frequency) and which had low amplitude. In a drowsy state of mind they would have slow waves (low frequency) of high amplitude. Alertness or arousal can of course be measured in more ways than by the EEG; but this instrument remains perhaps the most useful direct measure of this cortical property. Now, according to the theory which I have put forward, extroverts are characterized by poor arousal, introverts by high arousal; those with both extrovert and introvert tendencies are of course average on this scale.

Such an hypothesis permits of direct testing. Given an identical non-arousing situation, extroverts should behave on the EEG like drowsy persons, *i.e.* show slow alpha waves of high amplitude, whereas introverts should behave like alert persons, *i.e.* show fast alpha waves of low amplitude. This seems in fact to be true; several investigators have found differences in that direction, and quite marked in character. This finding (together with other perhaps less convincing ones concerned with evoked potentials in the EEG,* which also

---

*The EEG, as already noted, records brain waves from the scalp. These waves can be artificially produced by giving a sudden stimulus, such as a loud click. The response to such stimuli is called an "evoked potential." It is difficult to record and measure because it is not very much stronger than the surrounding "noise" of nerve cells firing anyway, and has to be averaged over a large number of separate occasions before becoming properly observable. Evoked potentials have been shown by Ertl to differ when comparing persons with high I.Q.s and persons with low I.Q.s; and there are

differentiate extroverts from introverts) seems to furnish us with the required link between the biological side and personality. Anatomico-physiologico-neurological structures like the visceral brain and the reticular formation, the strength of whose functioning in responding to environmental stimulation is largely determined by heredity, give rise to stronger or weaker autonomic reactions, and to greater or less arousal. These emotional and arousal reactions, according to their strength, determine the habitual behavior pattern of the individual—and this habitual behavior pattern is what we call "personality"—and measure in detail as extroversion-introversion, or neuroticism-stability.

MOST OF THE TIME these personality factors are independent of each other, but this is not always so. We are not often in a state of high emotion—fortunately perhaps. In peace time, at least, experiences of paralyzing fear or strong anger are relatively rare, and even somewhat milder emotions occupy no more than perhaps five per cent of our time. Now the visceral brain has the ability to alert the cortex, either directly or through the reticular formation. Hence when a person is in a state of high emotional excitement, he cannot simultaneously be in a state of low arousal. This will in any case seem intuitively obvious, and detailed physiological work supports it. While, thus, for most of the time these dimensions are independent, under strong emotional excitement they cannot any longer be regarded as such. Now states of high emotional excitement are the unfortunate rule for people high on neuroticism, and low on stability. They tend to live in a world of constant crisis, eternal anxiety, recurring emotion. These people then suffer not only from constant stimulation of

---

several indications that introverts and extroverts can also be differentiated (although not by the same measure as that which correlates with I.Q.). Introverts, to be more precise, have shorter latencies (respond more quickly) and greater amplitudes (respond more strongly), particularly to weak stimuli.

the visceral brain, but through this they are also typically in a state of high arousal. For them the independence of introversion (high arousal) and emotionality (strong visceral reactions) has broken down, and they are chronically dysthymic—highly aroused and highly emotional.

It seems unlikely on *a priori* grounds (and has indeed been found to be quite untrue) that psychological experiments and their effects and results should be independent of the emotional state or the cortical arousal of the subjects carrying out these experiments. It used to be thought that by reassuring the subjects in a general sort of way, and by interesting them in the project, a uniform state of low anxiety and high arousal could be produced which would be quite general for all subjects, and thus eliminate these factors as variables from the experiment. But clearly this is not so. Even such a simple experimental measurement as that involved in recording a resting subject's EEG produced evidence of great variations in arousal. Furthermore, these variations are predictable from our theory. It would seem that extroverts and introverts, emotional and stable subjects, would behave quite differently in psychological experiments, and that unless such differences are taken into account, the whole experiment becomes pretty worthless. Such effects are indeed often found, but to predict exactly what might happen calls for some thorough understanding of the psychological theory underlying the phenomena in question. I will give just one example, to make clear what is involved.

Suppose that I ask you to predict whether extroverts or introverts will remember better a series of paired nonsense syllables, like the following: *SIP—WOL*; *VIL—MUF*; *SEL—PON*. The list of seven such pairs is repeated until it is performed perfectly. All fourteen syllables are given accurately, by the subject writing down without prompting all seven stimulus words, and all seven response words, in the correct pairing. Groups are now formed of extroverts and introverts respectively. Some are tested almost immediately, others after one minute, others after five minutes, others yet after thirty minutes, and a last set after twenty-four hours. Care is taken to prevent rehearsal by giving subjects some other task to do during the waiting periods (except the twenty-four hour one, of course). Which group would remember the syllables better, the introverts or the extroverts?

At first blush one might say—the introverts, of course. They have the higher degree of arousal, and cortical arousal or alertness must facilitate remembering. True, but incomplete. What actually goes on when we learn something (nonsense syllables or Shakespeare's poetry or whatever)? Experimental evidence suggests that we have two kinds of memory. At first new material enters into short-term memory, which is envisaged as consisting of reverberating circuits in the brain. These quickly die out, unless transformed into chemical traces (probably the outcome of some form of protein synthesis, and involving ribonucleid acid). This transformation into long-term memory is called consolidation of the memory trace; and there is evidence to suggest that the length and strength of consolidation is a function, among other things, of the degree of cortical arousal present at the time.

So far, one would still consider it likely that introverts would do better. There is, however, one more complication. The process of consolidation of the memory trace interferes with reproduction—possibly because the same sets of neurons or cell assemblies are involved, and can only serve one purpose or the other. Consequently, while consolidation is still in process, memory will not be available for reproduction (remembering). This means that extroverts (poor arousal, little consolidation) would remember better, shortly after learning, than introverts (strong arousal, long consolidation) whose neurons would still be busy with consolidation, and therefore not in a state to produce the learned material ready for remembering. Conversely, after a longer period of time extroverts (poor consolidation, little remembering) would be expected to do rather poorly. Introverts, whose strong consolidation would have furnished them with a strong memory trace, would be expected to remember particularly well now. Thus, if we test different groups of introverts and extroverts after different rest periods, we would expect to find their scores crossing. At first, extroverts would be very superior, while at the end, introverts would be very superior—with a point of equilibrium in between. Figure 3 shows the outcome of the experiment.

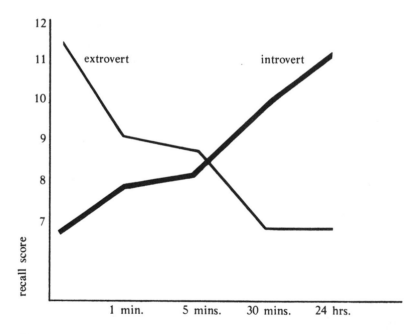

Figure 3   recall interval

After practically no rest, extroverts remember almost twice as much as do introverts. After five minutes, the two groups remember about the same amount. After twenty-four hours, introverts remember almost twice as much as extroverts.

This experiment is instructive in more ways than one. Consider, first of all, the outcome if we had adopted the usual experimental technique of disregarding personality variables. Averaging over all subjects would produce a straight line. It would seem as if length of recall interval did not affect recall at all! Yet this conclusion is obviously absurd—rather like the old British Navy rule, which says that because some sailors like two lumps of sugar in their tea, while others like none at all, therefore everybody will get one lump. You must not average dissimilar sets of data—so runs the first rule of scientific wisdom. Unfortunately it is broken every day by experimental psychologists willing to bury their mistakes in the absurdly inflated error term. Different people behave differently—even in the best controlled experimental situation. We simply have to recognize this fact, and that means recognizing the importance of personality, and allocating it a position central to all psychological research.

Consider another interesting feature of this experiment. Improvement of performance during a rest pause has been widely studied by psychologists under the heading of "reminiscence." Yet the outcome of numerous studies of verbal reminiscence has been so varied, some people finding evidence of such improvement, others not, that it became known as the "now you see it, now you don't" phenomenon; and interest in it has declined so much that for several years no studies have been published on it. Our Figure makes the reason for these discrepancies clear. Introverts show a beautiful instance of reminiscence; over a twenty-four hour period the score almost doubles! Extroverts instead show a beautiful instance of forgetting; over a twenty-four hour period the score is almost halved. Take both groups together, and the score does not change at all. No wonder "reminiscence" became so difficult to pin down. Results depended entirely on the personality make-up of your group. Include a majority of introverts, and you see it; include a majority of extroverts, and you don't.

EXPERIMENTAL PSYCHOLOGISTS who wish to exclude personality variables from their studies tend to point to the procedures of the hard scientists. These, they declare, work on the simple formula $a = (f)b$ which we have already encountered, and consequently *functionalism* must be the rule in psychology also. But this of course is a gross oversimplification of what physicists do; so gross in fact that it amounts to misrepresentation.

Take an example from cryogenics, the study of very low temperatures. It is well known that temperatures of a few degrees above absolute zero (K) produce superconductivity, *i.e.* a state in which no resistance to the passage of an electric current is offered by the metal or alloy so cooled. But can we write: Superconductivity = (f) Temperature? Certainly not. Some metals show superconductivity, others do not.

What characterizes each group? The formula would work for mercury, lead, tin, indium, thallium and gallium—all metals with rather similar physical properties, such as low melting points and softness. However, these were not the relevant properties. After some time Meissner discovered superconductivity in hard metals with high melting points, such as tantalum, niobium, titanium and thorium. Others were later added, *e.g.* aluminum, cadmium, zinc, osmium and ruthenium. But some metals did not show superconductivity. Among these are monovalent ones like gold or sodium, and a few divalent ones like magnesium and calcium. Other non-conductors are iron, cobalt, nickel and the rare earth metals. These all have high internal magnetic fields which are likely to suppress superconductivity.

Is the nature of the atom itself responsible? Apparently not. Neither gold (Au) nor bismuth (Bi) is superconductive, but the inter-metallic compound Au_2Bi is. It appears that the reason for superconductivity has to be sought in the gas of free electrons rather than in the nature of the atom. Furthermore, alloying and indeed any form of crystal imperfection tends to affect superconductivity adversely. As Felix Bloch said: "Every theory of superconductivity can be proved wrong!" Thus, for the physicist the notion of treating all elements alike for the purpose of his functional equation simply does not make sense. The table of the elements, and their well-known properties, takes the place of the dimensions of personality in psychology. No physicist would average results over different elements and alloys; he would consider the very notion as insane. Why should psychologists not follow the same path to wisdom and treat unlikes separately?

THROUGH THE CONCEPT OF PERSONALITY, we have thus been enabled to trace a path from the physiological to the experimental side. This path leads on, needless to say, to the social side. The greater learning potential of the introvert so demonstrated would obviously be expected to influence his success at school and university. Indeed there is much evidence to show that introversion correlates positively with scholastic achievement beyond the primary school. This particular cause is almost certainly not the only one to produce this effect, but it is very likely one of a whole set of different causes, some of which we will encounter later on. Let me note just one more thing which may be explained in terms of our hypothesis. Stimulant drugs, like caffeine and nicotine, increase cortical arousal, and hence consolidation; no wonder students smoke and drink coffee when they are studying! And no wonder that extroverts smoke more, and drink more coffee—they stand in greater need of arousal.

Another chain of argument is probably particularly important; but as I have dealt with it in some detail before I will merely mention it now. Pavlovian conditioning was discovered by Pavlov himself to be dependent on cortical arousal; and later, more sophisticated work has borne out this hypothesis. Hence my prediction that introverts would condition better. There is much evidence that indeed introverts form conditioned responses more quickly and more strongly than do extroverts. This is particularly true when circumstances are unfavorable to the formation of conditioned responses, *i.e.* when the stimuli are weak, and the time-interval between them relatively short (*e.g.* 300 milliseconds). When stimuli are very strong, and time-intervals rather long, the position may be reversed. The arousal produced by the stimuli is so strong that, combined with the natural degree of high arousal present in the introvert, it pushes the person concerned beyond the optimum degree of arousal. This, in fact, is another important general discovery of experimental psychology. The relation between arousal and performance is not linear, but shaped like an inverse U. When arousal is low, increasing it improves performance; but only up to a point. Arousal beyond this optimum produces disorganized performance, and hence the person performs less well as arousal is increased even further. Pavlov already established these ideas when he talked about the "law of strength"— performance increasing with increasing arousal, and "protective inhibition"—*i.e.* the cortex protecting itself from overstimulation by shutting down partially when stimulation became too intense. This general law (known as the Yerkes-Dodson law, after two American psychologists who first discovered it in the early years of this century) has one additional qualification: the optimum point of arousal is lower for complex and difficult tasks, and higher for simple and easy tasks. This is, perhaps intuitively, obvious. The ability to solve difficult mathematical equations is more easily disrupted by overstimulation than is the ability to run fast, or to hit hard.

However that may be, I have argued that the ease of conditioning which characterizes the introvert makes him more vulnerable to neurotic disorders, which may be conceived as conditioned emotional reactions. Similarly, the failure of the extrovert to generate quick and strong conditioned responses makes the development of a "conscience" in him more difficult—conscience, in terms of psychological theory, being simply the sum of conditioned anxiety reactions to doing things labelled "wrong" or "naughty" in childhood and adolescence. I have argued these points at some detail in my book on *Crime and Personality*, and will not elaborate them here; we will return to the general theory in the chapter on "Sex and Personality" later on. In any case, the evidence is quite strong that introverts with high emotionality seem predisposed to become neurotics, whereas extroverts with high emotionality seem predisposed to become criminals.

Sir Cyril Burt's important follow-up studies of 763 children who had been rated by their teachers on extroversion and emotionality may serve as a good example. After thirty-five years, 15 per cent and 18 per cent respectively had become habitual offenders or neurotics. Of the former, 63 per cent had been rated high on emotionality; 54 per cent had been rated as high on extroversion, but only 3 per cent on introversion. Of the latter, 59 per cent had been rated as high on emotionality; 44 per cent had been rated as high on introversion, but only 1 per cent on extroversion. Here, then, is another chain linking the physiological and experimental side of our Figure 1 with the social side, through the intervention of personality variables.

YET A THIRD LINK can be made through the concept of preferred level of sensory stimulation. There is a general law in psychology which states that the best-liked level of stimulation is intermediate between sensory deprivation (*i.e.* too little stimulation) and too strong stimulation, which produces pain. The latter point is obvious. Extremely bright lights, extremely loud noises, very heavy pressures, all end up by being painful, and hence avoided. Sensory deprivation is a rather more recent field of experimentation, largely due to the need of knowing what might happen to astronauts shut off from many sources of ordinary stimulation. Put crudely, the subject of the experiment is shut up in a room which is soundproofed and dark. He wears padding over his hands and feet, so that he cannot feel anything. Or else he may be submerged under water, breathing through a tube; the water is of skin temperature, so that he can feel nothing whatever. Conditions such as these become unbearable very soon. The absence of stimulation is no more supportable than the presence of unduly strong stimulation—hence the terror of solitary confinement.

How is this linked with personality? Sensory thresholds are linked with cortical arousal—under conditions of high arousal you hear soft sounds, see subdued light, feel light touches more easily than when in a state of low arousal. Hence introverts would be expected to have lower thresholds than extroverts; an expectation amply borne out by many experimental studies. From this we would expect introverts to be more tolerant of sensory deprivation, extroverts to be more tolerant of pain. To the introverts the slight stimulation provided by the restricted environment is well above the low threshold of their sense organs, but to the extroverts it is below that threshold, and nothing is felt. Strong sensory stimulation is so far above the threshold of the introvert that pain is felt, when to the more robust extrovert the stimulation is only a little above threshold value, and no pain is felt. These deductions have in fact been verified quite a number of times, and thus lend support to this particular chain.

We can go one step farther and argue that as the optimum point of stimulation lies towards stronger sensory stimuli for the extrovert, and towards weaker sensory stimuli for the introvert, and as behavior would normally be directed to establishing an equilibrium at or near the optimum point of balance—so extroverts would be characterized by what has been called "stimulus hunger," i.e. they would search for and enjoy strong sensory stimulation, whereas introverts would shy away from it and prefer weak stimuli. In one illustrative experiment introverted and extroverted subjects, tested singly, were isolated in a dark room, and instructed to press a key against a spring. First, the mean strength of their press was established. Then they were "rewarded" for strong presses by three seconds of loud juke-box music coming on, and bright colored light illuminating the scene. If subjects kept pressing strongly, lights and music stayed on; if not, they went off again. As predicted, extroverts started pressing harder and harder, while introverts pressed less and less hard—the former to enjoy the strong sensory stimulation, the latter to get away from it! Thus even the Skinnerian notion of "reinforcement" is clearly tied to personality; or, as the Manhattan wit once put it, one man's Mede is another man's Persian. This experiment is relevant to the potential criminal's extroverted search for the "bright lights and loud music" of the city. Not only is the temptation stronger, but also, as we have seen, the resistance to temptation provided by his "conscience" is weaker. No wonder he slips and falls, where the introvert does not.

Let us consider a last chain between the two sides in our diagram (Figure 1). Wundt called the extroverted person "changeable"; and the evidence certainly supports him there. Extroverts move their homes more frequently, they change their jobs more frequently, they have less "brand loyalty"— and in addition, as we shall see in the next chapter, they change their sexual partners more frequently (and have divorces more readily). Why is the extrovert more changeable? The answer may lie in a kind of behavior studied in the laboratory under the heading of "alternation." Let a rat loose at the bottom of a T-maze, and put pieces of food at the two arms of the T, in such a way that the rat cannot see them when he reaches the top of the stem, and has to move right or left. Suppose he goes right, finds and eats his meat, and is put back again to the starting point. Will he go right or left next time? You might think that having been rewarded for going right, he will go right again, but this is not so. He is more likely to go the other way. In human terms you might say he was driven by "curiosity" to find out what lay along the other arm of the T which he hadn't explored yet; but such an anthropomorphic term does not help us very much. There is much evidence that any perpetual or motor experience sets up some form of reactive inhibition, *i.e.* some tendency which works against that type of behavior being immediately repeated. This inhibition weakens the tendency to go right, and is stronger than the reinforcement which would otherwise pull the rat to the right; consequently the rat goes left. This is the essence of alternation behavior. Its putative cause is some form of reactive inhibition (which can of course be studied in many other situations, suitably quantified, and is no *deus ex machina* to get us out of our difficulties).

Inhibition, in general theory, is the opposite of arousal. Hence we would expect introverts to show less reactive inhibition than extroverts—a formulation for which there is much evidence. Inhibition can be experimentally manipulated so as to strengthen the fundamental point made. Stimulant drugs, like amphetamine, increase arousal and hence decrease inhibition; depressant drugs, like alcohol, have the opposite effect. And as one would expect, alternation behavior is increased by depressant drugs and decreased by stimulant drugs. We can now understand the very obvious pressure of extroverts for novelty, for change, for alternation. Their weak arousal cannot effectively oppose the growth of reactive inhibition, and hence the regular, the usual, the ordinary becomes anathema, and the search is on for new stimuli, as well as for strong stimuli. Artists, who are often extroverted, tend to show this tendency to extremes, and it has rightly become part of the Bohemian legend. Thus, where Wundt was content to describe the extrovert as "changeable," we can now explain just why it is that extroverts are more changeable than introverts. Perhaps the rat has, after all, a part to play in human psychology. . . .

CONFLICT BEHAVIOR may also be shown to find a close

relation with personality. Psychologists usually discuss conflict in terms of *approach-avoidance*. In other words, a given object has certain properties which make us wish to approach it, but also others which make us wish to keep away. An obvious example would be a sexually very attractive woman to a married man; there are equally clear-cut reasons for approach as for avoidance. What will happen? This depends of course (in part, at least) on the respective strengths of the two impulses, but in part it is also a question of the changing strength of the two impulses as the person approaches his goal.

This problem has been studied in great detail by Neal Miller. He measured the strength of approach and avoidance by making his rats wear little jackets to which was sewn a string which in turn pulled against a spring; hence the strength of the pull could be measured, as well as its direction. Direction (towards or away from the goal) was considered indicative of approach or avoidance. Strength of pull was considered as a measure of the intensity of motivation. It was found that both the strength of approach motivation and the strength of avoidance motivation increased the nearer the goal the rat found itself; however, the avoidance gradient was steeper, as shown in Figure 4. Thus, if we put a hungry rat in a long, straight runway, at the other end of which we place some food, he will get progressively more highly motivated the nearer he gets to the food. If we place a shocking device at the food end of the runway, he will get progressively more afraid as he approaches—if the anthropomorphic language be forgiven. Combining food and shock produces a typical *approach-avoidance* conflict. As shown in Figure 4, the approach tendency will be stronger when the rat is far removed from the goal, but gradually this superiority will diminish as he approaches the goal, until finally he will come to rest at some distance from the goal—just about where the two lines intersect. Increasing his hunger will elevate the

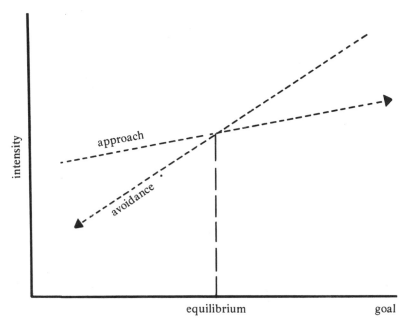

equilibrium   goal

Figure 4

approach gradient, possibly sufficiently to place the point of intersection beyond the goal; this means he will actually reach the food, get his shock, and eat it. Or the shock intensity may be increased, and the rat may now have his avoidance gradient raised so much that he will stay completely at the entrance of the runway, without moving along it at all. This model has been submitted to a considerable amount of experimental research, and has been found to give an excellent account of itself. There are of course other conflicts, such as *approach-approach* (you want to buy a hat and a dress, but you have enough money only for one or the other), or *avoidance-avoidance* (you don't want to do your homework, and you don't want to be punished, but if you don't do the one, you will get the other). But there is no point in entering into these complexities here.

Now the importance of these gradients for our immediate purpose is, of course, that we would predict that extroverts would have an elevated and/or steeper approach gradient than introverts. Introverts would have an elevated and/or steeper avoidance gradient than extroverts. Hence the generally outgoing, pleasure-seeking, aggressive, active behavior of the extrovert, and the generally inward-turned, harm-avoidant, submissive, passive behavior of the introvert. Emotionality, by acting as it were as a booster or an amplifier (by virtue of its function as a drive), would make these tendencies all the stronger and more obvious.

As an example, consider my experiment with the criminal and the neurotic rats. In this, we introduced a rule into our rat colony: it was forbidden to eat for three seconds after food had been dropped into the trough. Offences against this rule were punished by a (mild) electric shock to the forepaws. When three seconds had elapsed, rats were allowed to eat in peace. For this experiment we used a group of highly emotional rats, and another group of unemotional ones; these rats had been specially bred over many generations for this trait.

It was anticipated that extroverted rats would show "criminal" propensities, by eating during the forbidden period, in spite of being shocked; introverted rats would be so afraid of the shock that they would not eat at all, even when it was safe to do so. These tendencies correspond to an elevated approach gradient in the first case, and an elevated avoidance gradient in the second. Rats midway between the two extremes of extrovert and introvert would be capable of behaving in an integrated, normal fashion, *i.e.* wait until the three seconds were up, and then eat in peace. Emotionality would make this integrated behavior more difficult by boosting whichever gradient was higher, and thus reducing the proportion of rats balanced between approach and avoidance.

So it turned out. Emotional animals either behaved in a criminal, psychopathic manner, or else in a dysthymic, neurotic manner, while unemotional animals typically behaved in an integrated, functionally adequate way. Are the similarities between rat and human behavior implied in this experiment more than just analogies? Time alone will tell; certainly the possibility of making predictions of rat behavior from a consideration of human personality is a rather striking inversion from the usual habit of doing the opposite. An application of these principles to human sexual behavior is given in the next chapter. This may serve to suggest that a positive answer to this question may not be entirely mistaken.

SO MUCH, THEN, for this very brief account of some of the links which a theory of personality can forge between the two opposite sides of psychology. There do seem to be connections between electrophysiological measures, such as the EEG, on the one hand, and social activities, like criminal acts or neurotic breakdowns, on the other. Such connections would not be intelligible except through the mediation of such hypothetical constructs (or intervening variables) as *extroversion-introversion*, or *emotionality-stability*. It is, of course, not suggested that these are the only such intervening personality variables. Undoubtedly there are many others which in due course will be unearthed by patient research. But a beginning must be made somewhere, and beyond any doubt these two dimensions of personality are important and relevant to much that is being done in experimental psychology and in social psychology.

Ultimately what is being said here reduces to a very simple point. For some subjects of research, the subject matter is infinitely divisible—or almost so. Physics can subdivide its elements endlessly until the atom is reached (and now, as is well known, we can subdivide even that). Biology is not in this happy position, and psychology certainly is not capable of subdividing endlessly either the people it studies, or even the rats it experiments upon; even Solomon in his famous judgment between the two women claiming to be the mother of the baby did not seriously consider splitting it in two. Physiology studies sub-systems, such as the reflex arc. But when we deal with behavior, the laws of physiology—while extremely important and relevant—are constantly modified because the entities referred to are embedded in a context of other variables. In the physiological preparation the reflex arc is isolated as far as this is possible to achieve. In the functioning organism the working of the reflex arc is in part determined by the cortical arousal of the organism, by the activation of its autonomic system, and by many other variables which make the extrapolation of the rules of the physiologist to the living, intact organism of very doubtful value. This is not to say that what physiologists are doing is not worth doing. Far from it. Their work is absolutely essential to a proper understanding of the functioning of the organism; but it is not sufficient. The bits and pieces have to be integrated, and it is only when such integration has taken place that we can talk about behavior. And what is more, the laws of integration are not implicit in the laws governing the various sub-systems studied by the physiologist. They require to be discovered separately—by the psychologist. Hence, however important and fundamental the work of the biologist, psychology requires the concept of the intact organism. The notion of "behavior" goes beyond segmental analysis, and it postulates such notions as "personality."

Experimental psychologists often try to avoid the restrictions imposed on psychology by this restrictive but inescapable fact. They aim to discover the laws of learning— or of remembering—or of perceiving, without paying heed to the organism which learns, or remembers, or perceives. They attempt to do this by controlling the environment as much as possible; but obviously such control is at best only partial. Any experiment on persons, or rats, inevitably brings into the laboratory the person, or the rat. You cannot control or eliminate this disturbing factor. And the person, or the rat, brings into the experimental laboratory a cortex which works at a predetermined level of arousal, an autonomic system which is overtly reactive, or sluggish, or average, and a brain which is efficient, or poor, or mediocre. We have seen how memory works quite differently in extroverts and introverts. You do not get rid of these differences by averaging. We have seen how learning works quite differently in emotional and unemotional people. You do not get rid of these differences by averaging. And we have seen how neurotic and criminal rats differ in their reactions to our laboratory experiment. Even with such very simple organisms, personality obtrudes to a very marked extent. It would seem to be the course of wisdom to give in and accept the impossibility of eradicating in the laboratory all the myriad individual differences which interfere with our "perfect" performance on experimental tasks. Instead of treating such factors as "error," we should accept them as fact and study them in their own right. In this way we may hope to learn something about personality, and incidentally gain some measure of experimental control over this recalcitrant thing called "human nature." This message seems so obvious, and so reasonable—yet it is more honored in the breach than the observance.

Social psychologists, too, although they often pay lip-service to the virtues of personality research, do not often include it in their research designs. I have already drawn attention to the marked tendency of psychologists to ask "general" questions, answers to which would presuppose the existence of some universal notion of "human nature," uniform and unvaried, instead of the markedly heterogeneous and variable article which we see in the marketplace.

Kinsey, to take an example which we will analyze in more detail in the next chapter, is concerned with "population values": such as the proportion of men and women who have intercourse before marriage; or who have homosexual contacts; or who indulge in "perversions."

This may be of some interest, but surely it simply sidesteps the important causal question: What is it that causes some people to have premarital sex experiences, and others to shun such behavior? Who indulges in perversions, and who does not? What are the personality variables leading to the different types of sexual behavior so assiduously studied by Kinsey and his many followers? The fact that not all people are alike makes these purely statistical "population values" of very limited interest. We are simply averaging over dissimilar units, and the answers we obtain are of limited scientific interest. At most, social psychologists and sociologists "break down their populations by age and sex." These causes of breakdown are, to be sure, useful. But they usually do not reduce the error variance half as much as would the use of a reasonable measure of personality variables.

It would be wrong to think that the traffic between personality study and experimental psychology is one way. This is not so. If experimental psychology needs to take into account personality variables, so equally "personality theory" would be impossible in any realistic sense without the concepts of experimental psychology, physiology, neurology, and even anatomy and genetics and biochemistry. Such notions as *arousal* were, after all, introduced by the experimentalists. No rational predictions in the field of remembering could be made if we did not have such theories as those regarding consolidation of the memory trace, short-term and long-term memory, and the interference of consolidation with reproduction. In other words, I am not suggesting that in any sense personality theory is superior to, or independent of, experimental psychology. I am suggesting that only by working closely together, and seeking to establish a unified, unitary science can both hope to live up to their pretensions. And similarly, only by drawing on the accumulated knowledge of experimental and personality study can social psychology hope to become a true science and contribute in its turn to the development of general psychology.

For here, too, the traffic is not all one way. People clearly do not live in isolation, and the concept of personality has little meaning outside its social context. A weakness in this sphere must obviously mean a commensurate weakness in our knowledge of that biosocial concept, personality. Any advance in one of these fields means an advance in all the others. Psychologists assume too readily that it is sufficient for each scientist to work away in his little room, on his little problem, producing some little advance. If in doing so he loses sight of the larger goal—and overlooks major variables which affect his work, and must be measured or controlled—then his minuscule "advance" will look rather poor compared with the demands of a truly scientific spirit.

Psychology is the study of behavior of persons, or it is nothing. Personality is at the very root of its subject matter. We must combine the careful, step-by-step, experimental approach of those who work with rats with the far-reaching social interests, the concern with social issues, which characterize those who use the couch. If we link up these fields through modern concepts of personality theory, then psychology may really be said to be "on its way."

Sex and Personality

THE INVESTIGATION of sexual habits and practices is a relatively recent development. Scientific studies in this field are few and far between in the years preceding the well-known work of Kinsey and his collaborators. Yet Kinsey did have precursors—odd though some of these may have been.

One of the earliest was the mysterious "Walter," the semi-anonymous author of what must surely be the longest and most pornographic book in existence—*My Secret Life*. In this set of eleven volumes Walter (who was probably the famous Victorian bibliographer and collector of erotica, H. Spencer Ashbee) recounts the events of his sexual life, from his childhood around 1840 onwards. These are described in considerable detail, and extend to a surprisingly large number of female conquests—he himself estimates that he had intercourse with some 2,000 women. Most of these were of course "gay," *i.e.* prostitutes, or else servant girls who had little defense against his customary combination of threats and gold. He did not refrain from rape in cases of difficulty, and included both young children and old women among his "conquests." The book is revolting and revealing in equal measure; few writings bring home to the reader in such a clear if earthy fashion what life in Victorian days was like for the poor, and how downtrodden were members of the female sex. He also throws much light on the alleged "morality" and "puritanism" of those days. Clearly these terms applied, if at all, only to a small section of the population, namely the middle classes. Working-class girls were extremely unlikely to remain virgins much beyond the age of sixteen—in contrast to our own "permissive" times when the age (as we shall see) is much higher.

A married pair of American psychoanalysts, the Kronhausens, have published a book of extracts from Walter's writings, interspersed with their "interpretations" and comments. As one might have expected, they regard this animated penis as a kind of prophet of the permissive, Freudian society which, having shed its repressions, can now go forward to its existentialist heaven of sensual delight. They subtitle their book: "The English Casanova," thus clearly demonstrating their aesthetic and moral insensitivity; Casanova was an excellent writer, compared to whom Walter is just a bumbling and almost illiterate amateur, and he showed feelings of compassion and tenderness which have no place in Walter's arid soul.

We shall return to Walter in a later chapter; here let me merely remark that his overwhelming interest in women and sex generally led him to prepare what seems to have been the first questionnaire in this field, predating Kinsey by about seventy years. Like Kinsey, he seems to have learned the questions by heart, and asked them personally not only of "gay" women but also of "servants and young girls and nursemaids." This inventory starts off with questions like: At what age does a little boy's cock get stiff? When do you think a boy first feels pleasure in its stiffness? How old was the youngest boy who wanted to put his hand up your clothes or was curious about your sex? How old were you when you first felt randy? How old were you when you first frigged yourself? These are the preliminaries, put to all and sundry. Others are more recherché and only asked of "gay" women. Does sperm seem a nasty fluid to you? Do you generally spend* with men or with a man who is new to you? Were you ever buggered and do you like it? Which do you like best [sic]: having intercourse or being gamahuched?† Walter comments on his questionnaire:

These are leading questions. The replies suggest others. The answers given to them by *many* women will, coupled with a man's own wide experience and observation of women, leave him but very little to learn about them; and enable him to form sound opinions about their sexual tastes and habits, and the phenomena accompanying their lust and spending, as well as about the habits and tastes of men.

This seems doubtful, judging by Walter's own pronouncements, even though he supplemented his questionnaire by direct observation (through peep-holes in hotels and bordellos) and experiment. (He attempted to have intercourse under water; this appears to be very difficult. He also tried to see how many coins a female vagina would hold: eighty-five single shilling pieces. Was Walter one of the fathers of experimental psychology?)

Walter—and Kinsey after him—relied much on verbal evidence. They talked endlessly to the men and women who came forward (or were induced in some way) to *tell all*. Two points naturally arise. Were the people interviewed a reasonably random sample of the population? Did they tell the truth? On both points much skepticism has been

---

*To spend is the Victorian equivalent for having an orgasm—Walter, in spite of his 2,000 women, seems to have had some very odd ideas on the subject of female orgasm.

†*Gamahuching* is apparently the Victorian generic term for oral stimulation of the sexual parts, embracing both cunnilingus and fellatio; I have been unable to discover its etymology as dictionaries are rather coy about mentioning the word at all.

expressed, and no doubt such skepticism is right and proper. Walter, of course, knew nothing about sampling, and cared less; Kinsey was more knowledgeable, and tried hard to satisfy his critics. In the nature of things it is almost impossible to succeed in obtaining a really good sample when one is dealing with sexual questions, and furthermore it is equally impossible to know whether one has succeeded or not! One can only hope that different workers, obtaining different types of samples by different methods in different countries, will soon find whether results are congruent enough to say that the specific methods of sampling employed did not affect the outcome to such a marked extent that the results are in fact worthless. On the whole, repetitions of the Kinsey-type investigation have tended to show that many different methods of approach yield essentially similar results. I would be inclined to say that the percentage error in Kinsey's figures is slight. This does not mean that they are right but, rather, that they are not so wrong as to make their use absolutely pointless. Science proceeds by approximation; first measurements are seldom very accurate, but they are essential if any improvements are to be made. If an investigator finds that 29 per cent of his female student sample say that they have had intercourse, does it really matter that the "true" figure for the population in question is 25 per cent, or even 37 per cent? A rough statement like "a third" gives a good idea of the finding, and probably excludes estimates of, say, 68 per cent or 84 per cent. It would be nice to be able to be more accurate, but what would one do with the extra accuracy? The Nobel Prize winning physicist, J. J. Thomson, once said that he was quite happy most of the time to get his measurements right within 10 per cent. Should psychologists ask for more?

MOST LAYMEN are misled in this matter because they consider the measurement of such fundamental aspects of nature as time and space. These are indeed measured very accurately, but they are not typical. When we start talking about fields where active research is going on, the margins of accuracy widen alarmingly. When Millikan started his work on the charge of electrons in 1906, the value of the charge was uncertain by at least 50 per cent; furthermore, all the methods used measured an average of many electrons only. In addition, there was no real proof that all electrons have the same charge, or in other words that a natural unit of charge really exists. If psychologists tried to work with concepts and theories subject to such margins of inaccuracy, and experimented with phenomena so uncertain, laymen would laugh at them and contrast their work unfavorably with that of physicists. But they would be wrong. In a new field of research, whether in physics or psychology, it is idle to look for great accuracy, or certainty; when you have found those, it is probably time to move on to something else. The difference is probably that physicists can carry on all this early work behind the impenetrable walls of the laboratory, secure in the knowledge that nobody is interested in what they are doing, or would understand it if they were. Psychologists cannot hide so easily, and what they do is nearly always of concern—often of passionate concern—to a very wide public. Hence our earliest steps come under critical scrutiny—often hostile scrutiny— long before one would really like to expose them in this way. Psychologists of course are often plain wrong—as are physicists; but that is a different matter. All scientific measurements are in error. As long as one has some reasonable estimate of the size of the error, one can frame rational conclusions which take this into account. Some errors in psychological measurement are quite small—as in sensory thresholds, or psychophysics—and some are quite large; all this is true in physics too. Estimation of size of errors is a skilled job, and an important one. The simple existence of errors does not rule out the formulation of reasonable conclusions.

But do people speak the truth? This is a tricky question—it

implies for instance that we can know what the truth is. If we want to know how what a person says compares with "the truth," we must have some independent criterion. Often people assume that such an independent criterion can be found in action; actions speak louder than words. But do they? When I lived in Germany under the Hitler regime, I knew several people who outwardly, and by their actions, seemed to support the Nazi government; to me, whom they knew well, they confided their hatred of all Hitler stood for. One later escaped across the border in a Hitchcock-type ski-run down the Czechoslovak mountain tracks; another ended up in a concentration camp. Surely their words spoke louder than their actions, at the time at least. Under duress either actions, or words, or both, may cease to be representative of "the truth." We all lie at times, not only by word of mouth but by our actions too. Do not wives distrust husbands who suddenly remember to bring home flowers? Even if we accept the distinction (are not words actions, too, and often very powerful and important ones?) we must distrust both words and actions, unless we have good reasons for believing in either, or both. In the field of sexual activity we are almost entirely restricted to verbal information, although there are ways and means of linking these up with actions. When we come to discuss the new data here presented we shall come back to this point. There are other ways of making verbal information "respectable"; these too will be discussed in their turn. For the moment, let me just illustrate with a historical parable the difficulties which attend the direct observation and measurement of sexual activity.

THE STORY CONCERNS Prince Vincenzo Gonzaga, whose unconsummated marriage with Margherita Farnese, granddaughter of the Duke of Parma, had been annulled. The Medici Grand Duke of Tuscany was willing to give him his daughter's hand in marriage, but there was one difficulty: rumors were spreading that the Prince was impotent. This would of course prove a most difficult hurdle to overcome, as the provision of a son and heir was the main duty of Princes and Princesses in those days; any failure on that score might produce endless troubles, wars, and murders. Hence the Medicis' condition for continuing with the negotiations about the marriage was that Don Vincenzo should prove his virility—with a virgin, and in front of witnesses! The story is extremely complicated, with many religious and political threads intertwined; it is told with consummate mastery by Roger Peyrefitte in his book, *The Prince's Person* (*La nature du Prince*) from which I have taken my information. The story is also extremely funny—although the Prince might have disagreed. Here I wish to dwell only on the complexity of the actual proof required. Simple as it might seem to be to prove that someone is or is not potent, yet this one single item of factual information proved extremely difficult to obtain and rather costly. The story illustrates the lengths to which one might have to go if one decided that it is actions alone which are to be investigated, and that words are untrustworthy—as in this particular case they might very well be, of course!

Objections were made right away against the test being done on a virgin; the Holy Father, in granting Don Vincenzo permission to remarry, had not specified that this should be to a virgin; it might be a widow. But the Grand Duke only had a virgin to offer, not a widow; hence he would not agree to a lesser test. Moral arguments were also raised, but declared nugatory on highest authority. Finally, the matter was discussed in committee (on 12 December 1583, at a secret Consistory, when Gregory XIII created nineteen new cardinals), and voted upon; the ayes had it. The Prince was told to prove before witnesses his virility *in virginem*, and those who would have to take part in the proceedings were to be exempted from censure.

It remained to lay down the ground rules. These were as follows:

(*1*) The girl would be "seen and examined by two physicians, two nurses, and two matrons, in the presence of Don Alfonso, Don Cesare, and the knight Urbani." (*2*) Don Alfonso would guard her strictly "until she was approached by the noble Prince." She would be locked up in the Belfiore castle, near Ferrara, in a room with barred windows and only one door.

(*3*) The jousts would take place in a single night.

(*4*) The Prince, in his efforts, would use "neither his fingers, nor any instrument or contrivance, nor anything that is not solely of his virtue."

(*5*) Those who had testified to the virginity would verify its destruction.

(*6*) Don Cesare would "see with his eyes and touch with his hands, as much as he wishes, the noble Prince's person."

These rules are not without loopholes, but they seemed satisfactory at the time. It remained to procure a girl; the widow of the architect Ligorio was approached and agreed to allow her eldest girl to participate in the test. All was set. Then disaster struck; the eldest daughter eloped with Count Scipione del Sacrato.

This threw everything into the melting-pot. Arguments arose about the rules—the Prince did not want to be restricted to a single night, and it was thought that one physician, one matron and one nurse would do. There were arguments that the virgin provided might be too cold, or not attractive enough. Then the Prince left Ferrara, and it was decided to try the test in another town. Moves were made to prevent the test from taking place. Great political moves and upheavals were made, or threatened. The bride came to hear of the rumors, but was somewhat incapacitated as far as her understanding went by ignorance of what "virility" and "impotence" meant; her confessor found it difficult to enlighten her. Finally an orphanage was found which was to provide the sacrificial victim, but again the fairness of the girl to be selected caused a rumpus. The Prince still objected to the time limit—he wanted to have three nights, not one. A choice was finally made; twenty-year-old Giulia was given a bath and prepared for bed. She was examined, and found satisfactory for the test by emissaries of both parties. The time limit too was settled; not one night, but twenty-four consecutive hours. Conditions were again discussed. "The noble Prince must go in alone, undressed, a night robe over his nightshirt." He was to allow the examiners to verify that "he had only his natural instruments, and he was properly developed, well-proportioned and complete." His Most Serene Highness's minister must see him with his eyes, and touch him with his hand, while he is at work." Venice was to be the new venue. When all was ready, Giulia started her period. This delayed matters.

On Sunday at four o'clock in the morning, the Prince presented himself for the test; his charger, he explained, galloped better at that time. Giulia "had been washed and made alluring from head to foot, and would have brought a block of marble to life." The Prince's person was examined, and it was verified that he had no instruments with him. Then he was packed off with the girl between sheets; he went to sleep and snored. In the morning he suddenly felt violent stomach pains, and was sick into the canal—he had eaten too many oysters. "I am just as I was," said Giulia, somewhat sadly.

The noble Prince kissed my lips, stroked my neck, ran his hands over my body, and felt my fig. Then he dropped off to sleep, with his face close to mine. He woke up a few minutes before seven o'clock, pressed me in his arms, lay on me without anything happening, and climbed off again. Then he started trembling so violently that he shook the bed, while the bells were ringing for mass. Then he started moaning and went out of the room.

When told that he would do in the evening what he could not do in the morning, she burst out laughing and said: "What do you want me to do? I didn't even feel his person. Don't talk to me about *that* any more." Great to'ing and fro'ing ensued, and greater arguments. The Prince pleaded illness. On Wednesday he finally returned to the fray. At five o'clock he lay down beside the girl; half an hour later he called the knight who supervised the game.

The noble Prince raised himself, leaning on his elbow, and my hand went between their two bellies till I could touch H. H.'s pubic region and clasp his solid person, which the girl had inside her body. It was evident that she had it inside, for she was groaning, but not with pain alone.

The Prince, proudly, said: "Now that you have touched and felt, and have informed yourself, leave me to my business." Strictly speaking, his business was of course over by this time; or was it? There were three canonical conditions for virility— *erectio, introductio, and emissio*; the last had not in actual fact been made subject to a test. A lengthy examination (verbal!) was made of Giulia; she seemed satisfied. So even in this "experiment" verbal accounts had the last word! The Holy Father was notified of the success achieved by the Prince. The marriage was arranged. It resulted in eight children. To these should be added the one begotten in his trial jousts.

IT WILL BE APPRECIATED that the ethical climate was different at that time. It is not likely that nowadays such a "trial" could take place within the jurisdiction of any Christian church. But looked at simply from the scientific point of view, the "experiment" seems rather amateurish; it established nothing. The Prince could easily have hidden an "instrument" on his person; the search was not very rigorous. He could have used his fingers; reliance was placed on the word of the girl, who might have been bribed. *Emissio* might not have taken place; there was no real evidence.

Sex is not easy to experiment with; this simple result seems the only one safely drawn from all this gallimaufry. Walter too seems to have been mistaken in his observations and experiments a good deal of the time. The "gay" girls of Victorian England were too much for him. Two American physicians, Masters and Johnson, have bravely taken up the cudgels, and have enlisted the help of modern electronics in their search, constructing artificial glass-tipped penis-like structures, lit internally and equipped with film cameras to take pictures of the interior of the female sex organs during simulated intercourse. Their volunteer subjects seem to have had a ball, but of course they were extremely unrepresentative of the general population which, even in these permissive days, might have objected to have scientific observers crowding round them to watch the details of their love-making.

On the whole, perhaps, the more acceptable method of investigation is the usual approach through the questioning, either in person or by inventory, of a more or less representative sample of the population, and results have certainly been fairly replicable in most respects. But there is one doubt which must remain in dealing with all the Kinsey and post-Kinsey works. Did these investigators ask the right questions? By this I do not mean to suggest that their method of investigating their subjects' sex life by suitably chosen questions could have been improved by choosing different wordings, or different questions; only marginal improvements are possible in this respect. My concern is rather with the fundamental questions which the investigators tried to answer through their research. They wanted to know what are fundamentally statistical facts, facts descriptive of the population. These range from such things as the proportion of boys and girls who have intercourse by the age of eighteen to the number of married women of forty who have indulged in extra-marital affairs. These questions seem very interesting at first sight, and scientifically important, but after wading through several close-printed volumes full of tables setting forth the results, most people experience, as I did, a certain amount of satiation. Enough is enough, we moan. Facts alone do not make a science—we also need theories, unification, laws.

There are of course some generalizations, usually relating to the method of "breaking down the population by age and sex." We are told (as if we did not know) that women are less prone to sexual adventures than are men; among unmarried students only one third of the men are virgins, but two thirds of the women. We are told that people participate more in sexual adventures as they grow older. And we are told some interesting differences between middle-class and working-class people. These, again, most people whose acquaintances are not confined to one class would have been able to guess. I am not carping. The Kinsey estimates are obviously more accurate than the kind of thing one might have guessed, even though the two are not all that far apart in most cases (this is possibly one reason why the Kinsey figures were so quickly and so widely accepted). I am only saying that these are grains of sociological sand, empty of psychological significance. Psychoanalysts have made the criticism that Kinsey concentrated on "sexual outlets" and orgasm in particular; they feel that he should have investigated the rather unsubstantial unconsciousness of his respondents. This is not a reasonable criticism. "Sexual outlets" are important, even if not all-important, and the study would not have gained anything by complicating the factual data-gathering by insubstantial investigations of the kind suggested. But there is a very relevant question which introduces psychological principles into this field in a rather more substantial form; this is the question: What kind of person does this, that and the other? Some students have intercourse and some do not— what are these different people like? Some women have extramarital affairs—what makes the difference? Some people always use the "missionary position" in sleeping together, others experiment—why? These are psychological problems, and unlike the psychoanalytic ones, they are in principle soluble. This chapter is concerned with questions of this kind, and will attempt to provide some semblance of an answer.

How would one approach questions of this kind? Baconians would proceed purely inductively, picking (say) virgin and non-virgin students and then collecting all sorts of information about them, in the hope that some might be relevant. This is not a good way of doing things, even though much research, so-called, is done this way. It seems more rational to state some theories which have some reasonable hope of being on the right lines, and then collect evidence which should support or disprove these theories. In this way only relevant facts have to be sifted. What kinds of theories can we appeal to?

Consider the discussion in the first chapter. It suggests that inherited physiological and anatomical differences predispose people to interact with their environment in certain specifiable ways, giving rise to extroverted or introverted, emotional or stable personality types. From the theories associated with these types, and from the facts known about their behavior in laboratory situations, we can make predictions about their likely behavior in relation to persons of the opposite sex, and about their attitudes to such persons, as well as to sexual practices, habits and rules. The reader may like to look back to the last chapter and try his own hand at the game; he can then check his success against the facts provided below.

Let us consider extroversion first of all. Extroverts are outgoing, dominant, changeable, sensation-seeking, relatively amoral. What sorts of behaviors would we expect of them in the sexual field? We may perhaps set down explicitly a number of expected behavior patterns which seem to follow from these characterizations, and from the experimental and theoretical background given in Chapter 1.

(*1*) Extroverts are more likely than introverts to have pre-marital intercourse.

(2) Extroverts are more likely than introverts to have extra-marital intercourse.

(3) Extroverts are more likely than introverts to have intercourse very early in life.

(4) Extroverts are more likely than introverts to have intercourse with several different people over a given period of time—say one year.

(5) Extroverts are more likely than introverts to have affairs with more than one person at the same time.

(6) Extroverts are more likely than introverts to have intercourse in more than one position.

(7) Extroverts are more likely than introverts to indulge in "perverted" practices, like fellatio and cunnilingus.*

(8) Extroverts are more likely than introverts to get along well with persons of the opposite sex.

(9) Extroverts are less likely than introverts to resort to homosexual practices.

(10) Extroverts are less likely than introverts to resort to masturbation in order to gain sexual satisfaction.

Readers may be able to think up several more predictions, but for the moment these will do; they give sufficient indication of the sort of prediction which our theory makes possible. All deal with extroversion, because this personality dimension seems the most relevant, but similar ones can be made with respect to neuroticism or emotionality.

---

*The term "perversion" is put in quotation marks because, although it is often applied to sexual practices of this kind, these are indulged in so commonly that the connotations of the term "perverse," *i.e.* that which is unnatural, abnormal, or wrong, would appear much too strong. Unfortunately there are no other terms which could be used instead to denote sexual practices which to many people smack of the forbidden, or which are regarded as degrading by them. All I can do here is to insist that the term is used in this book as simply a synonym for cunnilingus, fellatio, 69, and intercourse in positions other than the "missionary" one. I do not wish to brand these practices as abnormal or unnatural, or pass any kind of moral or aesthetic judgement.

I will not state these in equal detail. Obviously the strong aversive properties of fear and anxiety so easily mediated by the autonomic system are likely to keep the emotional or neurotic person at a safe distance from the (real or imaginary) dangers associated with intercourse. Instead of dealing with emotionality-stability, I will consider in some detail a third dimension of personality on which hitherto not very much research has been done: the dimension of *P* or *psychoticism*.

As is well known, there are two main varieties of mental illness—the neuroses and the psychoses. The former comprise disorders where emotional upset plays a dominant part—anxieties, depressions, obsessions, phobias, hysterical reactions, and many more. People scoring high on neuroticism questionnaires are similar in many ways to such neurotics, although not necessarily suffering from a clinical form of neurosis. The psychoses (which means essentially schizophrenia in its various forms and manic-depressive illness) tend to be more serious in their consequences. They are characterized by inappropriate emotions, emotional flatness, thought disorders and various other symptoms. There are certain personality traits common to all (or at least most) psychotics, and these can be discovered in "normal" people as well. Just as there is a continuum from the most normal, unemotional person to the severest neurotic, so there is a continuum from the most normal person to the psychotic. It is this continuum which we designate "psychoticism," and which can be measured by questionnaire, just as can neuroticism-emotionality, or extroversion.

What are people like who have high scores on this inventory? They are solitary and do not care for people. They are troublesome and do not fit in. They tend to be cruel and inhumane, and are characterized by lack of feeling and insensitivity. They are sensation-seeking, always on the lookout for an "arousal jag." They are hostile to others and aggressive. They like odd and unusual things, and have a disregard for danger. They like to make fools of other people, and to upset them. They are foolhardy. Mentally and physically, they tend to be slow to react; they do poorly on tests of reaction time and of vigilance. This is a brief description of some of the most characteristic traits of the high P scorer.

How would such a person behave sexually? He would tend to be impersonal in his relations and in his love-making, and might even be hostile to his partner. He would be readily aroused by sexual stimuli, and only too willing to indulge in the promised "arousal jag." He would care little for virginity, or the other social niceties of sexual conduct. He would indulge in masturbation and other vices and "perversions" quite readily. The thought of pre- and extra-marital sex would not worry him, and he would not be bothered by his conscience. He would delight in "blue" movies, pornographic novels, voyeurism and orgies, but his sexual attitudes would have a definitely pathological tinge. Walter, in addition to his extroversion, obviously had a lot of P in him—it seems regrettable that we cannot recall him and administer a personality inventory to him!

NOW FOR THE FACTS. Before turning to my own studies, mention must be made of a large-scale investigation done with German university students by the late Hans Giese and Günter Schmidt, who were working at the *Institut für Sexualforschung* in Hamburg. Some six thousand students were questioned by these workers, through questionnaires, but although most of these were unmarried, some were not; this and other factors reduce the numbers for various comparisons. The authors also used a very short personality inventory, which they validated by correlating it against one of my own; they are satisfied that it measures more or less the same extroversion and emotionality (E and N) variables as my questionnaires do. It should be noted, however, that with a longer, and hence more reliable, inventory the observed differences and correlations would undoubtedly have been much greater; inventories only containing four questions, like the authors' E scale, are inevitably unreliable. The theories on which they base their reasons for inclusion of these questionnaires are those stated in the first chapter of this book. Their deductions are very similar to those given above. In presenting their data, they subdivide their men and women groups into three: low N scorers, medium N scorers and high N scorers ($N1$, $N2$ and $N3$), or low, medium and high extroversion rating ($E1$, $E2$ and $E3$). Percentage "Yes" answers for each question are then given against each of these groups. What did Giese and Schmidt find?

As far as emotionality (N) is concerned, not very much. High N scorers masturbate more, and earlier, than medium and low N scorers; that is about the only significant finding as far as their sex life is concerned. High N scorers wish significantly more for coitus, and consider their libido strong; shades of Freud! Females who have had intercourse have progressively less capacity for orgasm the higher their N scores; the more neurotic, the less orgasm. Males who are high on N have more spontaneous erections and more pollutions than males who have lower scores. Women high on N have trouble with their menstrual cycles; they tend to be irregular and menstruation tends to be painful. All very much as expected, but not terribly informative—or perhaps emotional stability has less to do with sexual behavior than the psychoanalysts think. We will come back to this point after considering our own data.

The significant data concerning extroversion are so numerous that I have concentrated them into a table (Table 1). This shows that, as expected, extroverts masturbate less; they start petting earlier and do so with more enthusiasm at their present age. Extroverts start having coitus earlier, and they are more likely to have had experience of coitus at the present time than introverts. The median frequency of coitus is twice as high for extroverts as for introverts, and they have a much larger number of different coital partners. Extroverted males indulge in longer pre-coital sex play than introverted males; for women there is no such tendency, but this is hardly surprising because it is men who tend to determine these things in our society (and perhaps in others as well!). Cunnilingus and fellatio are more frequent among extroverts than among introverts; so is the assumption of a large number

	MEN			WOMEN		
	*E*1	*E*2	*E*3	*E*1	*E*2	*E*3
1. Masturbation at present:	86%	80%	72%	47%	43%	39%
2. Petting at 17:	16%	28%	40%	15%	19%	24%
at 19:	31%	48%	56%	30%	44%	47%
at present age:	57%	72%	78%	62%	71%	76%
3. Coitus at 17:	5%	13%	21%	4%	4%	8%
at 19:	15%	31%	45%	12%	20%	29%
at present age:	47%	70%	77%	42%	57%	71%
4. Median frequency of coitus per month (sexually active students only):	3.0	3.7	5.5	3.1	4.5	7.5
5. Number of coitus partners in last 12 months (unmarried students only): 1	75%	64%	46%	72%	77%	60%
2—3	18%	25%	30%	25%	17%	23%
4+	7%	12%	25%	4%	6%	17%
6. Long pre-coital sex play:	21%	25%	28%	21%	16%	18%
7. Cunnilingus:	52%	62%	64%	58%	69%	69%
8. Fellatio:	53%	60%	69%	53%	59%	61%
9. More than 3 different coital positions:	10%	16%	26%	12%	18%	13%
10. Experience of orgasm— nearly always:	—	—	—	17%	32%	29%

Table 1. Sexual behavior of students with low [E1] medium [E2] and high [E3] extroversion rating

of different coital positions. (Again women do not seem to bear this out, probably for the reason indicated above.*) Last, experience of orgasm in women is more frequent in extroverts than in introverts. These results are all very much in line with what was predicted, and they tend to bear out the results of our laboratory experiments on alternation behavior, conditioning, sensory thresholds, etc. Clearly extroversion determines to a considerable extent the way human beings behave in the sexual situation, the age at which they initiate sexual behavior, the types of behavior they indulge in, and the satisfaction (orgasm) they get out of it.

THE STUDIES I myself carried out were done on smaller numbers, but they went into much greater detail. Four hundred male and 400 female university students, all unmarried and under twenty-five years of age, constituted the sample; most were in fact nineteen or twenty years of age, with only a few older ones. These were given personality questionnaires to fill in, as well as an inventory of sexual practices and one of sexual attitudes.* Each student was also given a stamped, addressed envelope for returning the filled-in forms to the Maudsley Hospital. The study aroused considerable interest in the universities and colleges where it was conducted. The experiment was introduced to groups of students by means of a short talk emphasizing the scientific nature of the study, and the complete guarantee of anonymity for each respondent. We must, later on, look at such evidence as there may be concerning the randomness of the sample,

---

*One would deduce from this that women who indulged in cunnilingus, fellatio and different coital positions would be less likely than men actually to *like* these sexual practices. This has been shown to be so. Over ninety-five per cent of men indulging liked what they were doing, but less than fifty per cent of women.

*Many of the questions in this inventory were adapted from a much larger one published by F. C. Thorne; other writers suggested other questions; a number of new questions were added.

and the veracity of the respondents. Here let us suspend our doubts until we come to consider these two points. The actual questionnaires used are reproduced below; first the sexual attitudes inventory, which in point of fact came first, and then the sexual practices inventory. The personality inventory is not given here, but the descriptions given of the respective personality types scoring high and low on P, E and N will be sufficient to enable the reader to follow the discussion.

Before going on to the next part of the text, readers may like to do two things. They may first of all like to look at the items in the sexual attitudes questionnaire and ask themselves how these would group themselves if we put together items answered in the same direction by many people. And they might ask themselves how these groups of items would be answered by high and low scorers respectively on our various personality dimensions. Our analysis was carried out in an attempt to give a scientific answer to these questions. It may be of some interest to readers to see how closely they can anticipate the correct quantitative answer. Note that the version of the inventories given is the male one; the female version was suitably changed in respect of those questions requiring rewording. Thus Question 76, "I get very excited when touching a woman's breast" becomes: "I get very excited when men touch my breasts." Similar changes were made in the sexual practices questionnaire.

Following each of the questions in the Inventory of Attitudes to Sex was a "Yes," a "?" and a "No." Instructions were to underline the correct answer, *i.e.* that which applied to the person answering. It was made clear in the instructions that there were no right or wrong answers in any absolute sense. The "?" answer was only to be used if the person filling in the inventory just could not decide. Respondents filled in their sex, age and married/single status; only those who were single were included in the survey. As there are very marked differences between men and women, the percentage "Yes" answers given by the two sexes have been included in the inventory as here printed. Only the first ninety-four questions lend themselves to this treatment, and no percentages are given for the last four questions; they will be discussed separately. It should be noted, however, that whereas two of these questions refer to impotence and ejaculatio praecox for the men, the corresponding questions refer to frigidity and frequency of orgasm for the women.

INVENTORY OF ATTITUDES TO SEX		
	Percentage "YES" Answers	
	Male:	Female:
1. The opposite sex will respect you more if you are not too familiar with them.	38	59
2. Sex without love ("impersonal sex") is highly unsatisfactory.	49	80
3. Conditions have to be just right to get me excited sexually.	21	43
4. All in all I am satisfied with my sex life.	40	60
5. Virginity is a girl's most valuable possession.	16	24
6. I think only rarely about sex.	4	13
7. Sometimes it has been a problem to control my sex feelings.	46	44
8. Masturbation is unhealthy.	7	21
9. If I loved a person I could do anything with them.	55	46
10. I get pleasant feelings from touching my sexual parts.	61	37
11. I have been deprived sexually.	25	8
12. It is disgusting to see animals having sex relations in the street.	5	6
13. I do not need to respect a woman, or love her, in order to enjoy petting and/or intercourse with her.	43	12
14. It is all right for children to see their parents naked.	64	74
15. I am rather sexually unattractive.	10	5
16. Frankly, I prefer people of my own sex.	3	2

	Percentage "YES" Answers	
	Male:	Female:
17. Sex contacts have never been a problem to me.	35	41
18. It is disturbing to see necking in public.	12	23
19. Sexual feelings are sometimes unpleasant to me.	11	16
20. Something is lacking in my sex life.	50	26
21. My sex behavior has never caused me any trouble.	43	36
22. My love life has been disappointing.	39	23
23. I never had many dates.	36	26
24. I consciously try to keep sex thoughts out of my mind.	2	7
25. I have felt guilty about sex experiences.	29	41
26. It wouldn't bother me if the person I married were not a virgin.	˙68	73
27. I had some bad sex experiences when I was young.	15	13
28. Perverted thoughts have sometimes bothered me.	28	18
29. At times I have been afraid of myself for what I might do sexually.	19	26
30. I have had conflicts about my sex feelings towards a person of my own sex.	16	9
31. I have many friends of the opposite sex.	71	80
32. I have strong sex feelings but when I get a chance I can't seem to express myself.	23	12
33. It doesn't take much to get me excited sexually.	66	31
34. My parents' influence has inhibited me sexually.	30	25
35. Thoughts about sex disturb me more than they should.	12	7
36. People of my own sex frequently attract me.	4	4
37. There are some things I wouldn't want to do with anyone.	53	47
38. Children should be taught about sex.	94	97
39. I could get sexually excited at any time of the day or night.	88	69
40. I understand homosexuals.	44	35

	Percentage "YES" Answers Male:	Female:
41. I think about sex almost every day.	84	52
42. One should not experiment with sex before marriage.	7	21
43. I get excited sexually very easily.	60	27
44. The thought of a sex orgy is disgusting to me.	18	65
45. It is better not to have sex relations until you are married.	6	31
46. I find the thought of a colored sex partner particularly exciting.	24	3
47. I like to look at sexy pictures.	61	8
48. My conscience bothers me too much.	18	26
49. My religious beliefs are against sex.	7	13
50. Sometimes sexual feelings overpower me.	32	27
51. I feel nervous with the opposite sex.	25	15
52. Sex thoughts drive me almost crazy.	6	2
53. When I get excited I can think of nothing else but satisfaction.	24	15
54. I feel at ease with people of the opposite sex.	66	80
55. I don't like to be kissed.	2	3
56. It is hard to talk with people of the opposite sex.	12	6
57. I didn't learn the facts of life until I was quite old.	26	23
58. I feel more comfortable when I am with my own sex.	24	16
59. I enjoy petting.	92	78
60. I worry a lot about sex.	22	13
61. The Pill should be universally available.	84	65
62. Seeing a person nude doesn't interest me.	11	43
63. Sometimes thinking about sex makes me very nervous.	16	20
64. Women who get raped are often partly responsible themselves.	57	53
65. Perverted thoughts have sometimes bothered me.	26	18

	Percentage "YES" Answers	
	Male:	Female:
66. I am embarrassed to talk about sex.	9	8
67. Young people should learn about sex through their own experience.	34	23
68. Sometimes the woman should be sexually aggressive.	88	64
69. Sex jokes disgust me.	4	22
70. I believe in taking my pleasures where I find them.	44	7
71. A person should learn about sex gradually by experimenting with it.	52	42
72. Young people should be allowed out at night without being too closely checked.	68	54
73. Did you ever feel like humiliating your sex partner?	20	12
74. I would particularly protect my children from contacts with sex.	5	9
75. Self-relief is not dangerous so long as it is done in a healthy way.	74	56
76. I get very excited when touching a woman's breasts.	57	45
77. I have been involved with more than one sex affair at the same time.	32	14
78. Homosexuality is normal for some people.	74	70
79. It is all right to seduce a person who is old enough to know what they are doing.	73	35
80. Do you ever feel hostile to your sex partner?	37	40
81. I like to look at pictures of nudes.	63	10
82. Buttocks excite me.	42	8
83. If you had the chance to see people making love, without being seen, would you take it?	41	12
84. Pornographic writings should be freely allowed to be published.	59	32
85. Prostitution should be legally permitted.	62	32
86. Decisions about abortion should be the concern of no one but the woman concerned.	52	47

	Percentage "YES" Answers	
	Male:	Female:
87. There are too many immoral plays on television.	6	13
88. The dual standard of morality is natural, and should be continued.	32	26
89. We should do away with marriage entirely.	9	2
90. Men marry to have intercourse; women have intercourse for the sake of marriage.	7	3
91. There should be no censorship, on sexual grounds, of plays and films.	63	39

Please underline the correct answer

92. If you were invited to see a "blue" film, would you:
   (a) Accept   (b) Refuse   80   37
93. If you were offered a highly pornographic book, would you:
   (a) Accept it   (b) Reject it   76   40
94. If you were invited to take part in an orgy, would you:
   (a) Take part   (b) Refuse 61   4
95. Given availability of a partner, would you prefer to have intercourse:

(a) Never   (d) Twice a week
(b) Once a month   (e) 3-5 times a week
(c) Once a week   (f) Every day
                     (g) More than once a day
96. Have you ever suffered from impotence:

(a) Never   (d) Often
(b) Once or twice   (e) More often than not
(c) Several times   (f) Always
97. Have you ever suffered from ejaculatio praecox (premature ejaculation)

(a) Very often   (d) Not very often
(b) Often   (e) Hardly ever
(c) Middling   (f) Never
98. At what age did you have your first intercourse . . .

Overwhelmingly outstanding among items giving marked differences between the sexes are items relating to pornography (47, 81, 84, 91, 92, 93); orgies (44, 94); voyeurism (83, 62), and prostitution (85), closely followed by impersonal sex (2, 13). Sexual excitement is close behind (33, 41, 43, 46, 82, 3, 39). In all this of course males have higher rates of endorsement than females. Pre-marital sex is also favored more by the males (45, 70, 79, 42), as is promiscuity (77). But contentment in their sex life is more marked among women (4, 20, 11, 22), perhaps unexpectedly. Masturbation is more a male pastime (10, 8), and men are also less prudish in general (18, 68, 69, 59), and feel less guilt (25). Most of these differences are not unexpected, although one should not over-interpret them; some of the replies may represent little but widely held views unthinkingly endorsed. The only unexpected feature of the study is the apparent satisfaction of the women with their sex lives. It used to be thought that the "permissive" society favored men, as did the Victorian era. Possibly the clue lies in the greater sex drive apparent in the men, and in difficulties which this strong drive must give rise to when confronted with the stark reality that over half the women in our sample were still virgins, and apparently intent on holding on to this status. In this sellers' market, women clearly have the upper hand, and may enjoy this position. Again, the nature of our sample may be responsible for a finding which is not likely to be duplicated for older men and women. There is an interesting finding in Schofield's book in which he showed that female adolescents who had had intercourse were not very attractive on the whole, while male adolescents who had had intercourse were. The explanation presumably is again in terms of the sellers' market—men must be attractive to get a girl, but a girl who is attractive does not need to exchange her virginity for male attention. Specific research devoted to a clarification of these relations might be of considerable interest.

INVENTORY OF SEXUAL BEHAVIOR

Here are brief descriptions of sexual behavior patterns which people indulge in.

Indicate by putting a cross (x) in Column 1 whether you have ever indulged in this type of behavior.

(Note: Manual=by hand; oral=by mouth)

	Column 1 Males: Females:	
1. One minute continuous lip kissing	95%	92%
2. Manual manipulation of male genitals, over clothes, by female	71%	65%
3. Kissing nipples of female breasts	81%	68%
4. Oral manipulation of female genitals	34%	40%
5. Sexual intercourse, face to face	69%	45%
6. Manual manipulation of female breasts, over clothes	92%	80%
7. Oral manipulation of male genitals, by female	33%	35%
8. Manual manipulation of male genitals to ejaculation, by female	53%	55%
9. Manual manipulation of female breasts, under clothes	89%	73%
10. Manual manipulation of male genitals, under clothes, by female	69%	69%
11. Sexual intercourse, man behind woman	21%	22%
12. Manual manipulation of female genitals, over clothes	75%	70%
13. Manual manipulation of female genitals to massive secretions	63%	46%
14. Mutual oral manipulation of genitals to mutual orgasm	8%	6%
15. Manual manipulation of female genitals, under clothes	79%	67%
16. Mutual manual manipulation of genitals	69%	64%
17. Oral manipulation of male genitals to ejaculation, by female	18%	15%
18. Mutual manual manipulation of genitals to mutual orgasm	42%	32%
19. Mutual oral-genital manipulation	17%	21%

Percentages above are of male and female students, aged 19 and 20 combined, answering "Yes."

THE INVENTORY of sexual practices gave results which were much simpler than those furnished by the longer questionnaire, and consequently they may with advantage be discussed first.

When analyzed statistically, the items grouped themselves clearly into three groups or factors: (*1*) a petting factor, including such items as kissing and fondling breasts; (*2*) an intercourse factor, including manual manipulation of the partner's sexual parts; and (*3*) a "perversion" factor (for want of a better term), including the various items concerned with fellatio, cunnilingus and intercourse in unusual positions. These factors were not independent, but sequential; in other words, our subjects graduated from petting to intercourse, from intercourse to "perversion." The higher the age, the farther had they advanced on this road, but this proved only true on the average. In fact age did not play all that important a part, accounting for not more than at most 10 per cent of all the variability in conduct encountered. As age is not correlated with P, E or N among students, we may dismiss this obvious but uninteresting finding from our further analysis.

Extroversion was positively correlated with all the items, but particularly those making up factors 1 and 2. In other words, extroverts take a prominent part in kissing and petting, and in normal intercourse, but as a whole they are not anything like so prominent with respect to the more advanced or "perverted" practices. These are more likely to be attempted by high P scorers, who are less prominent in factor 1 type activities; presumably to them kissing and cuddling is pretty tame stuff. High N scorers tend to be characterized by lack of activity in any of the factors—they pet less, have intercourse less, and indulge in fewer "perversions." Overall, these correlations are higher for men than for women, presumably for the same reason as in the Giese and Schmidt research— men tend to take the more active line in love play and lovemaking, and therefore their personality features determine more closely just what is going to take place. These results are very much in line with our expectations, and with the results of the German student inquiry.

Below are given the actual percentages of 18-year-old students indulging in various sex practices; also given are similar percentages from the well-known study carried out by Michael Schofield and reported in his *The Sexual Behaviour of Young People.* This study of boys and girls still at school is of interest because Schofield was able to select and interview a sample of adolescents which is almost unsurpassed as far as random selection is concerned; from the sampling point of view his excellent work can hardly be criticized. Our own sampling of course leaves much to be desired; it is of interest therefore to see to what extent the two sets of figures are similar. If for adolescents of equal age (Table 2 contains figures only for his oldest group, the 18-year-olds, and for my youngest group, also 18-year-olds) the proportions should turn out to be similar, then one could argue that our less reliable method of sampling had not in fact resulted in too distorted a picture of actual sexual practices. No complete identity could of course be expected, for various reasons. Schofield's study was carried out by interview, ours by questionnaire. Schofield's subjects were schoolchildren, ours were university students. The actual questions asked were not identical, and neither was the setting. Nevertheless, any large discrepancies would give one to think.

In fact, the figures are remarkably close and the observed differences are not unexpected. Thus the male students are somewhat more active than the schoolboys; this may be a function of living apart from their families, having greater opportunities for staying out late, etc. Girl students are just slightly below the level of sexual activity of the schoolgirls; the difference may not be significant (it is very slight, and on such items as "intercourse" the figures are almost identical), or it may be due to selection—university girls are still much more

	Boys:	Students:	Girls:	Students:
1. Kissing:	93%	96%	96%	80%
2. Breast Manipulation:				
Over clothes:	80%	96%	80%	69%
Under clothes:	70%	91%	62%	57%
3. Manual genital stimulation:				
Active:	56%	72%	30%	30%
Passive:	44%	64%	45%	39%
4. Intercourse:	35%	55%	18%	19%

Percentage of 18-year-old boys and girls in Schofield sample, and 18-year-old students in present sample, who indulged in four main tupes of sexual activity.

Table 2

highly selected than are university men, and such selection is largely on the basis of past examination success, which is known to be correlated with introversion. However that may be, the figures do not suggest that our method of selection has resulted in a badly biased sample. If the Schofield sample and method of information extraction are as good as critical comment agrees they are, then our own results deserve similar acceptance, being in substantial agreement with his.

IT IS INTERESTING TO CONSIDER the evidence from these two studies in relation to the prevailing notions of our society as "permissive." Of the girls, less than one in five had lost her virginity by the age of nineteen (i.e. while still eighteen); this does not sound excessively permissive. There is little doubt that a similar study done in Victorian times would have resulted in a much lower figure for virgins; Walter estimates that among working-class and servant girls almost none would have retained their virginity by that age. He was of course what might be called an interested party, but one also feels that he probably knew what he was talking about; evidence from more academic quarters tends on the whole to support him. For boys our figures are higher; but even there Schofield's estimate is only one in three having had experience of sexual intercourse, and here his figures are obviously more relevant than the somewhat higher ones of my own study, his being derived from a random sample, mine from students only. Comparing these figures with those published by Kinsey and others over the years does not suggest any very marked change in habits. The proportions of sexually experienced boys and girls at these ages has not increased as it should have done if the notion of the "permissive society" had any real validity. "When all is said and done, more is said than done!"—this may be the slogan of the permissive society.

What happens after the age of eighteen? Figure 5 shows the incidence of sexual intercourse for girls (unmarried) at ages from fourteen to twenty-one, the figures for ages up to eighteen are taken from Schofield, those above from our own study. It will be seen that the curve up to nineteen shows a beautiful, regular progression; after nineteen it falls off. The broken line continues the formula of the curve up to twenty-one. The reason why the actual figures are so far below the imaginary ones is, of course, due to the fact that we have been concerned only with unmarried university students. If we are concerned with the sexual experience of all women, then to these should have been added all the married ones, who of course would in the overwhelming majority of cases have experienced intercourse. Up to eighteen or nineteen this difference does not matter as only few girls get married that early; after nineteen it begins to be very important. But clearly among unmarried university students, it is not until they are past twenty that even half experience sexual intercourse; up to that time over half are still virgins. For men the curve is similar, but of course at a higher level. For 19-year-olds the figure for sexual experience is 64 per cent, for 20-year-olds it is 73 per cent, and by twenty-two it has gone up to 86 per cent. It seems doubtful if figures of this kind really deserve to be called alarming, and it seems even more doubtful if they were ever much lower than this—even in Queen Victoria's golden days! Walter, I am sure, would have been shocked at this namby-pambyism of the modern generation; by the time he was eighteen he was well into double figures, and going strong.

The items in the table of sexual attitudes (Table 3) group themselves quite reasonably into fifteen groups, clusters, or factors, when the items are intercorrelated and factor analyzed. Each factor will be described briefly by listing the main items which characterize it. The names given to these clusters or factors are, to be sure, quite arbitrary; their main function is to give a general idea of the content of the factor, and to enable readers to recall the meaning associated with a factor when we go on to discuss the correlations of these factors with the personality scores. Other names may suggest themselves, and may be substituted if the reader prefers.

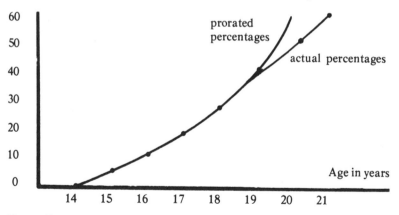

Figure 5

On the sex attitudes inventory, in spite of the marked differences in endorsement of many items, men and women tend to group together the same items into factors which are meaningful and recognizable. There are about a dozen of these factors. We will look first at the factors themselves, then go on to discuss the tendency of different personality types to endorse or reject the questions making up each of these factors. The first factor, *sexual satisfaction*, contains items such as: "I am satisfied with my sex life"; "I have not been deprived sexually"; "Nothing is lacking in my sex life"; "My love life has not been disappointing"; and "I don't worry about sex." There is only one item on which men and women do not agree: men who are satisfied sexually agree that we should do away with marriage, but women don't!

Our second factor is called *sexual excitement.* Items characteristic of this factor are: "It doesn't take much to get me excited sexually"; "Sometimes sexual feelings overpower me"; "I get excited sexually very easily"; "I get very excited when touching a woman's breasts"; "When I get excited I can think of nothing else but satisfaction." For such people "conditions don't have to be just right to get me excited sexually," and they don't "think only rarely about sex." It is interesting that the item: "I find the thought of a colored sex partner particularly exciting" has a strong connection with this factor only for women; for men there is none.

Sexual nervousness is the third main factor. This contains items like: "I don't have many friends of the opposite sex"; "I feel nervous with the opposite sex"; "I don't feel at ease with people of the opposite sex"; "I feel more comfortable when I am with my own sex." There is no reason to assume any tinge of homosexuality in this factor; we will encounter a proper homosexuality factor later on. For the moment, let us rather consider factor 4, which is *sexual curiosity.* Items here are: "I like to look at sexy pictures"; "Sex jokes don't disgust me"; "I like to look at pictures of nudes"; "I would take a chance of seeing people make love"; "I would agree to see a 'blue' film"; "I would read a highly pornographic book." These questions are all concerned with a liking for pornography and voyeurism, and a desire to have vicarious sex experiences.

Factor 5 relates to *pre-marital sex* (or virginity, if we look at the opposite side of the coin). Items here are: "Virginity is not a girl's most valuable possession"; "It wouldn't bother me if the person I married were not a virgin"; "One should experiment with sex before marriage"; "It is better to have sexual relations before you are married"; "I have had intercourse"; "The Pill should be universally available"; "It is all right to seduce a person who is old enough to know what they are doing"; "Women should be sexually aggressive."

Factor 6 might be called *repression*, (but not necessarily with the Freudian overtones this term has acquired). Characteristic items here are: "Children should not be taught about sex"; "I would particularly protect my children from contact with sex"; "I think only rarely about sex"; "Masturbation is unhealthy"; "I don't think about sex almost every day"; "My religious beliefs are against sex"; "Self-relief is dangerous, even when done in a healthy way"; "Men marry to have intercourse, women have intercourse for the sake of marriage"; "I have strong sex feelings, but when I get a chance I can't seem to express myself." This factor has an almost Victorian flavor; perhaps it ought to be called the Victorian factor.

The suggested name for factor 7 is *prudishness*. Items defining this factor are: "I don't like to be kissed"; "I don't enjoy petting"; "The thought of a sex orgy is disgusting to me"; "Sex jokes disgust me"; "It is disturbing to see necking in public"; "Sexual feelings are sometimes unpleasant to me": "I consciously try to keep sex thoughts out of my mind."

Factor 8 is a rather small one, with only three items prominently associated with it; it may be called *sexual experimentation*. These items are: "Young people should learn about sex through their own experience"; "A person should learn about sex gradually by experimenting with it"; and "Young people should be allowed out at night without being too closely checked."

Homosexuality forms the theme of factor 9. Items defining it are: "Homosexuality is normal for some people"; "I understand homosexuals"; "People of my own sex frequently attract me"; "I have had conflicts about my sex feelings towards a person of my own sex"; "I am embarrassed to talk about sex." No direct questions about homosexual experiences were put in the inventory as this might have been highly embarrassing to some respondents at least; it seems a pity that such consideration made it impossible to gather evidence on the frequency of homosexual activities.

Factor 10 is properly called one of *censorship*. Items connected with it are: "There should be censorship on sexual grounds of plays and films"; "There are too many immoral plays on television"; "Prostitution should not be legally permitted"; "Pornographic writings should not be freely allowed to be published"; "Young people should not be allowed out at night without close supervision"; "The Pill should not be universally available"; "It is disgusting to see animals having sex relations in the street." (No doubt this will be banned in due course.).

A very different picture is presented by factor 11, *promiscuity*. Items defining this factor are: "Sex without love ('impersonal sex') is not highly unsatisfactory"; "I do not need to respect a woman/man, or love her/him, in order to enjoy petting and/or intercourse with her/him"; "The thought of a sex orgy is not disgusting to me"; "I believe in taking my pleasures where I find them"; "I have been involved in more than one sex affair at the same time"; "I would see a 'blue' film, read a pornographic book or take part in a sex orgy." This is a fairly obvious and well-known constellation of attitudes, leaving little to the imagination.

Factor 12 has some pathological overtones; it might be called *sexual hostility*. There are only two items closely connected with this factor: "I have felt like humiliating my sex partner"; and "I have felt hostile to my sex partner."

Also somewhat pathological is factor 13, which may be called one of *guilt*. Items defining it are: "I have felt guilty about sex experiences"; "At times I have been afraid of myself for what I might do sexually"; "My conscience bothers me too much"; "Sometimes sexual feelings overpower me"; "Sex thoughts drive me almost crazy"; "I worry a lot about sex"; "Sometimes thinking about sex makes me very nervous"; "Perverted thoughts have sometimes bothered me"; "Sometimes it has been a problem to control my sex feelings." It should be noted that none of the respondents answered the question: "Have perverted thoughts sometimes bothered you?" with the classic phrase: "No, I enjoy them"; this must indicate the seriousness with which the inventory was filled in.

The final factor is 14, which may be called *inhibition*. Items relating to this are: "My parents' influence has inhibited me sexually"; "I didn't learn the facts of life until I was quite old"; "My sex behavior has caused me some trouble"; "Sex contacts have been a problem to me"; "Virginity is a girl's most valuable possession."

THESE, THEN, are the 14 factors which emerge from a statistical analysis of the interrelations between the items of our inventory. Note that the constellations of items which make up these factors are quite objective, and are entirely determined by the original data themselves. No human hand, one might say, has soiled the data from the time they were recorded on the inventories; they were transferred to punched card form, then sent to the computer, and finally the printed output of the Promax program landed on my desk, pristine and virginal. The interpretation and naming are of course to some extent subjective, as already pointed out; but the reader will be able to check for himself the reasonableness or otherwise of both.

We must now turn to the main question which concerns us here: to what extent are these factors determined by the personality of the respondents? Table 3 sets out the main findings; + and — signs refer to the direction of the relation between the factor and personality trait P, E or N, and the number of + or — signs refers to the strength of the relation.

Factor	P:	E:	N:
1. Satisfaction	—	+	— — —
2. Excitement	+	—	+ +
3. Nervousness	o	— — —	+ +
4. Curiosity	+ +	o	+
5. Pre-marital sex	+ +	+	o
6. Repression	—	o	o
7. Prudishness	+	— —	+
8. Experimentation	+	+	o
9. Homosexuality	+	o	+
10. Censorship	—	—	o
11. Promiscuity	+ + +	+ +	o
12. Hostility	+ + +	o	+ + +
13. Guilt	o	o	+ + +
14. Inhibition	+	o	+ + +

Relation between personality types *P, E* and *N*, and Sexual Attitude Factors. + and — signs indicate positive or negative relations. o indicates absence of any relation.

Table 3

Thus high *N* scorers (potential neurotics) have very little satisfaction in their sex lives, while high *E* scorers (extroverts) have a lot. An "*O*" means that there is no relation between the factor and the personality trait. This Table is a very rough-and-ready guide, but it will serve to set out the main findings from our survey.

Let us first of all consider the typical extrovert. He has no difficulties in making contact with members of the opposite sex, and is not nervous in his dealings with them. He is fairly promiscuous, and derives considerable satisfaction from his sexual life. He is not bothered by inhibitions, or repressions, takes an open interest in sexual matters, and opposes censorship of "pornographic" material. He shows no trace of homosexual leanings, believes that children should learn about sex by experience, and lacks all feelings of guilt. He is not prudish, and seems slightly "over-sexed," but not unhealthily so.

By comparison, the introvert seems to have made an equally healthy adjustment, but at a somewhat lower level of sexual arousal. He is slightly "under-sexed," but again not unhealthily so. He too fails to show any repressions or inhibitions, but he does have difficulties in approaching and getting on with members of the opposite sex; this probably accounts for his slight lack of satisfaction. He is somewhat prudish, does not approve of promiscuity, or of sexual experimentation and pre-marital sex. He is slightly in favor of sexual censorship.

Both the extroverted and the introverted personalities seem to have made a perfectly good and valid adjustment to sex; the former espousing the "permissive," sex-is-fun, libertine position, the latter the sex-is-sacred, restrictive, Puritan position. These terms of course somewhat exaggerate the positions taken, but they may serve to make them more recognizable. Few of our students, to be sure, take these positions to extremes. What we find are tendencies which for the purpose of description are somewhat purified and therefore seem more black-and-white than in ordinary life they would be found to be. It should also be noted that the descriptions given only apply to the particular age-group which we have studied. It seems quite possible that the introverted adjustment pattern is slightly less satisfactory for young students, but might be more satisfactory for middle-aged, married bliss; it is then that the philandering extroverts might show less satisfaction. Studies of older groups would throw much light on this problem.

If both extroverts and introverts have made acceptable and non-pathological adjustments to the problems of adolescent sex, how about the high N scorers, i.e. the potential neurotics? Textbooks are full of the sexual maladjustments of neurotics; in our perfectly non-pathological sample, do high N scorers behave rather like clinical neurotics? Theory would suggest that they should, and the figures seem to bear this out.

Such a person combines strong sexual excitement with equally strong nervousness when in contact with the opposite sex. His sexual curiosity is strong, but his satisfaction is absolutely minimal. He is prudish, full of feelings of hostility and guilt, and beset by inhibitions. Homosexual feelings trouble him a good bit. He is not in favor of sexual experimentation, pre-marital sex, or pornography, although he does not oppose these actively. One might say that high N scorers have strong approach and also strong avoidance tendencies towards the other sex. This inevitably produces a conflict which is quite apparent in the questionnaire entries, and comes out even more strongly in actual clinical cases of neurosis. In stable persons, *i.e.* persons scoring low on N, both the approach and the avoidance tendencies are considerably weaker, and consequently no great conflict develops. It is interesting to speculate on what might happen when high N scores are combined with high extroversion or introversion scores. When allied with the former, one might predict that the approach tendencies would win out; when allied with the latter, the avoidance tendencies. Clinical observation seems to bear out this observation. Dysthymic patients, suffering from anxiety, often require treatment for sexual difficulties; while psychopaths (high N, high E) often get into trouble for sexual offences of a minor nature—V.D. consequent upon promiscuous intercourse, illegitimate pregnancies, bigamy, and seduction. Major sex crimes seem to need an admixture of P; there is some suggestive evidence that sex criminals are characterized by extremely high P scores.

High P scorers are the most sexually outgoing group of all, but not in the non-pathological, socially more or less acceptable way of the extroverts. They combine an extreme degree of promiscuity with an extreme degree of hostility to their sex partners. Their sexual curiosity is unbounded, as is their appetite for pre-marital sex. They are in favor of gaining sexual knowledge through experimentation. Yet they are somewhat prudish, show some inhibitions, and tend towards homosexuality. On the whole, they are not satisfied with their sex lives; in this they differ considerably from the extroverts. The latter are happy-go-lucky libertines who take what comes along, while the high P scorers seem pathologically drawn towards sexual behavior which in the end does not satisfy them. They do not share the neurotic's guilt, and do not show any repression. Nor do they show the neurotic's nervousness towards members of the opposite sex. Looking through the inventories of high P scorers, one almost feels that they are addicted to sex as if to a drug, and that this addiction and dependence creates more difficulties for them than it solves. Walter seems to fall into this pattern perfectly. The descriptive pattern is clear enough; it remains to find out why high P scorers react in this way. Unfortunately the data do not suggest any obvious theory. At this stage of research one can only pose the problem.

IN LOOKING AT our three personality factors, it must of course be borne in mind that any particular person has a position on all three dimensions. He is not just an introvert or an extrovert, but combines his position on this continuum with a high or low degree of neuroticism, and a high or low degree of psychoticism—or, of course, an intermediate degree of one or both. All possible combinations occur, and the great majority will not be extreme on any one dimension—although showing tendencies one way or the other. Furthermore, in addition to the personality factors discussed, a person's sexual adjustment will naturally be governed by all sorts of additional factors—his upbringing, his good looks (or otherwise), the amount of money at his disposal (it is said that some women find a man's car the most sexually attractive thing about him), his intelligence, or lack of same, and even the simple level of testosterone secretion which heredity has endowed him with. Personality is only one factor affecting sexual adjustment, attitudes and behavior. Our analysis has been restricted to this factor, but it is not suggested that other factors are not important, or may more than balance a person's *P*, *E* or *N*. Yet our data certainly do show that these personality factors are important and relevant; moreover, they play their part in a predictable pattern. This pattern might change with increasing age; and it might be different in different social groups, or in different cultures. Only research devoted to the clarification of these issues can tell us to what extent our findings are generalizable to other groups, and other places.

Our discussion so far has not dealt with the four more clearly pathological items (96 and 97) dealing with impotence and ejaculatio praecox in the men, and frigidity and lack of orgasm in the women. Personality questionnaire scores for *P*, *E* and *N* were averaged for the men (or women) showing these pathological reactions, and compared with those of men and women not showing them. The outcome was very clear. Extroverts and introverts are not implicated in these four pathological reactions; neither are high nor low *P* scorers. But for all four, high *N* scorers showed the more pathological reactions significantly more frequently than did low *N* scorers. These results again agree pretty well with clinical knowledge, and demonstrate that our high *N* scorers are akin in many ways to actual psychiatrically diagnosed neurotics.

Before discussing some of the implications of our results, we must return to the all-important question of whether the results can be taken at face value. Is our sample sufficiently representative, and can we assume that they have spoken the truth?

There are two ways of checking on the former problem, that of representative sampling. We have already seen that with respect to the proportion in the sample who had had intercourse, our figures compared well with those given by Schofield, whose work is acknowledged to have been extremely careful, and indeed exemplary, as far as sampling is concerned. Much the same is true of the other figures quoted, for various kinds of petting. Similar considerations apply to personality. The actual mean scores for P, E and N in the general population, and in various sub-samples graded by sex, age and class are known. Our student sample does not differ to any marked extent from the standardization figures. In other words, our sample is representative both with respect to their personality scores, and also to their sexual behavior. As these are the two variables which we have brought into contact, it seems unlikely that our results are mere statistical artefacts.

The question of truthfulness is not capable of a direct answer; but there are a number of considerations which suggest that here too our study should not be dismissed too lightly.

(1) The inventories were lengthy, complex, and took a long time to fill in conscientiously. Under the conditions of anonymity prevailing it seems unlikely that any jokers would have deliberately (for what purpose?) falsified their statements. Checks were incorporated in the inventories, by asking the same question twice in somewhat disguised form. These did not disclose any obvious attempts to deceive, and it would have taken a joker quite some time to work out all the possible traps, and avoid them.

(2) The fourteen factors which were extracted from the attitude inventory, and the three factors which were extracted from the sex practices inventory, make good sense. This would not be so if many people had filled in the questionnaires arbitrarily, or with intent to cheat. It is one of the features of factor analysis that factors emerge from the *pattern* of answers. No single person could set about trying to forge his questionnaire answers in such a way as to create a "factor." To do this would need concerted action involving the majority of respondents. Coming as these did from many different universities and colleges such a notion is too paranoid to deserve taking seriously.

(*3*) Many respondents took the occasion to write in comments which indicated how seriously they took the whole thing, and how keen they were not to be misunderstood. Thus many girls who admitted to having had sexual intercourse wrote to say: "Only with my fiancé!" or "But not promiscuously." Several respondents included lengthy accounts of experiences or attitudes, indicating their sincere interest.

(*4*) Student friends and younger members of staff at some of the colleges used were asked to listen for comments regarding the investigation, particularly with respect to claims to have "fooled" the investigator. They found nothing but genuine interest and a desire to cooperate.

These are arguments; but there are also facts which point in much the same direction. If extroverts have intercourse more frequently than introverts, then we would expect that they would more frequently have illegitimate babies. It has indeed been shown in a study of mothers of such babies that they tended to be much more extroverted than mothers married in the orthodox way before conception. Prostitutes should be extroverted, in view of their impersonal and free indulgence in sexual behavior, and indeed empirical study has found this to be so. Promiscuous conduct easily leads to V.D., and a study of V.D. patients has disclosed them to be high on extroversion and also on *P*. Thus these factual consequences of "permissive" behavior fit well into the theoretical framework within which the present study was conceived.

THIS BRINGS ME to the most important consideration. Results reported in this chapter were not found in some vague Baconian, inductive fashion. They were predicted according to the dictates of the hypothetico-deductive method, by starting out with a quite explicit theory, and predicting the most likely consequences of that theory in the general field of sexual attitudes and behavior. Thus our results do not stand naked by themselves; they form part of a larger whole, parts of which at least are made up of carefully controlled laboratory investigations, such as those mentioned in Chapter 1. It is this pattern of results which is impressive and convincing; any single result, standing on its own, is always liable to be faulted in some way not easily forseen by the investigator, but scientific theories and results form a web, not a chain. *"Natura in reticulum sua genera connexit, non in catenam; homines non possunt nisi catenam sequi, cum non plura simul sermone exponere,"* wrote von Haller in 1768, anticipating the notion of validation of results in terms of nomological networks. The strength of such a network is not weakened much even though a single strand be torn.

Having indicated why it seems likely that our results are along the right lines, we may turn to a closer scrutiny of the possible social consequences of these findings. What is most striking, of course, is the great diversity of attitudes and practices. Some girls at twenty have not even been kissed, others have indulged in intercourse in many different positions, and in a variety of sexual "perversions" to boot. Some believe in the importance and continued value of virginity, others dismiss virginity with contempt. Some approve of orgies, of pornography, of blue films, while others regard all this with disgust. There is not one question on which there is unanimity. On most there is the utmost variety and confusion. This clearly poses a social problem: how can we have one set of rules, or mores, or laws to accommodate such a plethora of divergent attitudes and opinions? Laws, by their nature, cannot take into account human diversity—what is allowed (or prohibited) to one person is allowed (or prohibited) to all others. The only rational answer here would seem to be a lessening of legal concern with matters of individual conduct. Legislation should be kept to an absolute minimum, protecting the rights of babies, minors and others who cannot take care of themselves, but not interfering in the conduct of "consenting adults." Such an answer is easy, but it also raises complex and difficult problems; some of these are discussed in a later chapter ("The Uses and Abuses of Pornography").

I would think that more important than the legal consequences of the realization of human individuality in sexual reactivity would be the psychological ones. We tend to think of ourselves as, in general, very much alike. Some are a little brighter, others a little duller. Some are a little braver, others a little more fearful. Some are a little more serious, others a little more full of fun. But essentially all these differences are slight, and probably due to upbringing, or to events in a person's life. Under the skin all are much the same, Judy O'Grady or the Colonel's lady. But this easy and comforting illusion is often shattered when we read in the papers, or experience in our own lives, the impact which the huge differences in personality, intellect and behavior can have in the relations between different people. Newton; a psychopathic mass-murderer; our sexuopathic friend Walter; Shelley; Leonardo da Vinci; Buddha—these and many others are so far removed from the mean (along several different dimensions) that to consider them in terms of just a little more or less ceases to have any meaning. The sad truth is that human beings are innately diverse in many different ways—so diverse that it is difficult even to begin to realize just how large these differences are, or how impossible it is to argue from one's own behavior or reactions to those of another person— unless that other person happens to have a similar I.Q., degree of extroversion, score on P and N, and general educational and cultural background. This truth is sad because it takes away from our common humanity. If you have an I.Q. of 80 you will never appreciate Schubert's "Trout" Quintet, understand canonical algorithms, or take delight in a Barlach sculpture. Many people have by now accepted the great differences created by innate intellectual factors, although many others refuse to consider the evidence, for fear of what they might find. But it is in the broader field of personality that the idea has not even begun to sink in that people are inescapably different, innately diversified, and unimaginably unlike each other. Introvert and extrovert are like chalk and cheese; to group their behaviors and reactions together by some process of averaging is as absurd as to average chalk and cheese. But because these facts are in some way sad does not mean that we can refuse to pay any attention to them, or that we can pretend things are not as in fact they are. No sexual rules, no laws, no ideals will ever cover introvert and extrovert, neurotic and stable; one man's meat is another man's poison. This realization is the beginning of sanity.

Temperamental differences enter even into such relatively minute considerations as the choice of a girl friend on the basis of her physical attributes. We tend to think of women as "attractive" on a scale going from 1 at the bottom to 10 at the top. John Braine in his novel *Room at the Top* explicitly mentions such a scale, and argues that, in a particular area and class, men get girls with the higher ratings as a function of their own financial position—the poor have to make do with girls in the 1 to 3 range, while the very rich go in for 10s. This is obviously untrue—some rich men have very plain wives, and some quite poor men marry smashers. (I did myself.) But I am not concerned so much with the truth of the general law that there is a correlation between a woman's attractiveness and her husband's financial position. I am concerned with the assumption that a woman has a given "coefficient of attractiveness" which is equal for many different men. No doubt there is some agreement between men about the attractiveness of a group of girls; some are clearly more attractive than others. But in addition there are quite marked differences of opinion, and these are related to personality.

One of my colleagues, A. Mathews, collected fifty photographs of young women, ranging all the way from nude, buxom *Playboy* girls to fully clothed, thin models acting out their usual role of clothes-horse. These were then (by another of my colleagues) submitted to a sample of men to rate in terms of sexual attractiveness. As expected, extroverts tended to prefer the buxom nudes with their Marilyn Monroe-Jayne Mansfield figures, while introverts tended to prefer the fully clothed "nice" girls, with much less clearly marked secondary sexual characteristics. The relationship between attractiveness and size of bust is curvilinear (as befits this particular function); girls become more attractive as their bust size increases, but there comes an optimum beyond which any increase detracts from their attractiveness. Beyond a certain point they become vulgar and even comic. This optimal point differs from person to person, and our theory would suggest that it would come much earlier for the introvert than for the extrovert—as indeed it seems to do. The reason would of course be that identical stimuli, as we have seen in Chapter 1, produce greater arousal in introverts than extroverts; extroverts need bigger bosoms, more openly revealed, to experience equal arousal. (Take heart, ye girls with small busts; there is an introvert waiting to give you his soul!)

Another field in which there are pronounced personality differences is that of sex jokes. Here there is an interesting difference in theory between Freud and the views outlined in Chapter 1. For Freud, it will be remembered, laughter and amusement are derived from the escape, in the harmless form of a joke, of repressed material which had been relegated to the unconscious. It would be the inhibited, introverted person who would be more likely to have accumulated such repressed material, whereas the openly sex-oriented extrovert would have little such material to collect. Hence on Freudian argument introverts should delight specially in sexual jokes, whereas the very *raison d'être* for such amusement would be lacking in the extrovert.

On our theory exactly the opposite should be true. Extroverts show their delight in sexuality openly; sex jokes are just one of the many manifestations of such sexuality, and hence they would be expected to welcome it, and enjoy it. Introverts are much more censorious and more opposed to open sexuality; hence sex jokes should offend them, rather than amuse them. These contradictory predictions have several times been put to the test. The outcome each time has been the same—extroverts like sex jokes, introverts do not. On other types of jokes there are no such differences, hence the difference between extroverts and introverts does not arise from a defective sense of humor of the latter, or a facile endorsement of "very amusing" by the former. It is only with respect to sex jokes that extroverts show markedly more amusement. On all other forms of joke or cartoon material, extroverts and introverts give much the same reactions.*

BUT THESE ARE relatively unimportant corollaries of our general theory. The most important deductions perhaps concern marriage, and sexual harmony and conflict generally. If it is true that people show such profound differences in their sexual attitudes and behavior, then it would seem to follow that a successful marriage would be a very difficult feat to achieve. Such a marriage would have to be built not only on some congruence of physical attraction, similarity of intelligence, and reasonable closeness of background, but also on fundamental relationships in personality and temperament. An extreme extrovert, married to an extreme introvert, would not be likely to be happy, or to make his partner happy, even though all other signs and omens were set fair. The many combinations and permutations made possible by three dimensions (P, E and N), each having three degrees (high, medium and low), are likely to result in as many unions which have a poor prognosis as they are to result in unions

---

*This is not the only evidence against the Freudian theory. Practically all the empirical evidence that has been collected goes counter to it. It is no doubt for this reason that psychoanalysts and literary people still think so highly of it, and regard it as the only worthwhile psychological theory. Don't confuse me with facts, my mind is made up!

having a good prognosis. A period of engagement may weed out the most catastrophic combinations but experience, and the crush in the divorce courts, suggests that this is not inevitably so. There is always the (usually feminine) belief that men are changeable, and that a few months in her hands will make a new man out of the old Adam. Alack and alas! Such faith is seldom justified. Human nature is difficult to mold, and the divorce court is the graveyard of many such idle hopes, arrived at without benefit of psychological knowledge of the inheritance of personality.

Unfortunately very little is known about marital compatibility. There have been a few empirical studies, but these were carried out without the use of personality measures having any reasonable theoretical background or suitable validation. It is one of the wonders of modern society that governments will pay up to thousands of millions (sometimes dollars, sometimes pounds) for an airplane which is likely to make life hell for millions of people with its carpet of supersonic booms and bangs, and whose only purpose is to enable a few people to arrive in New York at 2 p.m. instead of 4 p.m., so that they can sleep away the internal upset created by the sudden time-change. Yet the same government will not pay one penny for research into the workings of the institution of marriage on which our whole society is built! Such research should in actual fact be neither impossibly difficult, nor impossibly expensive; its results could be of very great importance indeed. Unfortunately the chances of its being carried out are extremely remote. Governments never give money for sensible projects. (This is known as Eysenck's law in sociology; it is the only general law in sociology, as far as I know.)

How would such a project look? Well, first catch your hare. One would approach a thousand young engaged couples, obtain their agreement to take part in the study, and then administer to them a whole battery of tests, questionnaires and interviews, in order to get as complete a picture of their intelligence, personality, attitudes, sexual experiences, social and political views, psychiatric difficulties, social and cultural backgrounds as could be obtained through the use of objective methods. It would not be difficult to get volunteers; they could always be promised a *quid pro quo*, such as free medical and educational advice, and other help when needed. These young people would then be followed up for many years, interviewed and tested at regular intervals, and their whole marital history taken down assiduously. After ten or fifteen years, it would become possible to compare the happy marriages with the broken ones, or those not broken but clearly not happy. Gradually over the years a great mass of material would build up to document generalizations about marriages, about the importance and relevance of such factors as personality, or intelligence, or social and cultural background. We would at long last be able to base our advice, our opinions, our beliefs, on facts, rather than on surmise, hope and prejudice. Other parallel studies could investigate the causes of breakdown in other marriages, also with the aid of personality and other tests. We are at the moment spending quite considerable amounts of money on computerizing the selection of spouses; the marriage-broker nowadays speaks with the whirring of machinery in the background. This impresses many people, but of course the computer's output is only as good as the input. If the knowledge is lacking for writing a proper program which will mate like with like, then no computer can do better than chance. The advice given is no better than the theories on which it is based, and where the facts are lacking on which reasonable theories can be based, there even the almighty computer stands powerless!

But, of course, the main aim of such research into marriage as that suggested is not to open a computerized marriage-brokerage. It is to gain an understanding of the fundamental interaction between two people of different sexes. What we know about this is very little more than poets have known for thousands of years, and indeed most of our laws and our behavior patterns seem to be based on poetry, rather than upon sound knowledge—they certainly don't seem to work particularly well. There are, to be sure, always those who would want to do away with marriage altogether, from Plato onwards; but most of these iconoclasts seem to have little idea of what to put in its place (if anything); they too might benefit from a little empirical knowledge in this mass of surmise and guesswork. And, finally, there is the possibility that knowing something about these dyadic relationships might enable us to do some proper marriage guidance, i.e. apply the principles of scientific psychology to the mending of broken marriages. Attempts have already been made to use the "token economy" for this purpose (I am going to discuss these attempts in Chapter 3, which deals with the behaviorist technology).. But these attempts are of course very crude and simple. To make them more realistic and better adapted to the changing patterns of marital discord obviously requires a deeper understanding of just what the causes of these discords really are. Research is the lifeblood of action, and without such research all we are doing, or trying to do, is a mere stumbling about in the dark. The confession of ignorance is the beginning of wisdom!

Behaviorist Technologies in Psychiatry and Education

THERE are many differences between physics and psychology but none struck me more forcibly, when I reluctantly gave up my interest in the former to study the latter, than the lack of conscience of many psychologists about whether their theories actually worked or not. Physicists and engineers would be rather upset, in my experience, if the bridges they built kept falling down, or the ships they constructed kept going to pieces in the sea. You do not keep your job for any length of time if the tanks you build are found not to be capable of movement, or if the television sets you design give only a very distorted picture. There is usually an obvious, built-in feedback system which tells you whether what you are doing, or have done, is in fact working. Success or failure is in most cases only too obvious. The dam that bursts, and kills hundreds of villagers nestling beneath its supposedly impregnable walls, is not shrugged off lightly by those who constructed it; the designer of a new airplane that crashes will only, in the famous Arno cartoon smile, rub his hands, and say: "Ah well, back to the drawing-board." In real life he would be lucky to have even a drawing-board left! Psychologists often make far-reaching claims about their abilities to cure neurotics, improve educational practices, or help in the workings of industry. These claims are accepted by many people, and doubted by others, but the odd thing is that psychologists seem to show little interest in actually demonstrating that what they are advocating *actually works*. This curious trait is even more marked in psychiatrists and psychoanalysts: their enthusiasm for new methods of treatment is never equalled by a desire to demonstrate the actual effectiveness of these methods.

I had to learn this lesson the hard way when, during the last war, I was thrown into the general field of psychiatry and clinical psychology — by force or accident, and very much against my will. I found that psychiatrists were using a variety of different methods in treating what seemed much the same kinds of patients, and all were swearing by the particular methods they had become accustomed to using. I tried to discover on what basis they had selected their particular approaches, hoping to be referred to convincing experiments or clinical trials, but received no intelligible answers. This sent me to the textbooks, and the journals; here, if anywhere, the answer to my question would surely be found. I discovered that there was in fact very little interest in what was sometimes referred to as the "outcome" problem. Writers argued endlessly about what went on during the treatment sessions, or what should go on, or might be going on. They discussed what seemed rather remote psychic adventures which the souls of their patients might or might not undergo; and they argued about the desirability of strengthening the id and weakening the super-ego, or vice versa. But hardly a word about the proportion of recoveries and cures. Not a trace of properly designed clinical studies comparing the outcome of one method with that of another. I finally ended up with a rather meager set of papers and reports of the proportions of successes and failures which psychotherapists of different persuasions had published. These tended to vary considerably, but on the whole it seemed that about two out of three neurotic patients got better after two years of treatment. This looked pretty good, but it had to be compared with the "spontaneous remission" rate, *i.e.* the rate at which patients recover who have not had any kind of psychiatric treatment. It turned out that they too recovered at the rate of about two out of three in two years' time. In other words, there was in all this literature no real evidence to show that psychiatric treatment accelerated in any way the curative process which obviously tended to shift neurotics towards the "normal" end of the continuum, almost irrespective of what was being done to them.

Thinking that these facts would be of some interest to my colleagues, I mentioned them during a lecture I gave to the Annual General Meeting of the British Psychological Society in Oxford, some twenty years ago. At the end of my talk, a well-known professor of psychiatry, fists flying, came racing down the aisle, shouting: "Traitor! Traitor!" Only the timely interception of some persuasive friends managed to sidetrack him from attacking me physically.

I then published a short paper on these findings. The editor accepted it; but made the condition that the paper should be submitted to four well-known psychiatrists who would be permitted to answer the points made. (I agreed, of course; but finally the paper was published on its own; apparently no psychiatrists could be found to take up the cudgels on behalf of psychotherapy.

But during the next few years the dam burst, and dozens of angry and sometimes incoherent articles appeared purporting to invalidate my findings, and generally discredit the conclusions. Oddly enough none of these replies answered the points which I had made. They answered instead another argument which I had never put forward at all. "These studies reviewed by Eysenck are badly designed and badly executed; they do not provide evidence to show that psychotherapy is no good." That was the point made time and time again, and an excellent point it is, too. The quality of the work quoted (which was all the relevant work that had been published) was indeed very poor. If anyone in my department were to carry out and report sloppy, uncontrolled, and experimenter-contaminated work like this, he certainly would not last very long. That means that you cannot argue from the results that they *disprove* the effectiveness of psychotherapy. In any case universal negative conclusions of this kind are inadmissible. But I had argued something quite different, namely that the results *failed to prove* the effectiveness of psychotherapy; and this conclusion is not really in dispute. If the data are too poor to prove anything, then they are too poor to prove the effectiveness of psychotherapy. As no other data existed at the time, it follows that my conclusion must be correct. If the data mean something, then they clearly fail to demonstrate any particular effectiveness of the methods of therapy used. Heads I win, tails you lose — there simply are no data to prove the effectiveness of psychotherapy, and this fact has remained a fact in spite of all the arguments, the imprecations, and the shouting. There is only one way of showing that I was wrong —and a very simple way at that. All that psychiatrists or psychoanalysts had to do was to quote a single study which, using proper control groups and a proper method of assessment of outcome, demonstrated that psychotherapy worked. Nothing more was required, and nothing less would do. None of my critics has ever done this, and consequently I must conclude that there really is no such study. Until it comes along, the conclusion stands — there is no evidence to show that psychotherapy works.

THIS CONCLUSION has been challenged recently by some American writers who have argued that there is evidence showing that some psychotherapists actually help their patients, and accelerate their cures, while there are also other psychotherapists who have the opposite effect — their patients tend to get worse rather than better. These two types of therapists cancel out, and the overall effect is nil. They even describe the personality make-up of the successful therapist:

he is characterized by empathy, warmth and genuineness. These "therapy styles" are of course defined and measured with some degree of rigor. The unsuccessful therapist emerges in terms characteristic of the traditional, orthodox psychoanalyst — impersonal, purely interpretive, remote.

There is some evidence in favor of this theory, and provisionally one might perhaps accept it as reasonable. It does not, however, seem to contradict the generalization made from my material. I was concerned with the efficacy of the *method*; these results refer to the effectiveness of *individual persons*. What is being said is that irrespective of method, some persons (warm, interested, kindly) benefit mentally ill people by discussing their troubles with them. This I am quite prepared to believe. What I was doubting were the claims advanced in favor of certain theories about methods; in other words, that anyone trained to use the concepts and methods of psychoanalysis would, because of the inherent truth and superiority of the psychoanalytic method, be able to cure patients at a faster rate than anyone trained in other concepts and methods. If it is the person, not the method that is important, then again there is no force in the objection.

The lack of concern with outcomes revealed itself in many comments on my paper. Several well-known psychologists suggested, in so many words, that no attention be paid to these facts, and that they should carry on as before. This, in fact, was what most psychiatrists decided to do. Only gradually did the truth begin to seep in, until nowadays many young students take it more or less for granted that psychotherapy is pretty useless. I always saw my role in all this as being rather like that of the young boy in the fairy tale of the Emperor's New Clothes; it happened to be me who cried: "But look, he hasn't got any clothes on!" It is sometimes difficult nowadays to realize that at one time nearly everyone thought that the Emperor did in fact have on the most gorgeous raiment; *sic transit gloria*. . . . However, in science the old and discredited does not just fade away once its pretensions have been stripped off; something new and better must first be found to take its place. I suggested that if neurotic symptoms, so called, are (as they seem to be) nothing but conditioned emotional reactions to situations and objects that produce fear, generalizing to other, similar situations and objects, then it should be possible to make use of the vast store-house of knowledge about the acquisition and extinction of such conditioned responses, *i.e.* modern learning theory, and erect on this basis a better, more useful, and above all more effective system of therapy.

This system I called "behavior therapy," in contrast to psychotherapy, in order to highlight the main differences between the two. Behavior therapy concerns itself with observables. It attempts to change a person's behavior — including under that term such measurable aspects of behavior as emotion (fear, anxiety, anger). It pays no attention to speculative entities like Oedipus complexes, penis envy or super-egos, nor does it attempt to interpret dreams according to the gospel of Freud or Jung (two very different gospels, to be sure). And it is vitally concerned with the outcome of the treatment. It makes the question, "And did the patient get better?" the central theme of its investigations. This approach has scandalized psychoanalysts who were far more concerned with the hypothetical endopsychic conflicts between equally hypothetical entities which, like medieval demons, fought over the soul of the patient; but it rather attracted physicians who simply wanted to see their patients cured.

Many methods have been suggested for changing behavior. Behavior modification does not rest on a single principle or method. Two of the most widely used are the methods of desensitization and of aversion therapy; both derive essentially from the principles of Pavlovian conditioning. Other methods, to which I will turn presently, are derived rather from Skinner's principles of operant conditioning — of which more later. The so-called "token economies" are the most viable outcome to date of these theories. The term "behavior therapy" covers all these developments, and many others (like the use of "modeling" procedures) besides. The question immediately arises: Do they work? Does behavior therapy produce more and quicker cures than psychotherapy?

In this form the question is probably unanswerable. We must specify the type of patient treated, his symptoms and the length and severity of his disorder. We must specify the precise nature and dimensions of what is to be considered "cure." We must specify the precise nature of methods to be used under the headings of "behavior therapy" and "psychotherapy," and the amount of training and expertise required of the therapist. Finally, we should ideally have several therapists on each side so that we can evaluate the therapist's contribution to the variance as well as the method's contribution. Only limited steps have been taken to answer some of the questions included in this list. I will try to give some preliminary, tentative answers, based on the literature of the last ten years.

IN SUMMARIZING relevant studies, we must consider two ways of looking at the problem. The academic research worker is interested in the extension of certain general laws about conditioning and the extinction of habits, from their origin in the laboratory, to the clinic and the prison. The therapist is interested in the well-being and improvement of his patient. This difference affects many aspects of the problem; the type and rigor of the proof demanded, the type of experimental subject or patient studied, and the nature of the measure of change in behavior used by the investigator. Recognition of this difference in approach is important because many inconclusive and irrelevant arguments have arisen from it, arguments which simply illustrate that research psychologists and clinical psychiatrists do not necessarily share the same aims and concerns.

Certain neurotic symptoms can be observed in otherwise fairly normal persons. Indeed normality and neurosis constitute a continuum. Some of these symptoms (for example, simple phobias) provide an exceptionally clear-cut means of measuring the effects of the treatment. Fears of snakes, spiders, public speaking, test-taking, open or closed spaces, or heights, can be measured with great precision by actually placing the subject in a situation in which he is required to go near a snake, or go up a ladder. His behavior can be accurately observed and measured, and can be shown to be very reliable and stable over time. Physiological measures of fear can be taken, and correlated with behavior and self-ratings of fear. This makes possible accurate measurement of pre- and post-therapy behavior, and allows us to measure the effects of therapy, and compare different therapies. A dozen laboratory research projects since 1961 have used this method, and about half of these have also provided a follow-up period averaging eight to nine months.

The type of behavior therapy used in all these cases was Joseph Wolpe's method of desensitization — the gradual introduction of the feared object while the patient is in a state of relaxation. The feared object is introduced in "hierarchies," first in a form that is not much feared, later in a more direct or severe form. Control groups were tested after no treatment, simple relaxation, flooding or "implosion" of the feared object, suggestion and hypnosis, drug-placebo or insight therapy. In all cases the groups treated with behavior therapy showed greater change in behavior, in the direction of lessening of fear, than did the control groups.

Another advantage of this procedure is that it permits us to study which aspects of the method used are most important. Dr. S. Rachman's 1965 studies of relaxation without gradual use of hierarchies, hierarchies without relaxation, and combined hierarchies and relaxation may be quoted here. He found that combined hierarchies and relaxation gave the best results. P. J. Lang's 1969 studies on personal administration of desensitization therapy as compared with computer-administered desensitization therapy are also relevant. He found no difference. We may conclude from all these studies that desensitization unquestionably has the effect of lessening phobic fears of certain objects and situations to a strikingly greater extent than other procedures used; that both parts of the procedure (relaxation and hierarchies) seem necessary, and that impersonal methods (computer) work as well as personal methods, contrary to the hypothesis that "transference" effects are important.

Psychiatrists often object to experiments such as these, saying that monosymptomatic phobias are rare; that the subjects of these experiments are not neurotics of the kind referred to clinics; and that the relevance of these demonstrations to their day-to-day work is doubtful. Such relevance must, of course, be demonstrated. But it should be added that for Freud and his followers even mild errors in performance and minor misspellings were evidence of deep-seated complexes, and snake phobias in particular were explained along symbolic lines which linked them securely with his theoretical system. Indeed, it was for this reason that Lang and his associates selected snake phobics for their experiments. Psychoanalysts cannot therefore have it both ways. Either these phobias are typical of more severe neurotic disorders, in which case we may generalize from these results with some confidence; or their original views were mistaken. There is no doubt that Freud would not have predicted that the methods used by behavior therapists would succeed in effectively curing these disorders, minor though they may be. According to his set of hypotheses no permanent eradication of such fears (without relapse or symptom substitution) should be possible without "insight." The fact that results conclusively disprove this Freudian notion should not be allowed to go by default; it strongly argues against the whole psychoanalytic theory.

The fact that in these experimental studies monosymptomatic phobic patients have been used has given rise to the erroneous supposition (sometimes voiced as a criticism of behavior therapy) that these methods can deal *only* with monosymptomatic phobias. This is not true, as we shall see. The reason for concentrating on this type of patient is simply experimental convenience, and the possibility of accurate measurement of initial and final state. Mendel concentrated on wrinkled and smooth peas; but it does not follow that the laws of genetics he discovered only apply to wrinkled and smooth peas! Psychiatrists often fail to appreciate the value of having a convenient "test bed" for investigating rigorously and quantitatively the deductions from one's theories. Behavior therapy has for the first time made this approach feasible in the field of psychotherapy. This insistence on taking previously inaccessible problems into the laboratory is perhaps the major contribution of behavior therapy to psychiatry.

Proof of the effectiveness of behavior therapy *using patients as subjects* is, of course, much less easy to give, particularly as psychoanalysts have been remarkably coy in refusing to take part in joint experimental studies comparing the effects of different types of therapy. However, a number of such studies have now been carried out, all of them at the Institute of Psychiatry of the Maudsley Hospital, and we can at least have a preliminary glimpse of the likely results of such comparisons.

The work done by John Cooper, Isaac Marks and Michael Gelder covers over 110 patients treated with desensitization-type behavior therapy. It included follow-ups of about twelve months in every case, and used various "controls" (groups with similar conditions but differently treated, for subsequent comparison, ranging from simple hospitalization to mixed treatment, hypnotic suggestion, and insight psychotherapy). Some of these were retrospective studies in which matching was attempted from case records. These showed that isolated phobias responded significantly better to desensitization than to control treatment; complex phobic disorders such as agoraphobia (fear of open spaces) did rather better, but not significantly so. Obsessive neuroses and a group of other miscellaneous neuroses did no better (but also no worse) with desensitization than with control treatment. In looking at these results it should be borne in mind that the behavior therapy in question was done by psychologists experimenting with new methods of their own devising; these were pioneer efforts undertaken by untrained workers.

Furthermore, patients selected for behavior therapy were usually only referred as a last resort, after all other methods had conspicuously failed. It is impossible to match for this feature. The fact that in spite of all these difficulties behavior therapy emerged as significantly superior in most cases, and inferior in none, must count as a startling success.

Studies designed to provide a control group demonstrated again the significant superiority of behavior therapy in out-patients with focal phobias or agoraphobia. Not only did the phobias improve, but Marks and Gelder report "once the treated phobias diminished, improvements also followed in work and leisure adjustments that had formerly been hampered by the phobias." With a group of severely agoraphobic in-patients desensitization failed to do better than the control condition, but again it did no worse. The value of desensitization was found to be inversely proportional to the amount of severe free floating anxiety in these cases. The more anxiety the less successful the treatment, as compared to the control treatment.

Two recent and as yet unpublished studies have been carried out by Ph.D. students in my department, working under the direction of S. Rachman. In the first of these Jim Humphery allocated on a random basis successive child guidance cases suffering from neurotic disorders to treatment by either behavior therapy or psychotherapy; a non-treated control group was also available. Improvement was judged by two independent psychiatrists, ignorant of the treatment received. A ten-month follow-up was also provided. Behavior therapy took much less time — eighteen weeks as compared with thirty-one weeks for psychotherapy on average. Success of behavior therapy in improving the psychiatric condition of the child was significantly greater, in spite of the shorter time required. Unfortunately the children in the behavior therapy group, although matched by random procedures, were more seriously ill than the children in the psychotherapy group; this statistically significant difference partly invalidates the comparisons.

A similar, but rather more extensive study was done on adult patients by Patricia Gillan. Her patients were all out-patients suffering from serious and complex phobic anxieties. There were no monosymptomatic cases among her patients, many of whom in fact had difficulties in coming up to the hospital for treatment. She formed four groups of eight patients each, on a part random, part matching basis. Those in group 1 were given desensitization treatment with relaxation. Those in group 2 were given the hierarchies, but no relaxation. Those in group 3 were given relaxation, plus pseudo-therapy, but no hierarchies. Those in group 4 were given dynamic psychotherapy by a psychiatrist. Patients were rated by the therapist involved, and also by an independent psychiatrist uncommitted to either approach, who formed his judgment "blind," *i.e.* in ignorance of which treatment had been administered. Physiological measures were taken of the amount of fear produced by the phobic object or situation, both at the end of therapy and after a follow-up period of three months.

The results of this work clearly favor behavior therapy. The combination of relaxation with hierarchies is the most successful form of treatment, with hierarchies without relaxation somewhat inferior, but not significantly so.

Psychotherapy and relaxation without hierarchies are both significantly inferior. These two studies of random samples of neurotic children, and adults with serious disorders, suggest that the work reported from laboratory experiments can be replicated with psychiatric patients, and that we are justified in extending our conclusions from the one field to the other. This is an important advance.

The relatively high success of the method of using hierarchies, even without relaxation, fits in well with another hypothesis I have put forward, to wit that when psychotherapy is effective (though less so than behavior therapy) it is so because it incorporates some of the principles of desensitization. The permissive atmosphere produces a lowering of anxiety (relaxation). Discussion ranges around the presenting problems, and in the hands of an experienced psychiatrist naturally centers on problems towards the lower end of the hierarchy because these arouse only anxieties which under the circumstances are tolerable, to be followed later by discussions involving problems higher up the hierarchy.

Thus psychotherapy may often approach, though rather inefficiently because unintentionally, the procedure of hierarchy construction and working through, rather like Gillan's second method (giving the hierarchies but no relaxation). Support for this notion comes from the demonstration of C.B. Truax and R.R. Carkhuff, already mentioned, that while some psychotherapists can be shown consistently to help their patients, others equally consistently not only fail to help but actively retard recovery. What is of interest here is their description of the personality qualities and "therapy styles" of these two contrasted groups of therapists. As will be remembered, they find empathy, warmth and genuineness characteristic of successful therapists. Absence of these qualities, and in particular the presence of the opposites, is found in therapists who actually hurt and harm their patients. This is very much in line with my view of successful psychotherapy as embodying behaviorist principles. Empathy, warmth and genuineness generate an easy, relaxed atmosphere in which to develop the hierarchies which carry so much of the burden of successful therapy, while cold, "interpretive" and purist behavior on the part of the therapist has the opposite effect, *i.e.* preventing relaxation and increasing anxiety. On this theory, then, relaxation is usually present in interviews with "good" therapists and does not have to be created artificially by training, although such training may be necessary with some patients.

It may be worthwhile to pursue this theory a little further. The hypothetical process of "deconditioning" or extinction of habits involved in behavior therapy implies the formation of new conditioned responses, whether in behavior therapy or in psychotherapy. One might predict that subjects who form conditioned responses easily and quickly would do better in therapy than those who do so poorly and slowly. It has recently been shown by I. Martin in our laboratories that those who quickly acquire eye-blink conditioned responses in the laboratory are much more likely to do well with both behavior therapy and psychotherapy. This strongly supports my view, as well as suggesting more widespread use of this test as a prognostic device. Certainly no projective or other widely used test has to my knowledge ever succeeded as well as this in predicting success of therapy.

I have concentrated on desensitization methods, for the simple reason that trials using control groups are almost non-existent, outside this field. There are isolated exceptions, such as a paper by I. G. Thompson and N. H. Rathod dealing with aversion therapy* in heroin addiction. Using scoline

---

*In aversion therapy an undesirable item of behavior (smoking, drinking to excess, homosexuality, transvestism, drug addiction) is paired with some painful stimulus, such as an electric shock. The behavior may be actual, such as drinking alcohol in the laboratory, or it may be imagined by the patient, or it may be shown in photos or films. What is important is that it

injections which produce muscular paralysis and fear of suffocation as the unconditioned response, they elaborated a conditioning procedure in which self-injection with heroin just prior to paralysis constituted the conditioned stimulus. This method worked very well, as compared with the not too satisfactory control group. The severity of the effect of using scoline is justified by the poor prognosis of the heroin addicts — after five years untreated addicts are likely to be dead. The study needs replication, of course; but in view of the well-known lack of effect of other types of treatment, the results must be considered as extremely promising — eight out of ten patients did not use heroin after treatment, as checked by frequent urine analysis carried out without prior warning.

In their book *Aversion Therapies and Behaviour Disorders* Dr. S. Rachman and John Teasdale make the point that in most disorders where aversion therapy is attempted (alcoholism, homosexuality, fetishism, transvestism, drug addiction) the spontaneous remission rate, and the success rate of other methods of treatment are reasonably well known, and are both so low that any sizeable number of "cures," even though they may need booster doses of treatment, may be regarded as highly suggestive although proper proof with use of control groups must of course remain one's ideal. They demonstrate that aversion therapy can be made to work extremely well *provided* that the laws of established laboratory procedures for conditioning and habit extinction are not flouted in the process — as is too often done by psychiatrists not too knowledgeable in this field, and eager to apply methods whose rationale they comprehend only imperfectly.

---

must be followed by some form of negative reinforcement (shock or some other painful stimulus). Plutarch reports the first application of aversion therapy, when he recounts how Demosthenes, who suffered from a shoulder tic, suspended a sharp sword over his shoulder; when the tics jerked his shoulder upwards the sword pierced the skin. A few repetitions resulted in a complete cure!

A summing-up at present must be tentative. It is important to note that in all the twenty or so studies using control groups, whether dealing with experimental analogue "patients" or with real psychiatric cases, behavior therapy did significantly better than psychotherapy, or any other alternative method, in almost every case; it never did worse. When you remember that the behavior therapists in question were usually psychologists with little training in the method, and little experience (often Ph.D. students who had just a few hours of instruction) or else people experimenting with new and not yet worked-out methods, then you may begin to feel, as I do, that this result is really astonishingly positive and almost incredible. There is nothing like it in the history of psychiatry. It is possible to find fault with details or individual studies, and to suspend judgment in the case of others. It is very difficult to look at the evidence as a whole (which, of course, is what a scientist should do!) and come to any conclusion other than that behavior therapy not only has been shown to work, but that it is the *only* method of therapy for which this can be claimed.

This seems to me the one conclusion which has been very firmly established. We do not as yet know which types of patients it works best for (although some indications for this have been mentioned). We do not know which of several theories regarding the method of working of desensitization is correct (although some evidence is beginning to come in). And we do not know how to predict success or failure (although the work on eye-blink conditioning has laid a firm basis for research in this field). These may seem a large number of "don't know's," but in view of the youth of the methods of behavior therapy we may perhaps rather congratulate ourselves on the fact that its clinical and scientific value and usefulness have been so firmly established.

SO MUCH FOR desensitization and aversion therapy. How about Skinner's methods? Where Wolpe is concerned with the elimination of conditioned anxieties and other fearful emotions (as in desensitization), or where aversion therapy tries to associate such conditioned anxieties with certain disapproved forms of conduct, Skinner does not aim at the manipulation of emotion at all. Faithful to the law of reinforcement — which states that actions which are immediately followed by positive reinforcement or reward will be repeated—he has worked out a system of shaping conduct which has been very effective with certain types of psychotics and "autistic children."

Perhaps a few homely examples will be useful in setting the scene. You are trying to train your dog to come when you call. He doesn't. When he finally does come, you punish him. This is a useless and nugatory way of reacting; the dog will simply form the association: "Come to master—get beaten," and will be less likely to come next time. Such a reaction on the part of the trainer may relieve his impatience, but it will not help in training the dog. Now consider mother busily cooking dinner. Her little son wants her to play with him. She pays no attention, until finally he starts being naughty—he shouts, breaks a window, and in other ways attracts her attention. Now she does attend to him — either by scolding him, or by shouting at him, or in some other way. She thinks that such reproof will make him less likely to repeat his undesirable actions, but this is not so. For him the sequence of events is: "Play nicely and quietly — mother pays no attention." Followed by: "Be naughty—mother comes and pays attention." Next time the little boy wants attention, he is more likely to be naughty; his mother is simply training him in disobedience and naughtiness. To follow Skinner's dictates she should pay attention to him, praise him and play with him when he is well behaved, and pay no attention when he is naughty. This may be beyond human nature to achieve, but if we want to make our children behave, this is what we would have to do.

Now apply this to a group of patients in hospital. They too want to attract attention. They try to do this by behaving oddly, in a manner which they know will bring the mental nurse running, or by talking about their symptoms, which again the nurse has been trained to reward by lending an attentive ear. Traditional psychiatric methods of reaction, which are taught to student nurses, reinforce the odd and undesirable behavior of the patients; Skinner suggests exactly the opposite. In his system, the nurses would be trained to interact with patients as long as they behaved in a rational manner and talked innocently about everyday topics. The moment the patient starts to talk about his symptoms, or behaves oddly, the nurse is instructed to leave him and go to another patient. In this way rational, reasonable conduct is reinforced; irrational, "psychotic" conduct is not reinforced, and gradually dies out.

Does it in fact get eliminated? The answer, from a lot of research reported in the literature, is yes — the method seems to work. It is interesting that nurses find it very difficult to adapt to this new regime. Having been taught all their lives by psychotherapeutically oriented psychiatrists that they should listen to the patients' troubles, interpret their stories and weird sayings, and observe their odd actions, they cannot quickly switch over to exactly the opposite line of attack. They are so concerned with the putative "mental," endopsychic events supposititiously taking part in the minds of their patients, that they are not at all concerned with the effects their attention may have on the behavior of the patients. By reinforcing the wrong kinds of response they actually make the patients worse — just as mother encouraged the wrong type of behavior in her little boy. Nurses are often "do-gooders." This is of course not meant as a criticism — the world would be a better place if everyone in it wanted to do good to other, less fortunate beings. But to do good one must know just what the consequences of one's actions are. To assume such knowledge, and go ahead blithely without checking on the actual effects is likely, as in this case, to make things worse rather than better. It is not the intentions of the nurses (or mothers) which are being criticized; it is the outcome of their actions. A little knowledge can indeed be a dangerous thing. Human nature is not so simple that we can assume without proof that what we feel like doing is necessarily the right thing.

Skinner has worked out the details of "shaping" behavior in his experiments with rats and pigeons. First specifying precisely what behavior he wanted to produce, he would then administer reinforcement (food) whenever the animal made movements even approximately in the right direction. Gradually he would thus build up the animal's repertoire until finally the rat, or the pigeon, would dance, play ping-pong, or demonstrate a lengthy and complicated set of actions.

But surely people are not rats or pigeons, you cry out in dismay. No, they are not. But may there not be *aspects* of their nature and behavior which resemble those of rats and pigeons sufficiently to make the same methods worth trying? This is an empirical matter, subject to experimental study. It cannot be settled simply by armchair argument (although many people have tried to do just that). Take a completely mute, withdrawn schizophrenic. How would you make him talk after many years of complete silence, and after any number of psychiatrists and psychoanalysts have given him up? In one of our experiments, using Skinner's approach, the experimenter first ascertained what would constitute a positive reinforcement for the schizophrenic in question; it turned out that he liked sweets. She now watched the patient intensely. Whenever he made a movement with his mouth which even vaguely resembled the kind of movement which one might make in speaking, he was given a sweet. Gradually the movements were required to be more and more like speech, and finally he was given sweets only when he actually produced a sound. Now the requirements were upgraded again, until actual speech sounds were produced. Finally, the patient began to speak words, then phrases, and at long last whole sentences.

There are many such examples in the literature. Beyond any doubt, these methods work with both adult psychotics, even the most hopeless and chronic cases, and with autistic children, even when all other methods have been given up as useless. It is not suggested that these are cures. There is much else wrong with the patient apart from his failure to speak, or whatever specific behavior we may be concerned with. But sometimes we may be concerned with strategic behaviors, *i.e.* behaviors which cause the patient to be referred to the hospital as a psychotic, as a person who simply cannot get on in his everyday life environment. In those cases getting rid of the offending behavior may amount in effect to a cure—the patient can return to his everyday habitat. In any case, the reactions of these patients (and of normal people, too, when exposed to such "shaping" exercises in the laboratory) are surprisingly similar to those of rats and pigeons. This similarity is a fact; what deductions we make from it are of course a different matter. Nothing is here asserted to suggest that human nature is "nothing but" rat nature writ large. Any such statement I would regard as nonsense! All that I am saying is that methods developed in the animal laboratory may with advantage be tried out, with suitable safeguards, on mentally ill patients, in the hope of improving their status when everything else has failed. To refuse to do this because of prejudice seems to me inhuman. Why condemn our schizophrenic, or our autistic children, to prolonged suffering, just because we do not like to be reminded of our common animal ancestry? After all, what do we have to be proud of? Rats and pigeons do not make war, commit rape, or threaten to end all life on earth through pollution or atomic explosions. Perhaps we should learn from them in more ways than the one suggested here.

"SHAPING" BEHAVIOR in this fashion is a lengthy and

difficult job. The possibility needs to be considered whether it might not be possible to use this extremely potent method on whole groups. This has in fact been done, and the method of the "token economy" is one of the most intriguing and promising in the whole armory of behaviorist technology. This method, to be described presently, has been used in recent years with chronic schizophrenics and with criminals (two groups notoriously resistant to any form of behavior modification). Its success there augurs well for a wider usage, and it also raises hopes that chronic psychotics and convicts will not remain forever what they have all too long been — subjects of custodial care, with no hope for rehabilitation. It is sad for me to note that this method is being used ever more widely and imaginatively in the U.S.A., not at all in my own country; sad not only because British needs are at least as great as those of the Americans, but also because (contrary to the impression often created by the non-historical writings of the leading behaviorists) the method was actually pioneered and shown to be practicable and valuable by a British penologist, Alexander Maconochie. His life has been made the subject of a fascinating biography by John Vincent Barry, a Justice of the Supreme Court of Victoria, Australia; he also reviews in detail the origin and effectiveness of Maconochie's "mark system of prison discipline." Only a brief account of this remarkable man is possible here. Like all true originators, his genius was not recognized in his own time, and only gradually is justice being done to his memory.

MACONOCHIE came to Van Diemen's Land as secretary to his friend, Sir John Franklin, when the latter became Lieutenant-Governor in 1837. He was asked by an English humanitarian society to investigate the convict system, whose inhumanity and callous cruelty, stupid and self-defeating as we now know it to be, led him to condemn it vigorously. He also formulated far-reaching proposals for its reform. His reward was dismissal. The establishment, then as now, does not appreciate criticism, however justified. But in 1840 he was appointed superintendent of Norfolk Island, one of the most cruel and soul-destroying of all the convict settlements. To understand the philosophy governing these settlements, and prisons in general, one may perhaps quote a famous sentence by the Reverend Sydney Smith, who in 1822 declared that a prison should be:

> a place of punishment from which men recoil with horror — a place of real suffering, painful to the memory, terrible to the imagination . . . a place of sorrow and wailing, which should be entered with horror and quitted with earnest resolution never to return to such misery; with that deep impression, in short, of the evil which breaks out into perpetual warning and exhortation to others.

Maconochie's view was the very opposite:

> I think that time sentences are the root of very nearly all the demoralization which exists in prison. A man under a time sentence thinks only how he is to cheat that time, and while it away; he evades labor, because he has no interest in it whatever, and he has no desire to please the officers under whom he is placed, because they cannot serve him essentially; they cannot in any way promote his liberation . . . Now these . . . evils would be remedied by introducing the system of task sentences.

In other words, Maconochie contrasted the idea of rehabilitation with that of revenge. In this he was only one of many whose humanity was revolted by the vicious, savage and inhuman way in which society treated those unfortunates who, often without any great fault of their own, fell foul of rules which had little to do with any modern conception of "justice." But he went farther than any other reformer of his century. Some of his numerous innovations are listed by Sheldon Glueck in his foreword to Barry's book:

> He foreshadowed modern ideas of the indeterminate

sentence; he prepared prisoners for return to society by means of progressive stages of discipline and self-discipline; he used group-influence to good effect in the reformative process; he contributed to modern ideas of classification of prisoners; he recognized the merit of inmate-participation in the conduct of penal institutions; he realized the value of evidencing a personal interest in the problems of the individual offender; he permitted direct contact with the superintendent rather than through intermediaries . . . he established a school program with "marks for efficiency," and he employed prisoner-teachers; he permitted prisoners to cultivate small gardens of their own and to sell the produce; he sought to make the regime resemble free life in order to counteract the inherent dilemma of trying to "socialize" human beings by means of an abnormal social matrix such as a prison. In a word, he regarded the true function of a prison to be a "moral hospital." As Maconochie himself wrote, "vice is a disease and penal science just moral surgery. The means it employs must often be painful; but its object should always be benevolent — always the speedy discharge of the patient."

This idea was to be given greater publicity and more paradoxical formulation by Samuel Butler in *Erewhon*, where criminals are sent to hospital and the medically ill are punished by prison; but its origin was in the fertile mind of Alexander Maconochie.

In order to achieve this end, Maconochie proposed the substitution of a task rather than a time sentence. Instead of being sentenced to imprisonment for a period of time, the offender should be sentenced to be imprisoned until he had performed a specified quantity of labor. To specify and quantify this amount of labor is, of course, difficult. Maconochie suggested that the prisoner should be ordered to earn by labor and other forms of good conduct a fixed number of "marks of commendation," and thus his period of detention should end only when he had done so. On first entering the prison, the offender would suffer a short period of restraint and deprivation. This would shortly be followed by a second stage during which he could earn privileges, as well as shelter and food, by the earnings from his labor and good conduct. Purchases could be made by computing the value of the good in "marks," and setting them off against the "marks" earned by the prisoner. As Barry puts it:

The performance of allotted tasks would enable him to earn a daily tally of marks, for example, ten marks, but by frugal living, constant industry beyond the allotted task, and exemplary behaviour and demeanour, he could add to the daily tally. Disciplinary offences should not be punished by the customary prison methods of violence, deprivation, or enforced labour, but by fines expressed in marks, and by the withdrawal of privileges.

In due course, prisoners were permitted to join with other prisoners, and engage in the performance of joint work projects in which misconduct of one member is punished by loss of marks by the whole group.

As a prisoner progressed through the system, the restraints upon him should be lessened, and the final period of his detention should resemble as much as possible the conditions likely to be encountered on release, the expressed purpose of this stage being to prepare him for the release which the whole system was devised to enable him to achieve by his own efforts. The fundamental principle was: nothing for nothing; everything must be earned. Throughout the period of detention anything that tended to degrade the prisoner, or to deprive him of the character of a social being should be avoided. Brutal punishments, such as the use of leg irons, the wearing of chains, spreadeagling, the gag and the lash, should not be used.

These ideas are not entirely original; Richard Whately, Archbishop of Dublin, and the Quakers James Backhouse and George Walker had already suggested some quantitative system of withdrawal of privileges as a substitute for the use of punishment. Maconochie was the first to put them into a usable form, and try them out in an actual experiment.

Was the experiment successful? Before trying to answer this question, let us first of all list some of the reasons why it could not possibly have worked.

(1) The prisoners in question were all felons regarded as beyond reclamation; the scum of the whole prison population. No worse group could have been imagined on which to try out any new system. If Maconochie's many enemies had selected with the greatest care a group certain to prove incapable of improvement, this is the group they would have chosen.

(2) These prisoners, whatever their original state, had been brutalized to a degree which nowadays we would simply refuse to believe. Barry's descriptions of the foul conditions under which they lived, and the savage punishments to which they were exposed, have to be read to give even an inkling of the lives lived by these poor people.

(3) Maconochie's powers were much more limited than he had thought. Thus he could not assure his convicts that even when they had accumulated their share of marks, they would be released. Over half of all the convicts were officially regarded as outside even the attenuated scheme he was trying to introduce.

(4) He had little or no help from the Home Office, but instead received constant discouragement and reprimands. Finally he was dismissed long before his plans could have shown their value. He had to work against, not with, his superiors. He never received the support to which he felt himself entitled.

(5) His subordinates, who had to administer the scheme,

were old-fashioned prison officers, out of sympathy with his views, and dedicated to the ideas of "instant punishment." They did not see the convicts, as he did, as human beings, and even at best their support was lukewarm.

(6) Australian colonists were up in arms against his "soft" methods, and constantly called for his recall and dismissal. It was amongst these people that his prisoners, having served their sentence, or received sufficient marks to go free, would have to earn a living. The bitter hostility to Maconochie was also directed at his charges, and instead of helping them rehabilitate themselves, the colonists did their best to make the experiment a failure.

(7) Physical conditions at Norfolk Island were so primitive that it was very difficult for Maconochie to introduce many of his ideas. Communications with England were extremely poor and slow, and his demands were not met with much enthusiasm by the Home Office.

These are but a few of the difficulties which Maconochie encountered. It will be clear that his task was not an easy one.

In forming a proper evaluation of the success or failure of the experiment, one must consider the prejudices of those who have reported on it. The hatred and dislike of Maconochie and all his works which prevailed among senior officials, governors and the like, had to be seen to be believed. Having made his task well-nigh impossible, they blamed him for not succeeding within the space of two or three years in turning devils into angels. Having imposed the most brutalizing methods of treatment on the convicts, they seemed astonished that the leopard did not change his spots overnight. For a full account, Barry must be consulted; here let me just note a few accounts given by eye-witnesses, some hostile to Maconochie but not irreconcilably so.

First Maconochie's own evaluation: "I found the island a turbulent, brutal hell, and left it a peaceful, well-ordered community . . . the most complete security alike of person and property prevailed. Officers, women and children traversed the island everywhere without fear." Barry adds: "All the reliable evidence confirms his statement." The Rev. T. B Naylor was Church of England chaplain on Norfolk Island during Maconochie's administration; he wrote: "I am heartily and fully persuaded that under God's blessing, the system of "marks," or rather more generally the self-reformatory process is above all other means the best, if not the only means of uniting the conflicting interests of the criminal and justice." And in a letter quoted by Barry, he amplifies this statement as follows:

In thinking over all our Norfolk Island experience, I do not mean to say that some errors were not committed, but I am sure that infinite good was done, that nothing like his administration there has before or since worked so much good . . . I can prove that at no period was there so little crime, or anything like the tone of improved feeling which characterized the period of his residence there, and I am willing to stake all my credit upon the assertion that if he has a fair field and fair play, his cause will be triumphantly established. That he had neither on Norfolk Island is, I believe, very generally admitted even by his opponents. I *know* how insurmountable were the difficulties thrown in his way, and instead of now wondering that he did not do more, I am astonished that he did anything. I never, I should add, met a prisoner who does not confirm my conviction of the improving tendencies of the efforts he made.

What of the conduct of the prisoners once they left prison? "The conduct of your Norfolk Island men generally has been most exemplary; they have shown that a reformation far greater than has been hitherto effected in any body of men by any system either before or after yours, has taken place in them. With scarcely an exception, the whole are doing well, and some are in a respectable way of business, advancing far to prosperity. They are a credit to the name they commonly bear of Captain Maconochie's men." Thus a former prisoner, whose statements are fully confirmed by the Roman Catholic Bishop of Hobart, who was well familiar with Norfolk Island. The conclusion from these and other similar witnesses is difficult to avoid. The experiment in spite of extreme difficulties and a real determination on all sides that it should fail, was a marked success. Both within the prison and in outside life after prison the conduct of the convicts improved well beyond anything known at the time. The absence of quantitative comparisons make it difficult to go further than that, but so much seems established. It is an interesting comment on human nature that even now, 120 years later, there are still no official experiments under way to investigate these claims. We still argue endlessly about prison reform, but refuse to establish beyond doubt the efficacy of a method both humane and apparently effective for the rehabilitation of criminals. It is difficult at times to believe that such rehabilitation is what in fact we are striving for!

Maconochie was recalled in 1844 and, in view of official reports of unusual untruthfulness and distortion even for such documents, found that his experiment was considered a failure among the powers that be. He was given another chance (or perhaps half-chance would be a better description?) when he was appointed governor of Birmingham prison. But this too was an appointment without the necessary powers to introduce his methods in their proper form, and again he was soon ousted from his position by the implacable enmity of all the old, ferocious, narrow-minded haters of innovation. He wrote voluminously, and became widely known among prison reformers. He died in 1860, at age seventy-three —twenty years after his Norfolk Island experiment had begun. He was a great man, a leader of thought well ahead of his century; like most prophets, he was not honored in his country. It is only now that we are remembering him, and that his methods are being given a new lease of life by being linked with modern psychological theories, particularly those of Skinner. It is to these modern innovations that we must next turn.

MACONOCHIE had already elaborated the main principle on which modern "token economies" are based, but it may be worthwhile to restate these in rather less archaic language. The first principle is that explicit punishment, particularly in so far as it is based on the infliction of pain, is out. Modern research has shown that such punishment is not necessarily ineffective, but that it leads to the suppression, not the elimination, of the undesired type of response. When the imminence of punishment is removed, the suppressed activity emerges again; rehabilitation has failed. Furthermore, punishment has unpredictable consequences. It is often difficult to tell what these consequences will be, even in the short run. In addition, there is evidence that punishment brutalizes and leads to aggressive behavior. Take two rats and place them in a box. They will take little notice of each other and live together peacefully. Electrify the floor grid of the cage, thus giving them an electric shock — and they will turn and attack each other. By inflicting pain you can make a peaceful rat a vicious, aggressive brute. It does not seem unlikely (and there is some statistical evidence in support of this view) that you can do the same with human beings. Again, human beings are not rats; but they share a common bestiology with them. It seems foolish to run the risk. It is also inhuman.

The second principle is that positive reinforcement should be used whenever possible. This term is not identical with "reward," and I will continue to use it in spite of its awkwardness. *Reward* is something desirable awarded as a consequence of good behavior at some point of time not closely connected with the act in question. *Positive reinforcement* is the administration to the person who is being reinforced of something known to act as a reinforcer (*i.e.* which has previously been shown to motivate him) immediately after the act for which he is being reinforced has been done, so that he (or rather his nervous system) can immediately recognize the contingencies involved: *i.e.* behavior ⟶ reinforcement. It is the stress on temporal contiguity which is the main characteristic of reinforcement. Reward given at some other time, and not experienced as contingent on the behavior in question, is not positive reinforcement. It is this combination of reinforcement and contingency which comprises the essence of the token economy method.

The third principle involved is that the target behavior should be clearly identified, and not loosely described, as is so often the case, in such terms as "good behavior" or "obedience" or "politeness." Behaviorists often go to what appear to be ludicrous lengths to define the particular behaviors they wish to strengthen. However, such detail is absolutely necessary if incoherence in administration and confusion in reinforcement are to be avoided. Not only is this degree of specificity necessary in order that everyone concerned with the program should administer reinforcement along identical lines, and on identical occasions; only in this way can we measure the changes which take place in the behavior observed. Two people can disagree violently about whether a boy has developed the habit of cleanliness, and to what extent. There is no such room for disagreement when you specify whether he has or has not put the soap in its proper place on the basin, has or has not taken a bath, and has or has not washed his hands before dinner. Such precise specification also has the additional virtue that we know what we are talking about. We are so used to discussing things like "honesty" or "pornography" or "cleanliness" in the abstract that we never realize how differently different people interpret these terms. When we are forced to be specific we begin to identify areas of agreement and disagreement. Even if the reader of such a report disagrees with the analytic description of a given abstract term, at least he knows what was in the minds of the writers, and can, if he wishes, duplicate their experiment.

The fourth principle has already been alluded to; it is that the occurrence of the target behavior(s) should be recorded accurately before the beginning of the experiment (*i.e.* before you try to modify behavior, you want to know just what is going on in this area — what people are doing without interference). It is only against such a background that the effects of your experimental treatment can be evaluated. By preference you would have another group, behaving in a similar manner to your experimental group, but left without benefit of the treatment given. And often, of course, you would wish to remove the treatment after the experiment is over, to see how permanent the changes you may have produced might prove to be. Measurement is essential to the advancement of science. Qualitative changes can often be observed with the naked eye, as in the case of Maconochie's experiment, but these can be argued about, and disagreed with — and indeed, malicious "officials" did in fact claim that his work ended in abysmal failure. Only measurement, properly applied and meaningfully interpreted, can help us to compare in any precise fashion the claims of rival theories and practices. Hence the provision of such basic data is an essential part of the behaviorist's theoretical position. It is in relation to this proviso that he differs so profoundly from most other groups, from criminologists to psychoanalysts, from educationalists to lawyers, interested in these areas.

The fifth principle refers to the rewards actually given, and the frequency with which they are given. It is a fundamental law of learning that the frequency of reinforcement is much more important than the magnitude of the reinforcement. You will learn better if you are rewarded a million times by one dollar, than if you are rewarded once with a million dollars! Hence rewards should be small but numerous. Don't reinforce your subject by allowing him to view television for a week, but rather for half an hour; there are so many occasions you would wish to reinforce that otherwise you run out of reinforcers. Many but small is the motto. In this way, you avoid the interference of strong emotions with your procedure. If someone fails to gain his half-hour television permit, he won't mind so much. If he loses a whole week, he will be very upset, and that strong emotion interferes (or may interfere) with the process of conditioning. The people you are dealing with — psychotics, or criminals — are characterized by the fact that they do not have a proper sense of contingent behavior, *i.e.* the sequence of correct conduct → reward. The more frequently they are made to practice this, the more likely they are to learn it, and to modify their behavior accordingly.

There are, to be sure, many other principles, and even those mentioned above are, obviously, deliberately simplified to make them intelligible. A thorough and well written treatment of the whole field, with fascinating accounts of the application of these methods to psychotic hospital patients, is given in a book by T. Ayllon and N. Azrin, *The Token Economy*. This is well worth reading by the interested layman — the authors have succeeded admirably in their purpose of making the procedure clear to all those many people who might be concerned with behavior modification of this type, but who are not trained psychologists. Still, an example is often worth a sackful of theories in making clear what is involved in a new method, and I shall take such an example from some unpublished work on young delinquents, carried out by Montrose Wolf and his colleagues at Kansas.

The boys involved could earn points (tokens) for appropriate behavior, and lose points for inappropriate behavior. The points could be traded for privileges — such as use of a bicycle, tools, games, television, allowances, snacks, freedom to go downtown, or home for a visit. The point system is so arranged that if a youth accomplishes certain tasks expected of him while losing a minimum of points in fines, he will obtain all the privileges without having to perform any extra jobs. Each boy needs about 1,000 points a day to live comfortably. Points are earned by engaging in designated social, self-care and academic behaviors. At the end of each day the earned and lost points are tallied and recorded on a weekly point-sheet. The boys, thirteen to fifteen years of age, have a history of aggression, thieving, truancy and failure at school; they come from low-income families with histories of criminal behavior. They are looked after in groups of about five, in "a home-style, community based, treatment facility." All the boys had been committed by the county juvenile court. The treatment program is administered by the "house parents" who apply and measure the effects of the corrective reinforcement procedures.

The daily routine is similar to that of many families. The boys get up around seven o'clock, shower, dress and clean their bedrooms and bathrooms; after breakfast there are kitchen clean-up duties to perform. School follows, and then the boys return and do homework. Dinner and clean-up chores are followed by free time. Within the limits of their "points" they are free to use it as they please. Parents who have found it difficult to get their non-delinquent, well brought-up children to keep their rooms and themselves clean and tidy, and to help in the kitchen, might ask just how this miracle was accomplished. Consider "cleanliness."

By carefully defining a "clean room" reliable measurement was made possible as well as providing the boys with explicit instruction about the cleanliness criteria. A list of instructions and criteria described how the furniture should be arranged, the closet kept and the beds made. Admittedly, some of the definitions sounded like the army's training manual. For example, a wrinkle was defined as a disconformity of the bedspread which exceeded one inch in height, one inch in width, and twelve inches in length. Observer agreement regarding the cleanliness measure averaged 99 per cent. The reinforcement contingency involved points being earned for each item accomplished when the overall score was 80 per cent or above. Points were lost for each uncompleted item when the overall score was below 80 per cent.

At various times the "points" system was interrupted, and alternative methods tried, such as substituting instructions, or threats, or demands. All of these led to a marked drop in efficiency of cleaning behavior. When the "points" system was reintroduced, it was found to reinstate the desired behavior almost immediately. Finally, the number of days on which reinforcements were applied was reduced to one every two and a half weeks, without loss of effect. This was accomplished by gradually increasing the gap between days on which contingencies were applied.

Other experiments were tried, in order to investigate the effects of different conditions. Consider the introduction of "managers."

"It was possible to arrange the contingencies for aggressive verbal behavior and for bedroom cleaning behavior to relate directly to the behavior of each individual boy. There were other self-care behaviors which were difficult to handle on an individual basis. We first tried contingencies arranged for the group of boys as a whole. However, group contingencies proved to be less effective than other arrangements. A very effective contingency arrangement involved making a single boy responsible for the behavior of the other boys in the group with authority to give and take away points. In this manner, a very effective *managership system* was established.

"The manager was one of the boys who purchased the privilege of being manager and of administering points to his peers. His duties consisted of seeing that a specified list of tasks such as the taking of showers, the cleaning of the bathrooms, yard and basement were accomplished each day. The manager had the authority to give and take points depending on the quality of the job completed. In turn, the manager earned or lost points according to whether the tasks were accomplished or not and, whenever possible, as a function of the quality of work . . ..

"Figure 6 shows the relative effectiveness of the 'Manager system' with its contingencies and a 'group' contingency in maintaining bathroom cleaning behavior. As in the case of the bedrooms and all of these studies, explicit criteria were established for each item in the bathroom. For example, no objects were to be left on the sink, the soap was to be in the soap dish, the toothbrush in the toothbrush holder and all other objects in the medicine cabinet. Reliability of measurement between two observers averaged 97 per cent.

"As can be seen in this figure, under the 'baseline' condition, when the boys were simply instructed to clean the bathrooms, very few of the items were completed. When the 'manager' condition was put in for the first time it took about two weeks for an acceptable level of bathroom cleanliness to occur. The manager condition was then discontinued and point contingencies were placed on the entire group. As you can see various point values which were applied did not produce the level of tidiness that the managership accomplished. When the 'manager' condition was reintroduced the cleaning behavior again improved. When the 'group' contingency condition was put into effect the behavior deteriorated. And again when the 'manager' condition was reinstated the cleanliness of the bathrooms increased significantly . . .

"The next figure describes our analysis of the function of the manager's authority to give and to take away points for the bathroom cleaning behavior of his peers. The heavy lines represent the median scores for the last seven data points under each condition.

"The first 'baseline' condition shows the low rate of behavior when 'no manager' system and 'no point' contingencies were in effect. The 'manager' condition where the manager had the authority to both give and take away points from his peers was then put into effect and there was a dramatic rise in the cleanliness behavior. Of the point consequences administered by the manager 45 per cent of them were positive and 55 per cent of them were negative. It was our hunch that the authority to take away points must be critical for the system so in the next condition we discontinued the manager's ability to take away points. As you can see there was almost no reduction in the effectiveness of the manager system when the manager was only allowed to give points.

"In the fourth condition the manager could neither give nor take away points. As you can see, this had a marked effect on

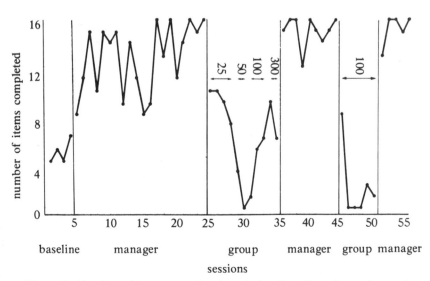

Figure 6. Number of items completed each day for all youths under each condition.

the bathroom cleaning behavior, reducing it significantly, although not down to the level which was reached when the next condition, 'no manager' and 'no points' was introduced. When the managership was reinstated with authority only to give points, but not to take them away, a high level of cleanliness was obtained. During the final period, when the manager had authority both to give and to take away points the level rose again to that reached during the previous period when positive and negative points were given. . . ."

THE POSSIBILITIES of investigating the effects of different reinforcement contingencies are endless, and the outcomes difficult to forecast. It is possible, for instance, to assess the performance of the whole group in cleaning the bathroom and award points to the group in consequence of their performance, but we can vary the way the assignment is made — either to the group as a whole, or specific assignments to specific boys. Would the reader care to predict which would be more effective? The answer is shown in figure 7. Group assignments clearly are less effective than individual

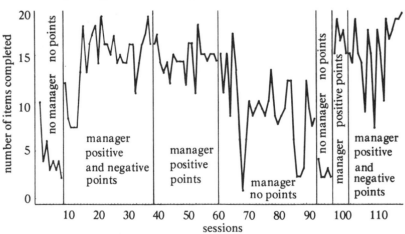

Figure 7. Number of items completed in two bathrooms each day for all youths under each condition.

assignments. In studying the effectiveness of these different systems, the investigators were concerned with four criteria. The system should be *effective* in producing the target behavior. It should be *preferred* by the boys. It should be *practical* and easy for the house parents to oversee. And it should be *educational* by providing the boys with experiences that would be useful to them in the future. No system seemed to meet all the criteria; that of appointing a manager, for instance, or having the boys bid (in points) for that office was not liked by the boys, although good in other ways. Finally the problem was solved by having the boys elect the manager! This made the system acceptable to them, without causing it to lose its effectiveness in promoting the desired behavior. Clearly much detailed work of this kind will need to be done, in many different circumstances and with many different types of groups, before far-reaching generalizations become possible. What is already obvious is that these methods can be made to work with astonishing efficiency, and without antagonizing those who have to work under these "contingencies."

Nor would it be true to say that only gross behaviors, such as cleaning the bathroom, can be manipulated in this fashion. The boys made many aggressive statements when they were first assigned to their groups. When these were made subject to "fines" in terms of points, their use fell drastically, as shown in figure 8; this shows the behavior of three of the youths. Figure 9 shows quite a different problem. One of the youths had difficulties in articulating properly. Four of his difficulties, involving the pronunciation of "ting," "th," "R," and "L" were made subject to "fines," and the outcome was a marked rise in correct enunciations. Clearly these methods cover quite a wide area.

Most impressive of all the applications of this particular

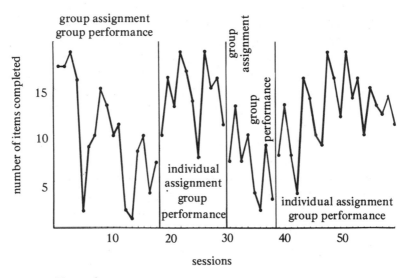

Figure 8.

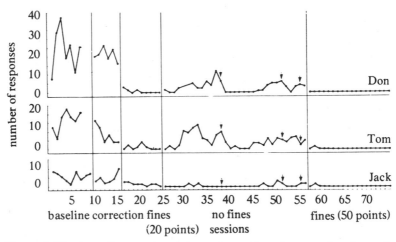

Figure 9. Number of aggressive statements per three-hour session for each youth under each condition. The arrows indicate threats to reinstate the fines condition.

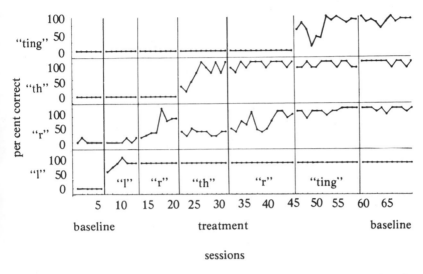

Figure 10. Percentage of correct articulations for one youth using four different classes of words where each class is treated in succession.

technology has been the use of "token economies" in mental hospitals; mention has already been made of the book by Ayllon and Azrin in which some of these are described. These writers took over wards full of chronic psychotic patients who had to all intents and purposes been given up as hopeless, and consigned to custodial care. They were living a vegetable existence and often unable to do anything for themselves. Quite counter to orthodox psychiatric views, Ayllon and Azrin argued that most of the behaviors characteristic of these patients were not the outcome of some "disease" process, but were rather produced by the psychiatric treatment itself. The reinforcement schedules employed stressed passivity, complaining, abnormal behavior and other undesirable forms of conduct by reinforcing these through added attention being given to patients behaving in this fashion. On the other hand, independence, activity, normal behavior generally were discouraged because they did not produce any sort of positive, reinforcing response. They argued, therefore, that by reversing this process, and by reinforcing positive, adequate, well-adapted behavior they would be able to bring out the latent "normality" of the patients.

This they tried to do by instituting a "token economy" rather like that described above, incorporating useful work done in the hospital kitchens, laundries, etc., as well as the use of simple skills (feeding oneself, cleaning oneself, etc.). They formulate their general approach, and its outcome, as follows. Noting the extreme types of symptoms that are seen in some mental hospital patients, they write:

One approach in dealing with patients has been to apply special treatment to these symptoms. The general philosophy that emerged from our efforts, however, was to emphasize the positive aspects of the patient's behaviour. Every attempt was made to bring the total environment to bear on building constructive and functional patterns of behaviour on the part of the patients, leaving until a later date the problem of eliminating symptoms. Surprisingly, it was found that once the procedures were effective in establishing functional behaviour, many of the symptomatic behaviours were no longer present and could not be studied. One can only speculate, of course, but it appears that the symptomatic behaviours by their very disruptive nature were reduced or eliminated because they could not exist side by side with the functional behaviours. In some instances, such as aggressive behaviour or stealing, where a symptomatic behaviour persisted, the treatment for such symptoms was made possible only after the constructive behaviours were established. The general procedure was to provide the patient with additional opportunities for engaging in constructive behaviour and obtaining extra privileges at those times when she was most symptom-free. Such a procedure was, of course, impossible until the patient was actively engaged in these functional activities and availing herself of the many privileges. The general philosophy here may be summarized as eliminating the negative aspects of behaviour by emphasizing the positive.

Both the difficulties encountered in these attempts and the successes achieved are graphically described in the book; it would take us too far afield to go into these in detail. What emerges is one of the most exciting and promising success stories ever to come out of the disappointing and frequently heart-rending field of human unhappiness. When people who have for many years lived a mere vegetable existence, requiring constant support and help in everything they did, suddenly become active, self-supporting and even able to leave the hospital and live independent lives outside, then clearly something important has happened. We know too well what the usual fate of "custodial care" psychiatric patients is to doubt for one moment that the intervention of the "token economy" program is responsible for the changes that have taken place in these patients, and the possibilities of extending this type of management to more and more patients of this type (who in fact take up about half of all hospital beds in Great Britain!) become extremely inviting.

I will not dwell on the obvious humane considerations; most readers may be able to imagine the difference such a transformation must make to the patients affected. Let me just mention the economic consequences of making quite large numbers of such patients effectively self-supporting— inside or outside the hospital. One would imagine (provided one was young and innocent enough) that hospital administrators, Department of Health officials and others concerned with these problems would immediately institute controlled clinical trials to determine to what extent these methods could be used in Britain, and how they could be used to lighten the tremendous burden which patients of this kind place on the national health service.

Older and more experienced heads would have been more realistic, and able to predict the true state of affairs. A stone thrown into the slough of despond could not have caused less response than the publication of this book, or of the many research articles dealing with this topic. As usual, no one cares; no one wants to know; no one is concerned. The thrilling possibilities of being able to help severely disordered, profoundly unhappy people — no response. The important possibilities of being able, in already over-burdened budgets, to save millions which could be used to much advantage in other fields of mental and physical health — no response. Administrators ambulate in their predestined circles. Analysts cling to their outdated and useless theories. Patients go on suffering. The tax-payer goes on paying.

Emerson was obviously wrong when he said that all you had to do was design a better mousetrap and the world would beat a path to your door — the vested interests of mousetrap manufacturers and vendors would effectively ensure that (a) no one would get to hear about your new invention, (b) any accounts would be either biased or unintelligible, (c) no action would be taken, however promising the new mousetrap, and (d) the public would be assured that existing mousetraps were the most perfect conceivable, in the most perfect of all possible worlds. We say that we want to cure mentally ill people. It is difficult to imagine that this is in fact true. It is certainly not our first consideration, which is to preserve the even tenor of our ways. No innovation must be suffered to interfere with what has always been and shall always be. Behaviorist technologies are far from perfect, and, needless to say, they always need further research, added proof and considerable improvement. But the evidence in their favor is strong enough to indicate that they deserve better than the complete neglect which has been their fate to date.

The use of such methods as the "token economy" is, of course, not restricted to psychotics and delinquents. If reinforcement is truly the important general principle which learning theorists claim it is, then it should be useful and indeed indispensable in all human affairs. Many applications have been made, and promising results published. Here I will only mention one such application to what one might call "normal" human problems.

This is the field of marriage, or, perhaps more accurately, that of marriages on the point of breaking up. This application is based on two fairly far-reaching assumptions. The first is that "the exact pattern of interaction which takes place between spouses at any point in time is the most rewarding of all the available alternatives." Thus R. B. Stuart, whose work in this field we will be concerned with. As he points out, "when a husband consistently fails to leave his friends in order to spend time with his wife, it may be concluded that his friends offer greater relative rewards than his wife . . ." The second assumption is that "most married adults expect to enjoy reciprocal relations with their partners . . ." These reciprocal relations are defined to mean that each party has rights and duties, and this in turn carries the behavioral implication that each party to such an interaction should dispense social reinforcement at an equitable rate.

Whenever one partner to a reciprocal interaction unilaterally rewards the other, he does so with the confidence that he will be compensated in kind in the future. For example, if the husband agrees to entertain his wife's parents for a weekend, he does so with the expectation that his wife will accompany him on a weekend fishing trip at some time in the future.

This reciprocity, according to Stuart, develops as a consequence of a history of positive reinforcement. There is ample experimental evidence that people are more attracted to others, and will reinforce these others more, if in turn they have previously been reinforced by them.

When disordered marriages are evaluated in light of this reinforcement-attraction hypothesis, it is seen that each partner reinforces the other at a low rate and each is therefore relatively unattractive to and unreinforced by the other.

This consideration leads to the third assumption, namely that "in order to modify an unsuccessful marital interaction, it is essential to develop the power of each partner to mediate rewards for the other." Thus we have here a prescription for happy marriages, and a method for improving unhappy ones.

When the mutual reinforcement game leads to too low a level of reward, either coercion or withdrawal is likely to develop. "In coercion, one member seeks to gain positive reinforcement from the other in exchange for negative reinforcement" — or perhaps, rather, in exchange for the cessation of negative reinforcement. Thus, take the case of a husband who wants his wife to show greater affection and more sexual compliance, but without providing the reinforcement for her which would produce the desired response. He would then be likely to respond to her refusals by becoming abusive, and accusing his wife of anything from frigidity to unfaithfulness. Cessation of this aversive motivation would then be contingent on his receiving the required affection. This is a clumsy and ultimately unworkable method; it can be observed time and time again in unhappy marriages in the process of going on the rocks. So is withdrawal. This leads in most cases to the discovery of other sources of reinforcement, from drink to mistresses, from drugs to lovers. In the unhappy marriage each partner requires reinforcement from the other, but is unwilling to provide it. What is needed is the realization that before the partner is likely to behave in a satisfactory manner, each person must himself invest in reinforcing behavior, and thus gain some form of control over the other's provision of reinforcements.

Through obvious emotional entanglements both parties are unable to take the first step. It is the task of the psychologist to break this deadlock and wean the marriage partners from their childish behavior. For this purpose Stuart recommends explanation of the situation, and the introduction of a token economy in which tokens are given for reinforcing behavior, to be exchanged for other types of reinforcing behavior. The way this works is as follows.

Each person lists three types of behavior which he would like to see the other partner demonstrate more frequently. These have, of course, to be specified with some precision. It is not much use for a man to say that he wants his wife to be more "feminine," as long as this term remains vague and undefined — presumably one of the difficulties is precisely that what she regards as feminine is not what he so regards! People often object that their partners should know what they want — they shouldn't have to be told. But partners are not clairvoyant, but often ordinary, somewhat insensitive people with their own troubles; they may indeed need to be told. A list containing these three types of behavior on each spouse's part is then posted up, and both are asked to record the frequency with which they are performed. When a baseline has been established of this "pre-therapy" behavior, tokens can be obtained by each partner from the other for the performance of the desired act, to be exchanged on some prearranged system for the performance by the other spouse of some other desired act. The basis is rather crude, of course — you talk to me when you come home for at least one hour, and I will let you make love to me tonight. To the outside observer the whole thing may even look ridiculous. But then observers are usually verbally fluent, highly intelligent people who cannot understand the verbal blockages which often prevent inarticulate people from communicating with each other. Lists such as those described do *something* to facilitate communication; and the performance of the desired behaviors, however artificial the contrivance which brought it about, *does* create reciprocal positive reinforcements.

This example has not been quoted because it illustrates an infallible method of preventing the break-up of marriages. There is too little evidence on the score of effectiveness to say more than that in a few isolated, and perhaps atypical, cases it seemed to work with marriages on the point of breaking up. Nor are the underlying ideas all that original. Do unto others as you would want to be done by — it is not exactly a novel command. It is rather the translation of these vague moral sentiments into a kind of technological program for action which makes the approach so interesting. Another point of interest is the contrast with the more usual purely verbal kind of advice given by marriage counselors. A clinical trial to determine relative effectiveness of these different approaches would be of great interest. Neither approach of course is likely to be effective with all marriage disputes; only a proportion, possibly a small one, is likely to be capable of being restored. However, if both partners could be brought to think along these lines before their marriage got on the rocks, prospects for a happy ending might be much brighter.

THERE IS ONE FIELD in which behaviorist technology has become rather more widely known, and where a beginning has been made on the needed research which alone can make it widely used. That is the field of the so-called teaching machines, or "programmed education." A brief consideration of this new development may fittingly bring this chapter to a close.

In a well-known article Professor B. F. Skinner has pointed out that:

Scarcely any area of human activity has been more resistant to scientific analysis and technological change than education . . . The methods whereby a teacher is supposed to impart knowledge to a room full of pupils have changed scarcely at all. Indeed, a number of critics are persuaded that there has been an actual decline in teaching effectiveness within the past thirty or forty years.

There is little doubt that, broadly speaking, Skinner is correct. There have, admittedly, been minor changes. Thus, some schools use green blackboards instead of the traditional black, and the more adventurous may occasionally use a half-hour of television to help instruct their pupils. Even these small advances have found no foothold in the universities, which still rely exclusively on lectures, seminars, occasional tutorials, and "private study" from textbooks. The university student transplanted miraculously from the year 1600 to our modern universities would be quite at home; and the student who had taken part in the Socratic dialogues at Athens might even feel that the standard of teaching has declined considerably!

There are, of course, many things wrong in the system we operate, and which might be improved without any radical revolution. We select university teachers without any reference to their teaching abilities, and without giving them any training in what is after all a complex and highly skilled trade. Recent complaints from students at many British and American institutions against the low standard of lecturing have been echoed in many other universities, and there can be little doubt that the average standard is deplorably low. Yet even if all of our lecturers were adequate and had received proper training in teaching methods, would this very much affect the applicability of the ancient tag about "facts passing from the notebook of the teacher to the notebook of the student without passing through the mind of either"?

Another problem which also could be solved — at least in theory, but which in practice bedevils all our efforts — is, obviously, the lack of teachers. Can any system of education work efficiently when at school a teacher may have to attend to between thirty and fifty children at any one time, or at a university when a professor may give a lecture to a group of a thousand students who then troop out, only to be replaced by another thousand who receive the same lecture again? The obvious remedy of training more teachers and professors runs into difficulties of finance (in order to attract more people into a profession you must raise their pay) and of distribution of relatively rare abilities (if more persons of high intelligence come into teaching they will be lost to other possibly equally important areas).

These, then, are our two besetting problems. What we are doing, we are not doing very well; and we are doing it under conditions which almost rule out any possibility of doing it well. Furthermore, we have no proper criteria of what "doing well" really means; and we have no scientific information about how we can set about improving things. I have mentioned the possibility of "training" university teachers in the art of teaching, but one would have to be very optimistic to imagine that anyone really knows what should be taught. Certain negative points are, to be sure, obvious. Some people mumble and speak so inaudibly that nobody can hear them. Some people have physical defects which should bar them from teaching. I once suffered for a whole year from a professor of Latin who had a cleft palate which made it impossible to understand a word he said; the lectures were, of course, compulsory! Some teachers have not done their homework and what they say does not make sense. All these are fairly obvious complaints which can be remedied in one way or another. But when it comes to more positive advice do we really know the answers to even the most elementary questions? The answer to this question at least is known. It is no.

Research into some of these problems might improve the position but it is doubtful whether it can drastically reform it. What is needed, as many psychologists now argue, is a complete break with tradition: a proper revolution in teaching methodology. Furthermore, it is argued that the essential breakthrough has already been achieved and that all that is standing in the way now is the usual array of traditional attitudes, sentimental wrong-headedness, and malinformed misunderstanding. What are the facts?

The revolution, as so often happens, began on a very mild note, causing scarcely a ripple of interest when Sidney L. Pressey in the mid-1920s designed the precursors of our modern automated teaching machines. These devices arose from Pressey's work with objective scoring techniques, which form such a large part of the American examination and intelligence-testing movement. Where thousands or even millions of people have to be tested, essays and other traditional type examinations are inefficient and time-consuming—apart from being extremely unreliable. It has often been shown that when the same set of papers is marked by independent examiners, their marks diverge very widely so that quite frequently students' passing or failing is determined far more by who the examiner is than by their actual knowledge and ability. Readers may remember the case recently where an enterprising school entered their children for two different but supposedly equivalent examinations held by different boards and authorities; there was almost no correspondence between passes and failures in these examinations, nor was there correspondence in the actual numbers passing and failing. Objective-type examinations while they have their own difficulties and drawbacks, at least are perfectly reliable and, if properly constructed, undoubtedly more valid than are essay-type examinations for those areas where *knowledge* is being tested rather than ability to write essays.

The typical objective-type examination asks a question and then furnishes several answers, only one of which is right. The student has to indicate which is the correct answer. Here, for

instance, is a typical item from such a test:
Teaching machines were pioneered by:
B.F. Skinner   S. Freud
S.L. Pressey   H. J. Eysenck
[Underline the correct answer]
In his work Pressey added one element which transformed these devices into teaching machines. What he did was to make use of a very important psychological principle which states that knowledge of results is an essential feature in learning. This has been demonstrated many times by experiments such as those of Thorndike who would show his subjects a line of given length and would then ask them to draw this line hundreds of times from memory. He showed that their ability to do so did not improve; but that when they were told after each line drawn whether it was too long, too short, or just right, they learned very quickly. Now one of the essential features of all examinations, whether essay-type or objective-type, is the failure of any feedback to reach the student. He may of course be told days, weeks, or even months later, that he has passed or failed. But he has no way of linking this information with individual items answered correctly or incorrectly. Thus, in the ordinary way, tests do not aid in the process of teaching. Pressey changed this by using a device about the size of a portable typewriter, which presented a question such as that given above to the student through a small window. The student had to press one of four keys corresponding to the four answer positions. If he pushed the correct key the roll of material behind the window moved on and produced the next question. If he pushed the wrong key the question remained until the right key had been pressed. In this way the student not only tested his knowledge but also acquired new knowledge. A few people became interested in the inherent possibilities of this type of device and compared its adequacy with regular classroom teaching; it was reported that results achieved with the machine were superior to those

achieved in ordinary classroom teaching.

However, for reasons which can only be subjects for speculation, Pressey's work did not catch on, except for isolated studies here and there. It was not until the late 1950s that the position began to change.

The change probably came about for two reasons. In the first place, Pressey did not have available a properly worked out set of theories, carefully tested in the laboratory, which could be used to construct teaching programs for his machines and which would lend his work respectability in the circles of theoretical and experimental psychologists. In the second place he did not possess the single-minded, crusading type of personality that has so often been found necessary to push new developments on to an unsuspecting, ungrateful, and potentially distrustful and hostile world. The person to do all this was B.F. Skinner. From his vantage-point at Harvard, Skinner directed a very successful campaign to make teaching machines a household word in educational circles in America.

To understand what Skinner did needs some understanding of his personality and his general attitude to life. Skinner believes very strongly that psychology holds the key to any advancement in, and improvement of, the quality of human life. He further believes that all change is brought about by the process of conditioning (to which I will turn in a moment) and that what is needed is a working out of fundamental laws of conditioning and their practical application to human affairs. He has gone so far as to predict his kind of conditioned Utopia in a novel *Walden II*, a title which will strike strange chords in the hearts of those familiar with Thoreau's original *Walden*. This book is still worth reading as a popular presentation of certain facts and theories in modern psychology, extended to deal with practical affairs and problems.

Making use of the knowledge gained in some thirty years' work with animals, Skinner took up the challenge of teaching machines, *i.e.*, the application of "shaping" to human learning. He first stated the purpose of a teaching machine: "To teach rapidly, thoroughly and expeditiously a large part of what we now teach slowly, incompletely, and with wasted effort on the part of both student and teacher." In order to achieve this aim he departs in several important ways from the original Pressey scheme.

Firstly, he pays little attention to knowledge of results, believing this is only important by virtue of the reinforcement that a correct solution produces in the student. In other words, he assumes that the signal which tells the student he is right is in some way equivalent to the grains of corn which serves to motivate the pigeon. This is an assumption which is difficult to prove; but it forms the basis of Skinner's approach.

Secondly, this emphasis on "stamping in" knowledge through reinforcement makes it desirable that such reinforcement should be given very frequently and, accordingly, Skinner stresses the construction of programs of learning which proceed by small steps and are accompanied by questions such as the average student will nearly always succeed in answering. Our little example of who pioneered teaching machines will show how this is done. By the time the reader reached this item he had already been given enough information to answer it correctly.

Thirdly, and leading to the same conclusion, Skinner believes that wrong answers are to be avoided at all costs. As he says: "Our ability to remember wrong facts—because we recall having read them somewhere—is notorious. Every wrong answer on a multiple-choice test increases the probability that the student will some day dredge out of his imperfect memory the wrong answer instead of the right one." This contradicts his stress on reinforcement—why should the student so tenaciously remember something which has *not* been reinforced? However, logical consistency has never worried Skinner very much, and the programs he has constructed certainly emphasize small steps and almost uniformly successful completion of each item.

Skinner is opposed to multiple-choice questions and prefers that "the student should compose his response rather than select it from a set of alternatives. One reason for this is that we want him to recall rather than merely recognize—to make a response as well as see that it is right." This is his fourth point of difference from Pressey.

Skinner and his followers have, accordingly, constructed and experimented with machines which are different from those previously employed. A question is exposed, and the student writes his answer in the proper space. He then pulls a lever which exposes the correct answer and also hides his written response under a sheet of celluloid so that he cannot go back and alter it. After comparing the two and seeing that he is right he then goes on to the next question, writes in his answer, etc. Skinner has also constructed somewhat more elaborate two-stage machines, in which the student writes his response and then uncovers not the correct response but additional information which enables him to correct his reply, if necessary, before uncovering the correct answer.

Skinner has actually used these machines in teaching his psychology course at Harvard, and he maintains that students "like the machine" and reports that they "learned more in less time and with less effort than in conventional ways." There is good evidence from published studies that these findings are fairly general. Both students and children become fascinated with the machines, like using them, find work with them easier than attending lectures or reading books, and learn more in comparable periods of time than they would otherwise do.

Many other workers have taken up this topic in recent years, and not all of them have followed Skinner in his theoretical analysis or in his practical methods of programming. There is, for instance, the so-called "branching" method in which the steps from one question to another are rather larger, so that more errors occur. Whenever the question is wrongly answered, however, the program branches so that the person giving the wrong answer is taken back over a series of steps that would finally enable him to give the right answer. Only then will he join the main program again and go on to the next question. This type of program has the advantage that the very bright can go ahead in large steps, as befits their ability, and are not bored by too small steps and repetitive questions. The not-so-bright can recapitulate whenever they go wrong and have a program prepared for them which is particularly suitable for their level of understanding. Which of these types of program is preferable will usually depend on the degree of variability in intelligence, previous knowledge, etc., existing in the group of students who are to make use of the program. If they are very homogeneous, branching programs may not be needed. If they are very heterogeneous, branching programs will almost be a necessity. It will be noted that, according to Skinner, branching programs should not work very well because wrong answers are frequently given; the evidence does not suggest that this interferes very much with learning.

Skinner concludes that "machines such as those we used at Harvard could be programmed to teach, in whole or in part, all the subjects taught in elementary school and high school, and many taught in college." I think the evidence supports Skinner's claim, and it also suggests that he is right in thinking that his machines will carry out the task more efficiently and in shorter time than would be true of human teachers.

LET ME ADD AT ONCE that the value of any actual comparisons that have been made is strictly limited. There are several reasons for this.

In the first place, there are obviously good and bad teachers, and there are good and bad programs. It is very difficult in any particular study to know whether the program was as good of its kind as the teacher was compared to other teachers. Indeed, one might almost say that the question at the moment cannot be answered. All that we can say is that the average teacher under present conditions will usually not do as well as the machine using a program of average excellence. This may not *necessarily* be due to any inherent superiority in the program. It *might* be due to the interest and the resultant drive produced by introducing some new toy into the school and allowing the children to play with it. In other words we may be dealing here with a new version of the famous "Hawthorne" effect. It will be remembered that industrial psychologists at this plant found that gradual improvement in working conditions produced considerable increase in output. It was at first attributed to the change in conditions. It was then found, however, that the improvement went on although the conditions had now changed for the worse. It is generally believed that improvement was due to a change in attitude on the part of the workers, produced largely by the personal interest shown in them by the investigators! Something of this kind might very well be active in many of the experiments that have been reported, although in other cases the machines have been used for a long enough period of time to make this explanation unacceptable.

Why, then, does a machine work better than the teacher? The answer, paradoxically enough, may be that it proceeds in a less machine-like fashion. A teacher faced with a class of fifty pupils or a professor faced with a class which may number several hundred has little or no chance of receiving any feedback from individual members of the class. They may understand what he says or they may not; he will not know until the final examinations are held. Very occasionally a given child or student may be asked a question by the teacher and the reply will provide some degree of feedback, and, if correct, an increment in reinforcement. But this occurs so rarely for any given child or student that it may for all practical purposes be disregarded.

In the case of the teaching machine, however, there is direct "personal" contact. The student is constantly active, receiving information this minute, answering questions the next minute, checking on the accuracy of his answer, going back over a branch line when his answer has betrayed a lack of understanding, and generally not proceeding until he has thoroughly digested all the information required. With some modern programs it is possible to have 10,000 individuals go through the machine in such a way that not two of them answer the same series of questions! In other words, there is here a degree of *individual* adaptation of teaching to student needs which could only be achieved if one human teacher were available for each student. Even then it is doubtful whether any human being could keep up this constant interplay for any length of time, or could proceed in a series of scientifically planned steps, tested carefully in many thousands of program hours.

This, indeed, is another outstanding feature of the man/machine interaction. A record of right and wrong answers is left behind when the teaching is finished, and this can be statistically analyzed to disclose those stages where questions are too difficult, where spacing is incorrect or where meaning is obscure. Programs can then be improved and rewritten until they are tailored to the needs of a particular group of students in a way that probably no human teacher could achieve.

Skinner claims that teaching machines provide a means of solving many of our educational problems in a completely revolutionary way. I have little doubt that in essence he is right. We may disagree with certain details of his own programs or even with major parts of his theory. This is completely unimportant because, like all scientific advances, these matters are self-correcting. Research is proceeding on a large scale at the moment in the United States (and to some extent also in Britain), and the answers to most factual problems will undoubtedly be forthcoming in the next ten years or so.

What arguments are there to put against these new developments?

MANY OPPONENTS SAY that not all subjects can be taught by machines, and this objection is certainly true at the moment but largely irrelevant. What can and cannot be taught adequately by machines is a matter for research and informed decisions, and already experiments are under way to teach such things as "sense of rhythm," inductive reasoning, and so on. Whether these and other topics can or cannot be taught will soon be known. But in any case the fact that some subjects cannot be taught does not invalidate the claim that others *can*, or the deduction that they *should*.

Another complaint is that these new methods will displace the teacher, and that this in some unspecified way would be a disaster. This, again, is not true. It is not suggested that teachers, professors, and others engaged in education should hand over completely to the machine. It is merely suggested that they should use the machine to relieve them of certain standardized routine types of duty which are boring in themselves and can be performed better by the machine. In most subjects—perhaps not all—there is a large amount of factual information that has to be mastered before any interesting or stimulating contact between student and teacher is possible. I am moderately sure in my own mind that my students can get something more out of a seminar in which we discuss the approaches of different learning theorists, or the methods of personality measurement used by different schools, than they could from any machine program. I am much more certain, however, that this interplay is only possible *after* they have acquired a great deal of factual information in all these fields which they can get very much better from a good program than from me. This is not a statement prompted by modesty. It is simply a statement of fact, based on a large amount of research.

This links up with another criticism which is often voiced: namely, that a good teacher can provide enthusiasm and an enlargement of the student's outlook which goes well beyond any facts that might be taught. I would be the last person to deny this. But, again, I think an inspiring teacher might if anything be helped if the drudgery of imparting elementary facts were handed over to a machine, leaving him free for his own much more important contribution.

Cost is a much more rational criticism. Here, again, I don't think it is a very convincing one. Admittedly some of the more complex machines are very expensive at the moment, but this is usually true only because they are not mass-produced. Mass-production—and simplification made possible by the universal use of such machines in schools and universities— would bring down the price abruptly to such a level that cost would have to be set against the saving in salaries which might be achieved, and also against the improvement in knowledge and qualifications following upon the introduction of such machines. It is quite impossible at the present time to lay out a balance-sheet of this kind. I doubt very much if cost should prove a decisive factor either way.

While I do not think that these criticisms and objections have very much value, there are a few comments which I think may be worth making. The first point is that the advocates of teaching machines *have* neglected a very important variable. All the research has dealt with averages, but there has been no effort to find out the importance or relevance of individual differences. It is reasonably well known that introverts prefer private study and reading, while extroverts prefer lectures and seminars; and it is possible that each type of person gets more out of the activity preferred. It does not seem likely that all types of personalities would benefit equally from machine teaching or from identical types of programs, and research along these lines would seem to be exceptionally important.

Unfortunately, nothing very much can be said about this as no one appears to have done any research into this problem. Even on Skinner's own principles one would have expected some interest in these matters. It has been shown, for instance, that introverts benefit from praise, extroverts from blame. Surely this fact must be relevant to the use, say, of "branching" programs? Indeed, we now know that in fact introverts benefit more from teaching machines than do extroverts; this type of knowledge is important but alien to Skinner's thinking.

Many other similar points could be made in criticism of the existing programs of research. But when it is remembered that serious work in this field is only about ten years old, I think that to ask for perfection is unreasonable. Instead of pursuing this line I would like to conclude by stating what to my mind, is the most important outcome of all this work. It is possible to argue, I believe, that the actual physical existence of teaching machines is the *least* important result of the work of Pressey and Skinner. What they have demonstrated is the importance of a tough-minded experimental approach to the problems of teaching and learning, and the value of using whatever principles (or laws) learning theory has to offer us in this respect. The man-in-the-street and the educationalist have not always realized the possible contribution the scientific approach can make to areas such as education which have traditionally been represented by non-scientists. The work here described has forced them to look for the first time at some examples at least of the scientific approach. Imperfect as these undoubtedly are, they are sufficiently challenging to arouse interest, and to call for further research.

This research may lead to unexpected directions. What we learn about ways of programing machines may help us to "program" teachers, if this use of the term be permitted. In other words, what we learn about the most efficient ways of teaching has general applicability and may furnish us with the knowledge needed to teach teachers to teach.

In many ways the advances I have described here are parallel in the educational field to the advances made by behavior therapy in the psychiatric field. In each case the application of modern experimental techniques and methods has led to a breakthrough which opens up exciting possibilities for the future. If these possibilities are to be realized it is important that the man-in-the-street should fully understand what is happening and should be kept informed of progress. This is only an interim report. I have no doubt that in a few years' time our understanding will be much more complete and a much more definitive report could then be written.

Teaching machines, and the programming of educational material, are not of course the only contributions which behaviorism has made to education. Some of the methods of "shaping," and some of the principles of the token economy, have been used with great success in the classroom, for such purposes as keeping discipline. Typically, many teachers (not unlike mental nurses, parents, and others concerned with discipline) make the fundamental error of applying reinforcement at the wrong time, and for the wrong type of behavior. The effect is only too often the opposite to that which they want to produce. The pattern of a typical example is, by now, familiar. Little Johnny is working well and quietly; teacher pays no attention. Little Johnny gets naughty and starts making a fuss; teacher pays attention, goes over to him, speaks to him—and reinforces his bad behavior, because human interaction is for most children a very reinforcing kind of activity. The fact that she tells him off is not very relevant. It is rather like the habit of some Sunday newspapers to publish pornographic stories under the guise of "exposing" some evil—usually the only evil in question is that produced by the paper itself! Similarly, a film which portrays the wonderful life led by some gangster hoodlum is not likely to elevate the moral tone of its audience by making him pay the supreme penalty in the last two minutes. It is the interaction with the teacher which lifts the child out of its boredom, and acts as a reinforcer; what she says goes in one ear and out of the other. Much better to overlook most petty naughtinesses, and punish the more serious ones by some form of banishment—with a minimum of interaction. Better still to reinforce good behavior, by noticing it, talking to the child, and praising him. Best of all, according to some research done in recent years, is to introduce some form of token economy in which children earn points, or tokens, or sweets for good behavior, and lose them for bad behavior.

As always, the behaviors in question must be rigorously defined, and a scale of rewards laid down. After a very short time, the effects are quite startling. Even very badly behaved classes have been found to simmer down, and to improve dramatically. The precise method of implementation needs a good deal of research in each case, of course; British children may not always react the same way as American; young and old children may differ, as may boys and girls. But the principle seems to work very well, and might be worth teaching to prospective teachers—what they learn about classroom management at the moment is not usually of much practical use. There are, however, some dangers in these methods, and oddly enough they appear in a form which recalls the joke about rats already quoted in the first chapter: "Look how well I've got my psychologist conditioned— whenever I press this lever he comes and feeds me!"

The experimenters in one of these studies decided to introduce control periods, *i.e.* periods when the token economy was suspended, so that the children could not earn points by good behavior. They arranged to have the morning sessions run along token economy lines, and the afternoon sessions without tokens. However, they had reckoned without the children. From a pre-experimental number of hourly "misdeeds" of about fifty, the introduction of the token economy soon managed to reduce the number to between five and ten. When the non-token afternoon sessions were introduced, however, the number of "misdeeds" rose to 120! In other words, the children, annoyed at being deprived of the opportunity of earning points (and all the goodies which could be obtained that way), proceeded to administer negative reinforcement to the experimenters, by misbehaving so badly in the afternoons that the experiment could not be continued (and the tokens had to be reintroduced in the afternoon also). This odd and true story raises the question, obviously, of *who* was the better psychologist—the experimenter or the children. I will not try to answer it here. Nor will I go into another question which will probably have occurred to many readers, namely that of the ethics of behavior manipulation. This, and the allied problem of "brain-washing," I will leave to a later chapter.

The Rise of the Mediocracy

IN 1958 Michael Young published his tragi-comic pseudo-historical account of *The Rise of the Meritocracy—1870-2033: an essay on education and equality.* He wisely cast it in the form of a novel, not only because this made the book more readable, but also because it enabled him to sidestep awkward questions which psychologists and educationalists might have asked about his many *obiter dicta.* In this way he also escaped the necessity of suggesting realistic alternatives to the selection methods in education which he attacked so vigorously — in particular, the method of selection by intelligence test. In this short chapter, I wish to look at two large and probably insoluble problems in education — selection and the prediction of educational success — and to suggest that we are at present taking a retrogressive path which is likely to lead to consequences which few people really desire. To say this makes it incumbent upon me to say what I regard as desirable. It is only when ends are agreed, or at least comprehensively identified, that discussion about means becomes realistic, and debate meaningful.

Jean Floud stated one desideratum of educational policy which I think most people would endorse, when she pleaded for a policy to "secure the adult citizen's right to have been educated to the limit of his natural capacities." This, of course, is a Utopian ideal, but one to which educational policy should always aim to approximate. It states, as it were, the individual's right *vis-à-vis* society: his just and inalienable claim which may at present be unattainable in full, but which should never be forgotten in the scramble for money, buildings, priorities, balance-of-payments crises, and political upheavals. Another desideratum comes from the needs of society. We cannot exist without a proper supply of teachers, doctors, engineers, economists, businessmen, mathematicians, lawyers, technicians, historians, writers, musicians—the list is endless, but each entry presupposes long and skilful education and training. We cannot hope at present to educate enough people to fill our needs in each of these categories—doctors are but one obvious example, as are mathematics teachers. There are economic difficulties here, as in building enough teaching hospitals, and there is a contradiction between society's needs and our first principle— not enough children seem to feel that their "natural capacities" include mathematical ability!

Taking these individual and social needs together, we must contrast them with a society's ability to invest sufficient money and time in education—primary, secondary and tertiary, to use these ugly and antiquated terms. In our lifetime, and in that of our children, we are unlikely to reach a point where enough educational facilities exist to enable all demands to be satisfied; even in the U.S.A., so much richer than the U.K., this point is still at a Utopian distance. Given these hard facts, which are not in dispute, there is an obvious need for some principle of selection. Where only a small proportion can be given places in the universities, as against the pressure of much larger numbers who wish to go, and/or who are needed by society to go, some form of selection is inevitable. The same is true (at least in Britain) of secondary education — it is impossible for everyone to go on to Advanced (A) levels, and selection is necessary. Just how much money is to be invested in education is a political decision, and it is not the purpose of this chapter to argue the point; all that is required is the acknowledgement of the fact that not sufficient money is likely to be available for all legitimate needs *whatever political party may be at the helm.*

SUCH SELECTION may be along one of two lines. The first kind we may call natural selection, or selection by successive hurdles. The child passes through successive stages in his education, and his relative success is gauged by examination results. Later stages depend on his success in earlier stages; no entry to university without success in several "A" level subjects, for instance. This "natural" system may not be universal. By going outside the selective system, *e.g.* by investing in education through fee-paying schools, some of these hurdles may be avoided, though not all. To most people this type of selection seems natural, and superior to the alternative, which makes use of special measures of that set of "natural capacities" Jean Floud referred to. Such measures are usually identified with I.Q. tests, although in actual practice no selection in terms of I.Q. only has ever been practiced in England. The 11+ examination for instance, used tests of English and arithmetic in addition to I.Q. tests in determining the 11-year-old pupil's standing, thus giving intelligence only one third of the total weight in deciding on his future schooling. Why add this "unnatural" hurdle to the others, and why regard its inclusion as a decisive step towards fulfilment of the great educational ideal of a democracy?

THE ARGUMENT is a very simple one. Nobody would seriously dispute that a child's chances of surmounting educational hurdles depends very much on the quality of the education he receives. The better his teaching, and the facilities of his school, the more likely he is to do well in his examinations. But it is well known that certain schools are better than others. This gives pupils in the better schools an undeserved advantage over those in the worse ones. Such advantages favor urban over rural children. They favor middle-class children over working-class ones. This is true even when we look simply at state-provided education; the disparity may become even larger when we include in our survey private schools of one kind or another. It is possible (we will look at the evidence in a minute) that measures of intelligence, such as the despised I.Q., may be less dependent than educational achievement on extraneous advantages enjoyed by middle-class children. If this were so, then we might use them to redress the balance and lay more stress on the children's "natural capacities," rather than on their acquired learning.

This notion of the intelligence test as an "instrument of social justice" owes much to Sir Godfrey Thomson, and a good deal can be learned by looking at the results of its first use in this capacity in the middle 1920s, when, in Britain, the Northumberland Education Committee introduced such a test into its scholarship examination for grammar school selection. Its main reason was to try to redress the balance between rural and urban children. Too few of the former had obtained grammar school places, and the reason in all probability was the poor schooling available in remote, rural schools, many of which were of the single-teacher kind, with poor equipment and few books. If rural children were disadvantaged in this way, and if I.Q. tests were less dependent on environmental and particularly school influences, then the introduction of such tests should increase the number of children from rural schools who had been excluded previously in spite of high ability. The result of the experiment was an immediate and spectacular rise in the number of rural children admitted to grammar school.

Note that it is not suggested that I.Q. tests are *pure* measures of innate cognitive or educable ability. It is merely suggested that their use *tends* to redress a balance upset by environmental forces which act in rather a gross manner on other even more imperfect ways of measuring which had been relied on in the past. Note that it is not suggested that I.Q. as measured is entirely *innate* and completely *immutable*; these notions have never formed part of any reputable psychologist's theories—least of all those of the late Sir Cyril Burt, who has probably done more than anyone to advance the scientific study of intelligence, and who has often been cast in the role of villain in these discussions.

In our argument the point that I.Q. tests are less dependent on school influences than are educational attainment tests is vital, and it may be useful to give some evidence for it. Consider a study carried out in Hertfordshire by two leading British sociologists, Jean Floud and A. H. Halsey. The Education Authority dropped the use of the I.Q. test, in response to attacks, and these investigators compared the social composition of the local grammar schools in 1952 and in 1954 — *i.e.,* before and after the I.Q. test had been dropped. The categorizing of children by parental occupation was less reliable in the later year, and they allocated "all doubtful and unclassifiable cases" to the working-class group; yet the proportion of working-class children fell from 14.9 per cent to 11.5 per cent! At the same time the percentage of children of professional and managerial parents rose from 40 per cent to 64 per cent. And remember that these changes occurred when the I.Q. test only constituted one third of the selection test. If selection had been only on the basis of I.Q. (which is not being suggested as desirable), then the number of working-class children admitted to grammar school would have been greater still than 14.9 per cent, and the number of children from professional and managerial parents smaller still than 40 per cent. Thus this example illustrates admirably the continued value of I.Q. tests as instruments of social justice.

Other investigators, like Professor E. D. Fraser in Aberdeen, and Dr. J. Douglas, have studied the relationship between environmental variables and intelligence and attainment tests. Both find (although in the latter's case one has to calculate the result from some figures given in another context) that the correlation is higher for the attainment tests than for the I.Q. tests — even though the I.Q. tests used in school selection (often called "verbal reasoning" tests) contain more education-related material than might be ideally desirable, and are more closely correlated with social class than are non-verbal intelligence tests. J. L. Daniels, for instance, found a difference of eighteen points of I.Q. between working-class children and middle-class children on a verbal test, and one of eleven points on a non-verbal test. Many other similar investigations in the U.S.A. have given similar results, leaving little doubt about the aid that I.Q. tests can give in redressing the educational balance in favor of the bright but underprivileged working-class child.*

These being the facts, one might assume that on rational grounds liberal and left-wing educationalists would welcome the I.Q. as a selection device, while conservative and right-wing ones would reject it. After all, its main effect would be to allow large numbers of able working-class children, otherwise debarred, to enjoy higher and better education than they would otherwise, at the expense of less able middle-class children who are at present favored through the environmental advantages they enjoy by virtue of their parents' affluence. This, however, has not been so. Left-wing educationalists, left-wing politicians and left-wing writers have mounted a strong attack on I.Q. testing, and indeed on the very concept of the I.Q. and its measurement, which makes up in vitriolic vituperation what it lacks in factual knowledge and logical argument. Michael Young, too, although much less vitriolic and much more knowledgeable than his colleagues, has joined the chorus (and perhaps even helped to inspire it).

---

*I have given special attention to the complexities (racial, especially) of the American stituation in my recent book, *The I.Q. Argument* (The Library Press, 1971).

Like them he seems to dislike the very notion of an elite, predestined and predisposed to intellectual leadership and to the enjoyment of the fruits of education. Such an attitude is reasonable when the make up of the elite is decided in terms of parental blue blood, or capitalistic ideas of "buying" the best education possible or available. It becomes meaningless when what is at issue is the very stuff of which education is made, namely the educable qualities of the children themselves. There is no doubt that these qualities are in large measure inherited — the very fact that using I.Q. tests for selection *increases* the proportion of working-class children and *decreases* the proportion of middle-class children chosen for more advanced education should make this point clear, even if the experimental evidence available were not as over-whelmingly strong as it is. Dropping I.Q. tests thus has but one obvious and clear-cut effect: it makes it less likely that bright children who are socially disadvantaged will obtain an education suited to their natural capacities, while dull children with social advantages will receive an education which they cannot properly appreciate, and which may cause them to emerge as failures, dropouts, or throw-outs. Can this be, one wonders, the intention of idealistic socialists trying to create a new Jerusalem in our green and pleasant land?

Those so criticized may reply that their notions are somewhat different. If some are disadvantaged as compared with others, then we should pour money into special educational measures to help the disadvantaged —whether their I.Q.s are specially high or not. Let us not worry, they say, about these innaccurate and not completely independent assessments of alleged inborn differences. Let us instead redress the balance of social advantage educationally, by giving special help to all those who come from poor homes, or go to poor schools, or who have suffered privations in other ways. This form of reasoning does more honor to the hearts than to the heads of those proposing it. For two reasons. The first reason is that it has been tried, and failed; the second is that *with limited resources* available for all of education, special help to some means less education for others. A brief paragraph will amplify these two objections.

The notion of "compensatory education" is not a new one. It has been bruited about a good deal in the U.S.A. and in recent years large-scale government programs have been instituted in several countries with the purpose of putting it into effect. As Professor Arthur Jensen pointed out in his famous paper in the *Harvard Education Review* which is still attracting much attention, "compensatory education has been tried and it apparently has failed." The whole paper is relevant to my argument and I have developed it at length in my book the *I.Q. Argument,* but here I will just quote one paragraph.

Compensatory education has been practised on a massive scale for several years in many cities across the nation. It began with auspicious enthusiasm and high hopes of educators. It had unprecedented support from Federal funds. It had theoretical sanction from social scientists espousing the major underpinning of its rationale: the deprivation hypothesis, according to which academic lag is mainly the result of social, economic and educational deprivation and discrimination—an hypothesis that has met with wide, uncritical acceptance in the atmosphere of society's growing concern about the plight of minority groups and the economically disadvantaged. The chief goal of compensatory education—to remedy the educational lag of disadvantaged children and thereby narrow the achievement gap between "minority" and "majority" pupils—has been utterly unrealized in any of the large compensatory education programs that have been evaluated so far.

This evaluation is borne out by the United States Commission

Report on Civil Rights in 1967, which said:
The Commission's analysis does not suggest that compensatory education is incapable of remedying the effects of poverty on the academic achievement of individual children. There is little question that school programs involving expenditures for cultural enrichment, better teaching, and other needed educational services can be helpful to disadvantaged children. *The fact remains, however, that none of the programs appear to have raised significantly the achievement of participating pupils, as a group, within the period evaluated by the Commission.*

The second point to be made is probably too obvious to require much discussion. The sum total of money available for education in even the richest countries of the West, is limited. In Britain it is well below minimum requirements for even the most essential needs of the children involved; if any large part of this is spent on programs of compensatory education, then less is available for all other types of education. If the probabilities of success for such compensatory education programs were high, then a reasonable argument could be put forward regarding priorities. When the evidence from large-scale, well-set-up and lavishly financed American studies is as clearly negative as seems to be the case, then only political prejudice outweighing all contrary evidence can persist in calling for expenditure of large sums of money on what must at present be regarded as a lost cause.

Jensen remarks that had the facts about inheritance of intelligence been taken into account, then the prospects of the "compensatory education" programs would have seemed much less bright; he gives an excellent discussion of the evidence concerning the heritability of intelligence. To his analysis might, with advantage, be added some estimates recently made in England by Professor J. L. Jinks and Dr. D. W. Fulker, respectively a geneticist and a psychologist, of the influence of hereditary factors on performance in I.Q. tests and in attainment tests. Heritability of I.Q. they find to be around 75 per cent; heritability of educational attainment they find to be less than 30 per cent. In the former they find "common family environment unimportant"; in the latter they find "common family environment very important and accentuated by effect of correlated environments." This agrees perfectly with Godfrey Thomson's view, and also with that of Cyril Burt. It bodes ill for any attempt to leave out of account in a nation's educational schemes the innate abilities and capacities of its children.

It is seldom realized to what extent these innate capacities are in fact wasted under our present system. When I.Q.s are measured of doctors and lawyers, miners and garbage-collectors, it is usually found that the brightest 10 per cent of the latter score *higher* than the dullest 10 per cent of the former; indeed, some garbage-collectors and miners score as high as any of the doctors and lawyers. The children of these two groups of middle- and working-class people overlap even more. But the fact remains that when equated for I.Q. the middle-class children have a much better chance of a good education than the working-class children. The bright street-cleaners and miners, and their children, are the victims of social injustice; the dull doctors and lawyers, and their children, are the beneficiaries. It has been calculated that while on the average, working-class groups have somewhat lower I.Q.s than middle-class groups, yet the *total* number of highly intelligent people is *as large* in the former as in the latter — due to the larger number of working-class people in the population. Society is the loser if bright working-class children are not educated to the limit of their ability, and so of course are the children themselves; greater, not less, use of I.Q. tests would seem to be the answer to this problem.

THERE ARE, OF COURSE, OBJECTIONS to I.Q. tests, and some of these have some merit. I.Q. tests are declared to be fallible; of course they are. All scientific measurement is subject to error; the size of the expected error has to be judged in relation to other errors involved in the total process of allocation and advancement. Thus we rely very much on examination results, yet it has been demonstrated over and over again that examinations are extremely unreliable — very much more so than I.Q. tests. Hartog and Rhodes, in their *An Examination of Examinations,* showed that even when the same set of papers is marked twice by the same examiner, marked changes in scores appear. These become much greater when the same set of papers is marked by different examiners. And when the same set of candidates writes two separate examinations, marked by different assessors, reliability sinks very low. I.Q. tests are constructed for maximum reliability, and achieve very high levels indeed. Examinations are not constructed for reliability — in fact, the very notion of reliability does not seem to enter the heads of those setting and marking them; when they are tested, they are nearly always found wanting. Thus, we are asked to rely on what are known to be unreliable instruments, and to reject what are known to be reliable instruments, for the simple reason that the latter are not quite perfect. This is curious reasoning. Human beings have to make important decisions many times a day, on the basis of knowledge and evidence which is not perfectly reliable; one should try to make the evidence as reliable as possible, not reject relevant facts because they are not perfectly accurate. The important thing to discover is whether these facts actually improve the validity and the accuracy of the decision; there can be little doubt that I.Q. tests do serve that function, even in their present imperfect state.

But are I.Q. tests not subject to coaching? Yes, they are; however, two or three hours of practice preceding the administration of the final test would wipe out all coaching effects, so that this does not present any great problem in a properly organized examination system.

How about late developers? Yes, they would seem to exist, but it is not impossible to predict which children will be late developers. Some recent work has shown that this tendency is associated with personality (introverts seem to be slower in development), and the relevant personality traits can be measured. Doing so would presumably increase the predictive accuracy of the I.Q. tests.

Does the I.Q. not change with time? Yes, it does, although mostly at ages below ten and eleven; the changes subsequent to the beginning of secondary education are much smaller, although in individual cases they can be quite marked. Research has shown, however, that certain types of tests and problems predict terminal I.Q. better than the usual tests which are more concerned with present status; it should not be impossible to construct measuring instruments which predict future I.Q. better than existing ones.

Has research not shown that instead of I.Q. we should be talking about different special abilities — verbal, numerical, perceptual, etc.? Yes, there is much evidence that a profile of abilities is more useful than the I.Q., which is more or less an average drawn through such a profile — if only educational authorities would use such tests, they are available in profusion.

Do not "convergent" tests, like traditional I.Q. tests, fail to measure important qualities like originality, which is better measured by "divergent" tests? Probably, but again it is up to the educational authorities to carry out research and use such tests if they are found useful; there is no problem in principle. The sad point is that (a) educational authorities have continued using the 1920s type of test, with little change, and have refused to pay attention to the many important developments in the psychological analysis of intelligence which have occurred in recent years; and (b) that educational authorities have shown little sense of responsibility for introducing proper research supervision of the working of their schemes, together with the provision of experimental introduction of innovations to keep them up to date. This is true of the various governmental Departments of Education, too, which ought to take a much more active part in investigating the precise effects of changing methods of allocation, and the possibilities of improvement emerging from academic research. Objections to I.Q. tests frequently made, such as those mentioned above, often have a real foundation and are by no means frivolous, but neither are they insuperable. Their import can be reduced considerably, or abolished altogether, by introducing a more scientific method of test construction and evaluation into the encrusted and old-fashioned system.

The experience in Britain is not insignificant, especially after the years of socialist policy under the Labour Government. Have then the British not escaped from the need for allocation, and therefore the whole worry about I.Q. testing, through the abolition of the 11+, and the (almost) universal introduction of the comprehensive schools? Such a belief, while widespread, is of course completely unrealistic. The 11+ type of examination is still retained, but in a disguised form, and with headmaster's recommendation exerting a decisive influence in border-line cases; children still take the examination, but are not told about it and may not know what the results have been. Inter-school grouping is certainly diminishing, but intra-school grouping is not. *Grouping in Education,* a book edited by A. Yates, lists nine separate methods widely used for this purpose. These are: (1) grading, (2) special classes, (3) tracking, (4) streaming and setting, (5) informal grouping, (6) planned heterogeneous grouping, (7) planned flexible grouping, (8) teachability grouping, and (9) intra-class grouping. To this should be added what might be called a disguised form of inter-school grouping. Even among comprehensive schools (as in American high schools) there are good and bad ones, using these terms to refer to the quality of the teachers, the provision of facilities, the qualities of the buildings, the average level of pupil ability, and similar relevant aspects of schooling. If the schools serve the same neighborhood, then the brighter children will tend to be "creamed off" by the better school — particularly the brighter children of middle-class parents who know what education is all about. Attempts are often made to avoid this by setting limits to the number of children each school can take in various broad ability grades, but such attempts are doomed to at least partial failure by the very breadth of these grades. As an extreme example, suppose we force each school to take 50 per cent of children above I.Q. 100, and 50 per cent below; the good school could take those above 115, leaving those between 100 and 115 to the bad school, and those between 90 and 100, leaving those below 90 to the bad school. The condition of equal allocation by grade would have been obeyed, but the mean I.Q. levels in the two schools would be quite different.

However this may be, no one would argue that the need for allocation disappears when we reach the level of university education. Selection at this level poses a very serious and difficult problem for all university teachers — and one which has certainly not been solved. There is almost no recourse here to intelligence tests, although the evidence suggests very strongly that *proper* use of *appropriate* tests could be of *considerable* help.* Intelligence tests can help, not only in the selection of students, or their rejection, but also in their allocation; tests of special verbal, numerical or perceptual

---

*Note the adjectives inserted in this sentence. Enthusiastic amateur psychologists have sometimes experimented with inappropriate tests used improperly, only to find the results disappointing. This is not surprising. Just as the ability to read the temperature of the patient on a thermometer does not enable the layman to diagnose the patient's disease, so the ability to administer a routine group test does not endow the layman with the right to interpret the results—quite apart from the question of how to choose the right test in the first place!

abilities may suggest better and more suitable courses of study than are often selected by students ignorant of the requirements of the courses, or of their own abilities. Again, I.Q. tests do not pretend to make perfect predictions — after all, ability is only one of the many prerequisites needed for academic success, and a high I.Q. by itself is not enough for outstanding achievement. But ability is certainly something that should be taken into account, and even a less-than-perfect estimate may be useful. Here again, our universities have lacked the initiative and boldness needed to carry out even the preliminary research which would tell them something about the applicability of these methods in relation to their needs; their whole approach has been a mixture of smugness and self-satisfaction hardly justified by the results.

THE ARGUMENT that "more means worse" (originally formulated by the novelist Kingsley Amis in an article in *Encounter*) is often cited in this connection. Slogans of this kind are not very helpful in dealing with a highly complex problem. They are characteristic of what one might be tempted, following C. P. Snow, to call the approach of the innumerate. Consideration of any mathematical model of selection suggests a frighteningly large number of parameters which must be borne in mind when considering the effects of any change in procedure, such as increasing the number chosen. W. D. Furneaux discusses some of these parameters in his book on *The Chosen Few*. Some of these are: the proportion of pupils chosen for further education; the number of dimensions into which the selection criteria can be subdivided; the correlation of these dimensions with ultimate success; the number of additional dimensions which should be taken into account but are not (such as I.Q.); the correlations of these additional dimensions with ultimate success; the degree of success with which accepted pupils are allocated (or allocate themselves) to different types of courses; the correlation of different types of test with the success of such allocation; the validity of the measurement of ultimate success, and its reliability.

Depending on the numerical values of these parameters, it is possible that "more means worse," or that "more means better," or that "more means more of the same." We cannot say without careful investigation — particularly when methods of teaching are changing, and standards do not remain steady either. But there is a strong probability that if the "more" are better selected than the few, then "more" may very well mean "better" rather than "worse." This is particularly so if under "selection" we include "allocation to particular courses of study." I have no wish to be dogmatic on this point; it would need much well-designed research to establish the true facts in this area.

To say this is not to condone the notion of "open enrollment" (the mass admission of students from local high schools) which is being demanded in the U.S.A. by many of the student leaders, particularly black ones. Nor would the argument presented favor the notion of ethnic quotas, also being canvassed in the U.S.A.; according to this, universities would be forced to take blacks in direct proportion to their numbers in the nation. In my view, such proposals are in nature racist, and counter to democratic principles. Furthermore, they would certainly contradict the statement of desirable objectives for education mentioned in an earlier paragraph, because for every dull and poorly educated Negro admitted under such a rule, a bright and well-educated white student would be forced to drop out. Such a process would indeed spell out the slogan "more means worse" with a vengeance! The fact remains that Negroes of equal intelligence to whites *are* disadvantaged in gaining access to higher education by virtue of the significantly poorer educational facilities which characterize American practices as far as colored citizens are concerned; here again the I.Q. would seem to provide a possible solution to an extremely intractable problem.

Why is selection necessary? At the university level the answer is obvious. Society cannot afford to spend enough money to educate more than a small minority at this level, and there are only a limited number of potential students with enough ability to benefit from such courses. But the need for selection at the secondary school level, or even at the primary school level, may not be so obvious. Here the answer often given is that classes homogeneous for ability are easier to teach, and that different ability groups can proceed at their own speed if properly segregated.

These reasons are often assumed to be true because their truth seems to be obvious, but such research as has been done does not entirely support the alleged superiority of homogeneous classes. The Yates book on *Grouping in Education,* already mentioned, and A. Morgenstern's *Grouping in the Elementary School* review some of the literature without suggesting that ability grouping is all that effective. But it would be a mistake to pay too much attention to research the quality of which is not very high; there are so many difficulties in carrying out research of this kind properly that results must be very doubtful. Teachers used to teaching a particular kind of class may not be able to make use of the opportunities afforded by having pupils of similar ability; they would require special coaching in appropriate methods before being able to make the best of the situation. Experiments are usually carried on for too short a time to enable marked effects to manifest themselves. The ability groups are not differentiated enough in capacity for clear effects to emerge — American work with exceptionally bright children, and English experience with E.S.N. children suggests that when extremes are taken, grouping does result in faster progress. But the fact that research so far has not been of very high quality does not mean that its results must be disregarded and the opposite of their conclusions assumed to be true.

Provisionally, at least, we should perhaps accept, albeit with qualifications, the fact that a general system of grouping on the basis of I.Q. does not necessarily improve achievement — as long as no special provision is made for the proper treatment of all brighter children.

This is an important provision. Bright children do not necessarily benefit by being separated from less bright ones when the whole system and philosophy of teaching remains the same, and when their teachers are not specially chosen, and trained, in terms of their ability to deal with exceptional children. Bright children may require different methods of teaching, laying emphasis on independence, individual projects, research, self-motivation and similar factors. When all they are offered is "more of the same" they may not react at all positively, but may instead rebel and "down tools." As the Educational Policies Commission says,

Because their intellectual interests and prospective future differ from others, and because they can learn more and learn it more rapidly, the educational experiences which gifted students should have in school and college ought not to be identical with the experiences of other students. Some of their education should be the same, but some should be different— different as to kind, quality and level of insight. Every teacher, school, school system and institution of higher learning should have systematic policies and procedure for the education of their gifted children.

As Hollingworth, a well-known expert in this field, points out,

We know from measurements made over a three-year period that a child of I.Q. 140 can master all the mental work provided in the elementary school, as established, in half the time allowed him. Therefore, one half the time which he spends at school could be utilized in doing something more than the curriculum calls for.

Hollingworth goes on to call attention to the many ways of "time wasting" which pupils impose on themselves because no proper use is made of this time by teachers; indeed, teachers often have to invent "busy work" in order to keep bright pupils occupied. "Few of these devices have the appropriate character that can be built only on psychological insight into the nature and the needs of gifted children." No wonder that Charles Darwin, Jonathan Swift, George Eliot, Sir Walter Scott, Daniel Webster, Schiller, Goethe, Shelley and Einstein were rated as failures by their schools. The ordinary process of schooling children of mediocre ability does not provide for the exceptionally bright.

Advocates and opponents of non-selective schooling both tend to argue in terms of certain psychological and educational preconceptions which have little support in reality. For the most part, the needed research simply has not been done at all, or where there is some factual evidence, it is usually so hedged around with qualifications as to make simple, uncomplicated political deductions impossible. This fact may lead to one of two rather different conclusions. Politicians and governmental bureaucrats usually assume that their particular views and preferences are so obviously true that no research is needed, and if none exists to contradict decisively what they want to see effected on other grounds, then they feel quite justified in going ahead. Psychologists tend to feel that before decisive changes in education (or any other social fields) are made, some good evidence should be collected from properly controlled studies to indicate the likely consequences of such changes. It seems absurd to them that conservatives, liberals, and socialists should discuss *ad nauseam* the question of selective grouping on the basis of unproven preconceptions, when research could be carried out to obtain factual evidence which alone can settle the question once and for all. (What is said here about this particular problem is *pari passu* true of all other educational problems, of course. Political arguments about psychological facts are not impressive or convincing; facts should be ascertained by experiment and research.) Both sides have fallen down on the job of instituting the required large-scale research which alone would enable us to give a proper answer to this important question.

THIS NEED FOR RESEARCH in education cannot be over-emphasized. In many European countries education has already overtaken defense as the biggest item in the nation's budget, yet the amount of research done is derisory and its quality undistinguished. Do the new methods of teaching youngsters to spell, or do math, indeed inculcate better and more original ways of approach in them, or do they simply serve to make them unable to spell or count? In England, Dr. J. Downing's Reading Research Unit, which was investigating the effects of introducing the Initial Teaching Alphabet as an aid in learning to read, and which was conducting a well-controlled series of experiments, was refused the sum of 40,000 pounds which was needed to follow 2,500 children right through their school career and had to close down, thus wasting all the time and money already expended. This is typical of the unscientific and doctrinaire approach of politicians to education. Problems of fact are decided in terms of political bias and social fashion, and the children (and ultimately society) are the sufferers. If only politicians, who prate about leading us into the twentieth century, technological breakthroughs and scientific advances, could be made subject to the law of estoppel! As things are, all the verbal fighting about the "new education" is going on in a thick fog; scientific advances and technological breakthroughs do not thrive in such a climate. The twentieth century is the century of empirical investigations and scientific proof; philosophical arguments about factual matters belong to the eighteenth century — as do, alas, most of our politicians.*

The experiments on "grouping" of children of similar ability together or in separate classes or schools have usually relied on a single I.Q. score. This is almost certainly not the optimum way of securing a proper system of "grouping." Different abilities are involved in different school subjects, and the high verbal-low numerical child and the low verbal-high numerical child may have a similar I.Q. but respond quite differently to teaching in English and mathematics, in line with their special bent. Before we can come to any reasonable conclusion we must introduce into our research, and our selection procedures, multi-factor tests measuring several of the better established abilities. A single figure for the I.Q. is not useless by any means, but it is clearly *not enough.* Such research, even if it were successful, would not necessarily lead to a reconsideration of the principle that inter-school grouping was not supported by the facts; it would probably lead to an improvement of grouping within the single comprehensive school.

The complexity of the factors involved in research on "tracking" are not usually realized, particularly by those

---

*In 1955, when the British controversy about comprehensive schools was at its height, the total education bill was 1,276 million pounds; about 250,000 pounds were being spent on educational research in England and Wales, *i.e.* one part in over 5,000! Compare this with the British Ceramic Research Association, which has an income of 294,200 pounds, with a government grant of 64,158 pounds. Where education gets a government grant of 20,000 pounds, baking research gets 28,000 pounds, flour research 25,000 pounds, hosiery research 28,000 pounds! We in Britain clearly care more for ceramics, flour and hosiery than about education, judging by the money we are prepared to devote to research. By now the total amount spent on education has risen, and the proportion devoted to research has failed to do so—truly a case of the blind not only leading the blind, but refusing stoutly to accept any help!

whose views for or against are based on political considerations. It might not be too counter to fact to say that we simply do not know what the facts are.

Consider just a few of the complications which arise, and have been shown to influence the outcome. (1) Teachers' attitudes are important; teachers in favor of tracking are unlikely to "work" a non-tracking system as effectively as a tracking one, and vice versa. (2) The mean ability, and the range of ability within a group, are both important; what is true of a fairly uniformly dull group may not be true of another group containing extremely bright and extremely dull children. (3) Social composition — what is true of working-class groups may not be true of middle-class groups of children or of groups containing different proportions of both. (4) Personality—introverts seem to take to tracking better than do extroverts. (5) Subject matter—for some subjects tracking seems to be superior, for others non-tracking. (6) Age—it cannot be assumed that because non-tracking is superior at one age, it will also be superior at another age. These are only some of the very real complexities involved.

Next consider the multiplicity of criteria. How are we to judge the superiority or inferiority of a given system — in terms of examination results? In terms of social adjustment of the children? In terms of long-range attitudes towards people of a different social class developed during school time? Or in terms of any other of the multiplicity of criteria which have been suggested, and might reasonably be made the objectives of education? The very question—Is tracking better than non-tracking? will be seen as meaningless. We must first seek answers to the questions: Better for what? and better under what conditions? Educational problems, as they are usually discussed by politicians and also by teachers and educationalists themselves, are often pseudo-problems. In the nature of the case, there cannot be any meaningful answers, and discussion engenders merely heat, but no light. Very, very few social problems and questions are uni-dimensional, *i.e.* capable of a simple "better or worse" answer. Most are multi-dimensional, so that any proposed solution may be judged better according to one criterion, worse according to another, and equivalent according to a third. Tracking might, for instance, lead to better educational achievement than non-tracking for bright, middle-class introverts of twelve years or more, in mathematics and English, when taught by a teacher of the same sex in single-sex classes. It might have the opposite effect in not-so-bright working-class extroverts of under twelve, in history and English, when taught by teachers of the opposite sex in coeducational classes. The effects on social integration might be in the opposite direction, and those on long-term class attitudes might be quite uninfluenced by tracking. It is facts of this kind which are required before we can really say anything about the desirability or otherwise of tracking; and it is precisely these facts which are largely missing.

Opinion in educational circles swings wildly from one extreme to the other — not on the basis of factual evidence, but on the basis of persuasion, impression, speculation, talk, political bias, and what have you. When will we learn that the very notion of "experts" has no meaning when the facts do not exist knowledge of which alone can make a person an "expert"? At the moment we are all fumbling, guessing and playing ducks and drakes with the education of our children throughout the West. We are arbitrarily changing conditions, but not experimenting in the proper sense because there are no proper controls, and no adequate measurement of effects or follow-up. *Quem deus vult perdere . . .*

THE READER MAY FEEL that if grouping children of similar I.Q. together does not improve their performance and achievement, then why practice selection at all? Consider the facts. Schools tend to draw upon their neighborhoods; a school in a working-class neighborhood will tend to have a predominantly working-class group of children, while a school in a middle-class neighborhood will tend to have a predominantly middle-class group of children. Stephen Wiseman, in his *Education and Environment,* draws a picture of some of the differences which may be found in these two schools. He asks us to consider two equally bright pupils, one of whom (*A*) is outstanding in a school in a poor area where 60-70 per cent of pupils are below a standard score of 85 (where 100 is average). The other (*B*) is an average pupil in a school in the outer suburbs with only 5 per cent or so backward pupils.

Consider the differences in their timetable. The first is likely to have many periods devoted to reading, to basic English, to elementary arithmetic; his other lessons, necessarily curtailed in number, are likely to be elementary in content and fairly formal in approach. His opposite number, *B*, will have little or no time devoted to reading (as remedial exercise) or elementary arithmetic. He will be *using* these skills in literature and in mathematics. His other fare—with much more time devoted to it—will have a great deal more variety, complexity and challenge.

In addition, of course, *A* would have come from a primary school where the large number of backward children would have made proper study difficult, while *B* would have come from a primary school not suffering from this disadvantage. In terms of achievement *A* would at all stages be inferior to *B*, simply because of his social background. If he is to be rescued from this background some direct measure of his I.Q., or better still of his total pattern of abilities, would seem the only way. Tracking might be suggested, but in the poorer school there may simply not be enough children to make up a track in which *A* could advance in accordance with his ability.

This problem is likely to become even more serious as the tendency for families of similar social status to live together in certain neighborhoods, and to send their children to the same school, becomes more and more developed. In the U.S.A. this has led to extreme and rather self-defeating moves, such as to collect children in one district and take them by bus to another, in order to overcome this tendency. Even in London at the present time such trends are noticeable. Two of my children went to comprehensive schools quite close together; one was like that described in connection with A, the other like that described in connection with B — in spite of the fact that the Education Authority set limits to the number of children acceptable in each ability group. If bright working-class children are to be given an education appropriate to their ability, something will have to be done to rescue them from this vicious circle, and only the I.Q. test suggests itself as a possible answer.

Other methods have, of course, been used elsewhere to redress the balance; these would probably not appeal to many British or American parents. Thus in the *D.D.R.* (East Germany) a law has been passed to ensure that half the grammar school places are filled by pupils of working-class or peasant origin; this enforced balancing act also applies to the universities. While not wishing to advocate anything of the kind, I would like to draw attention to the fact (predictable from genetic theories of I.Q. but not from environmental ones) that, far from diluting quality, this system, introduced by Kurt Hager, has achieved excellent results, and compares favorably with the West German system (where working-class children make up 67 per cent of the population, but produce only 7 per cent of the university entrants). In the recent mathematical "Olympics" the first three places were taken by countries from behind the Iron Curtain, with East Germany lying third — well ahead of West Germany (in spite of the much larger population of the latter country). The problem still remains, of course, of how the working-class children in the *D.D.R.* are selected who make up the balance of the grammar school entrants; but the point I wish to draw attention to is that by tapping the unused abilities of working-class children, the *D.D.R.* (for whose dictatorial practices I have no wish to offer excuses) has succeeded in building up a meritocracy whose education is based explicitly on the principle of "equality of opportunity for all." I.Q. testing offers us a more democratic opportunity to do the same.*

IT WILL BE SEEN that throughout I have seen the I.Q. test as a positive device for spotting talent where environmental conditions have conspired to bury the potentialities of the bright child. This view should be contrasted with that so widely held by disappointed parents of 11+ failures, who see it as an artificial hurdle which has kept back their children from the kind of education they wanted. This certainly is not the way Godfrey Thomson looked upon the I.Q. test, and I think that Professor Wiseman, with his impressive eponymous sagacity, hit the nail on the head when he said that a high score on an I.Q. test is indisputable evidence of high ability, while a low score may be due to other causes than dullness — from which he inferred, I think rightly, that we should pay far more attention to high scores than to low.

Let failure be determined, as hitherto, by school marks (preferably objectified and made more reliable); but let the I.Q. test be used to rescue bright children whose attainment, for reasons of environmental conditions, has not kept pace with their abilities. "Under-achievers," so called, may of course be suffering from personality defects and deficiencies which make it unlikely that in spite of their high ability they would

---

*It is interesting to note that a *higher proportion* of working-class children went to universities in Great Britain during the post-War years than in any other democratic country in Europe. It is probably true to say that in part at least this grand result was due to the use of I.Q. tests in selection at the secondary-school stage. It will be interesting to see whether this differential will be maintained once the I.Q. test is dropped.

ever succeed in achieving scholastic eminence in line with their capacities. But in many cases it is personal and parental attitudes which are at fault, and objective facts, such as are presented by I.Q. measurement, may be all-important in changing these.

If this is not the way society has hitherto used the I.Q., so much the worse for society. The I.Q. has been condemned, and commended, very often for the wrong reasons. By itself it is merely a scientific measure of something very important (not all-important!) in education and in life; how such measurements are used is, of course, quite a different question, but one which should not be answered, as it has usually been answered, without much knowledge of just what the I.Q. is and is not, and what it can and cannot do. Political argument is no substitute for informed discussion, and the paradox that American liberals and English socialists, imbued with a passion for social justice, should be rejecting with particular ferocity the only known instrument that would help to ensure precisely that instrumentation of social justice which they have asked for, indicates more clearly than anything the confusion which hangs over this whole field.

In suggesting that we should reconsider the banishment of I.Q. tests from polite conversation I would not like it to be thought that I am opposing the democratic change from different *types* of school to universal, comprehensive schools. Alice Griffin has shown that the predictions of scholastic disaster which accompanied the British switch-over to comprehensive schools have not been fulfilled. She found in her comparative studies of different types of school that (*1*) Midlands suburban comprehensive schools provided a stimulating environment for children of all levels of ability; (*2*) little difference was found in attainment in English between the three types of school organization; (*3*) brighter pupils expressed better attitudes to school in comprehensive schools than in grammar schools, this being particularly true in the case of girls; (4) the findings support the hypothesis proposed by Miller that the comprehensive school helps to overcome the disparity of esteem for different types of school organization, has a unifying effect on morale and appears to strengthen the holding power of the school. More research of this kind is of course needed; but the evidence seems strong — with the proviso that what is true of the particular comprehensive schools investigated is not necessarily true of all other comprehensives; there are quite vital differences between schools bearing the same label.

SUMMING UP what I have said, I would conclude that both our capitalist and also the communist type of society give rise to social classes. Members of these classes tend to differ in intelligence, although with considerable overlap. The children born into these classes also differ in ability, but less than their parents (due to regression to the mean, a well-known genetic effect). Children of working-class parents are handicapped in achieving scholastic success by environmental deficits, as well as by parental attitudes and acquired value systems which place education lower in the value scale than would be true of middle-class children. These environmental handicaps prove quite effective in preventing many working-class children from achieving a level of education commensurate with their abilities, thus denying them social justice (equality of educational opportunity) and robbing society of their talents, which are urgently needed in a culture dependent to a large extent on high intelligence. I.Q. tests may serve to spot unused talent in under-achieving children, and may thus draw social attention to a problem which would otherwise be swept under the carpet.

What special measures society should take to rescue these children from their likely fate of everlasting educational damnation is still an open question. Perhaps special monetary help should be given, in addition to using high I.Q. to balance, in the race up the educational ladder, not-so-high school marks. The purpose of this chapter is to draw attention to the problem of making the provision of equal educational opportunities more than a pious exhortation, rather than to provide cast-iron administrative suggestions. When educationalists and politicians begin to realize the value of I.Q. tests in this connection, then and only then are we likely to get the necessary informed public debate which may precede social action. And perhaps we will also get the needed impetus to better research, done on a much larger scale than hitherto, which alone can improve existing measures and reduce the error inherent in all scientific measurement. Without the help of I.Q. tests, advancement into the higher paid, better educated groups of society will be barred to many able working-class children, thus bringing to the top a large number of people of *mediocre* ability, while keeping submerged many people of *superior* ability. This rise of a new mediocracy in all the civilized countries of the West would be socially unjust, nationally disastrous, and ethically unacceptable.

To all these arguments many people reply with certain objections which should at least be heard, even though they may not be logically consistent or factually acceptable. Some voice an objection against the very conception of an educational or any other form of elite. They place equality before the other ideals of the French Revolution. But this notion of equality is wrongly conceived if it is meant to indicate that all people are born with equal abilities, equally strong and beautiful, equally healthy and swift. When all scientists are the equals of Newton and Einstein, when all musicians write symphonies like Beethoven and operas like Verdi, when all boxers fight like Dempsey and Joe Louis, or all tennis players play like Tilden or Laver, when you and I can sing like Caruso or Galli-Curci, make love like Casanova, have the charm of Rex Harrison, the sex appeal of Marilyn Monroe, the strength and agility of Cassius Clay, the oratorical gifts of

Cicero or Winston Churchill, the wisdom of Socrates, the humility of St. Francis, the intellect of Bertrand Russell, the courage of those who fight for freedom in authoritarian countries — then will be the time to speak of this type of equality. Equality, as it is referred to in the famous lines about all men being created equal, means equality in the eyes of God, equality before the law, equal rights and duties as far as the state is concerned. It was never meant to suggest the absence of innate differences. These innate differences constitute our most precious heritage, biologically speaking; it is they which enable us to adapt to changing circumstances by favoring one set of genes and disfavoring another. Absolute uniformity would guarantee a quick death for the whole human species; let us give thanks that we are not all like an endless array of uniovular twins.

Others argue against the notion of heredity, not by appeal to scientifically and experimentally ascertained fact, but rather by appeal to certain individual cases they have come across, "Look at this child!" they will exclaim. "He never had a chance . . ." A drunken, criminal father, a prostitute for a mother, taking drugs all day, and out all night; no decent home life, no books, beaten by his parents on the slightest whim — is it any wonder that his I.Q. is low, or his school performance poor? Let us consider the case dispassionately — reserving our passion for efforts to improve the circumstances under which all too many children have to grow up, even in our advanced type of society. What I have to say is in no way intended to suggest that such efforts should not be made! Indeed they *should* receive much more financial and legal support than they do at the moment. All I wish to question is the relevance of the case to the argument from heredity. When the fathers and mothers of such children are tested, they usually turn out to have I.Q.s in the 70s or 80s; heredity alone would ensure that in most cases children of such marriages would be dull and well below average, would do poorly at school, and never rise to any intellectual heights during their adolescent and adult lives. The wretched circumstances under which the child is brought up are merely accessories after the fact; they may pull the unfortunate child down even farther into the mire, but they are not alone responsible. There are lots of children born into families of this kind who nevertheless do better on I.Q. tests than do children born into loving, kind families who do everything for their offspring; how would the environmentalist explain these counter-examples? Instances where both heredity and environment pull in the same direction cannot help us to decide between the two theories in question; it is when they pull in opposite directions that the facts begin to be interesting. Dull parents provide a poor environment for the children, but they may carry in them genes for much higher potential than they themselves have ever shown; hence bright children coming from dull parents and poor environments demonstrate the importance of heredity.

Nevertheless, there is some justice in the claims of psychiatrists, social workers and teachers who come into contact with underprivileged children, and who say that they simply cannot believe the figures which declare that only 20 per cent or 25 per cent of individual differences in intelligence are caused by environmental factors. It should be remembered that these figures are an average, taken over a random (or reasonably random) sample of the population. What is true on the average is not necessarily true of every individual making up the sample. The fact that the average height of the English male is 5 ft. 10 in. does not mean that there are no giants 7 ft. tall or no dwarfs 4 ft. tall. Similarly, in individual cases, heredity may be much less important than the figures would seem to suggest, while in other cases, to make up the average value, environment may be even less important than in general. It is precisely children of the former kind who are seen by psychiatrists, social workers and clinical psychologists.

The average figures do indeed have less relevance for that highly unrepresentative sample of the population. This does not mean that the figures are wrong. It simply means that we have to interpret them carefully and not draw conclusions which go beyond our facts. In a small number of cases — small absolutely, but nevertheless *far too large* for comfort — environmental factors *have been so adverse* that they are responsible for a very large proportion of a child's backwardness! No geneticist would deny this for a moment. But this is no good reason for throwing out the baby with the bathwater, and suggesting that heredity plays "little part" in causing individual differences in mental ability in the whole population. Hard cases make bad laws, and selected instances do not disprove a general rule in science.

It must be admitted that however true these objections to the generalization of individual case studies may be, to many people these have an appeal which quite outweighs the whole burden of the scientific evidence. For this reason I shall conclude this chapter by also quoting a case study. This study is a true and well-established story which illustrates in some detail how a baby can live through extremes of environmental deprivation not only without damage but can grow up to become one of the world's great scientists; how in addition these childhood deprivations did not prevent this baby from growing up to be one of nature's great men — not in the scientific sense, but in the humanistic sense. I think this story is important. It should be better known than it is, and whole-hearted environmentalists may find something to ponder over when they consider it with all the care it deserves.

Our hero was born during the American Civil War, son of Mary, a Negro slave on a Missouri farm owned by Moses Carver and his wife Susan. Mary, who was a widow, had two other children — Melissa, a young girl, and a boy, Jim; George was the baby. In 1862 masked bandits who terrorized the countryside and stole livestock and slaves attacked

Carver's farm, tortured him and tried to make him tell where his slaves were hidden; he refused to tell. After a few weeks they came back, and this time Mary did not have time to hide in a cave, as she had done the first time; the raiders dragged her, Melissa and George away into the bitter cold winter's night. Moses Carver had them followed, but only George was brought back; the raiders had given him away to some womenfolk, saying; "He ain't worth nuttin'." Carver's wife Susan nursed him through every conceivable childhood disease that his small frame seemed to be particularly prone to; but his traumatic experiences had brought on a severe stammer which she couldn't cure. He was called Carver's George; his true name (if such a concept had any meaning for a slave) is not known.

When the war ended the slaves were freed, but George and Jim stayed with the Carvers. Jim was sturdy enough to become a shepherd and to do other farm chores; George was a weakling and helped around the house. His favorite recreation was to steal off to the woods and watch insects, study flowers, and become acquainted with nature. He had no schooling of any kind, but he learned to tend flowers and became an expert gardener. He was quite old when he saw his first picture, in a neighbor's house; he went home enchanted, made some paint by squeezing out the dark juice of some berries, and started drawing on a rock. He kept on experimenting with drawings, using sharp stones to scratch lines on smooth pieces of earth. He became known as the "plant doctor" in the neighborhood, although still only young, and helped everyone with their gardens.

At some distance from the farm there was a one room cabin that was used as a school house during the week; it doubled as a church on Sundays. When George discovered its existence, he asked Moses Carver for permission to go there, but was told that no Negroes were allowed to go to that school. George overcame his shock at this news after a while; Susan Carver discovered an old spelling-book, and with her help he soon learned to read and write. Then he discovered that at Neosho, eight miles away, there was a school that would admit Negro children. Small, thin and still with his dreadful stammer, he set out for Neosho, determined to earn some money to support himself there. Just fourteen years old, he made his home with a colored midwife and washerwoman. "That boy told me he came to Neosho to find out what made hail and snow, and whether a person could change the color of a flower by changing the seed. I told him he'd never find that out in Neosho. Maybe not even in Kansas City. But all the time I knew he'd find it out — somewhere." Thus Maria, the washerwoman. She also told him to call himself George Carver — he just couldn't go on calling himself Carver's George! By that name he entered the tumbledown shack that was the Lincoln School for Colored Children, with a young Negro teacher as its only staff member.

He was constantly ill during the winters, but he kept on studying all that the school could offer him. When he had exhausted its small fund of knowledge, he moved on to Fort Scott; and for about ten years he kept on going from school to school, supporting himself as best he could by doing odd jobs. All his spare time was spent working on his school lessons, reading, studying. But life was by no means tranquil; he was not done with traumas which would give nightmares to a psychoanalyst. One day he witnessed a lynching. A Negro was taken from gaol by a shrieking mob, drenched in oil and thrown into a great bonfire. This was an everyday event in this most Christian country; yet he became intensely religious and joined the Presbyterians.

When he was 18, he went to Minneapolis with an elderly Negro couple who had befriended him; there he entered secondary school, and also took on the middle name of "Washington" — so as to avoid being mixed up with another George Carver. His brother Jim died of smallpox—Jim who

had never learned to read and write, and who had no
intellectual interests whatever. Then came good news — a
letter of application to Highland College, a small Presbyterian
school in Kansas, had been favorably considered. He spent his
last penny getting there, but when he hopefully presented
himself to the Principal, he was brusquely turned down —
"We don't admit Negroes!" Bruised in spirit, he gave up the
unequal struggle, became a homesteader and claimed a 160-
acre piece of land on the Kansas frontier, built a sod house,
and started to set up as a farmer. For two years he fought
nature single-handed, and without money or help. Gradually
his spirit recovered; he began to read and to paint again, and
finally he mortgaged his farm and headed back to civilization
— or what passed for it. Eventually he ended up in Simpson
College, Indianola; although a white college, it accepted him,
and he studied etymology, composition, mathematics and art.
He earned his living by setting up a laundry and cleaning the
other students' clothes. He was clearly an outstanding painter;
his art teacher showed some of his work (a painting of a
cactus-grafting experiment he had set up) to her father, who
was professor of horticulture at the Iowa Agricultural College
at Ames. This man had heard of the young man's skill with
plants, and suggested he go to Ames to study agriculture.
George was past thirty; he wanted to give his learning back to
his people. Agriculture seemed the obvious way, and he
decided to go to Ames. Hard work finally brough him his
Bachelor of Science degree in 1894—at the age of thirty-two.

From here on his rise was meteoric, but his story loses
interest from our point of view. (It has been well told in a book
by Lawrence Elliott, *Beyond Fame or Fortune.*) He was taken
on as assistant by an eminent botanist, specialized in
mycology (the study of fungus growths), and became an
authority. The scientific world was at his feet, but then he
received a letter from Booker T. Washington, the foremost
Negro leader of his day. Washington was trying to build up a

Negro institute of learning, but he faced one outstanding problem. "These people do not know how to plough or harvest. I am not skilled at such things. I teach them how to read, to write, to make good shoes, good bricks, and how to build a wall. I cannot give them food. And he wrote to George Carver, 800 miles away: "I cannot offer you money, position or fame. The first two you have. The last, from the place you now occupy, you will no doubt achieve. These things I now ask you to give up. I offer you in their place work—hard, hard work—the task of bringing a people from degradation, poverty and waste to full manhood."

He accepted, and his heroic struggles to create an institute out of literally nothing are part of Negro history. He changed the agricultural and the eating habits of the South; he created single-handed a pattern of growing food, harvesting and cooking it which was to lift Negroes (and whites too!) out of the abject state of poverty and hunger to which they had been condemned. And in addition to all his practical and teaching work, administration and speechmaking, he had time to do creative and indeed fundamental research. He was one of the first scientists to work in the field of synthetics, and is credited with creating the science of chemurgy — "agricultural chemistry." The American peanut industry is based on his work; today this is America's sixth most important agricultural product, with many hundreds of byproducts. He became more and more obsessed with the vision that out of agricultural and industrial waste useful materials could be created, and this entirely original idea is widely believed to have been Carver's most important contribution.

The number of his discoveries and inventions is legion; in his field, he was as productive as Edison. He could have become a millionaire many times over but he never accepted money for his discoveries. Nor would he accept an increase in his salary, which remained at the 125 dollars a month which Washington had originally offered him. (He once declined an

offer by Edison to work with him at a minimum annual salary
of 100,000 dollars.) He finally died, over eighty, in 1943. His
death was mourned all over the United States. The *New York
Herald Tribune* wrote: "Dr. Carver was, as everyone knows, a
Negro. But he triumphed over every obstacle. Perhaps there is
no one in this century whose example has done more to
promote a better understanding between the races. Such
greatness partakes of the eternal." He himself was never
bitter, in spite of all the persecutions he and his fellow-
Negroes had to endure. *"No man can drag me down so low as
to make me hate him."* This was the epitaph on his grave. He
could have added fortune to fame, but caring for neither, he
found happiness and honor in being helpful to the world.

This brief story of a great scientist and a fine human being
raises some very fundamental problems. Every year colleges
and universities in the U.S.A. produce tens of thousands of
agriculturists, biologists, biochemists and other experts in the
fields in which George Carver worked. Every one of these has a
family background, an education, and a degree of support
compared with which Carver's would simply have been
nonexistent. His father dead before he was born; his mother
abducted while he was a baby; born a Negro slave in the deep
South, weak and ailing; growing up in a poverty-stricken
house with hardly any books, with the white people who
brought him up not far from illiterate; denied schooling
because of his color, having to piece together the rudiments of
an education while constantly hungry, and having to earn
every penny he spent by performing the most menial jobs imaginable; exposed all the time to recurring traumas because of
his color; troubled by a severe stammer assumed to have been
brought on by his early abduction under extremely unfavorable weather conditions (to say nothing of his emotional
reactions); having only the most elementary and poorest kind
of teaching; rejected because of his color by institutes of
higher learning; always having to work his way through

secondary school and college . . . This kind of handicap is practically unknown now—however poor the education given to Negro children in the U.S.A. today. And compared with the education of Negro children, that of the favored white boys and girls who present themselves with shining faces at the commencement ceremonies at American colleges and universities has been exemplary—incorporating all the advances that modern educational science has been able to think up. And all these educational advantages are linked with, in most cases, happy, peaceful childhood experiences under the wise guidance and care of loving parents.

On the basis of an environmentalistic hypothesis, what wonders would we not expect these prodigies to perform! Surely soon the world will be completely changed by their discoveries — each one of them many times as productive, as inventive, as sagacious as the poor, ignorant black boy with his botched education and his non-existent family life! But reality teaches us that out of all these tens of thousands of molliecoddled youngsters, with all their highly favored upbringing, their high standard of education, their impeccable family background, not one is likely to achieve even a tithe of what the untutored, self-taught George Washington Carver managed to do. Something, one cannot but feel, has gone seriously wrong. If environment is so all-powerful, then how can the worst imaginable environment produce such a wonderful human being, so outstanding a scientist, and how can the best type of environment that oceans of money can buy and the top brains in education conceive, produce so vast a number of nonentities, with perhaps a few reasonable scientists sprinkled among them?

Or consider the physical equipment which was given to Carver, and that which even a young student nowadays commands. When Carver arrived at Tuskegee Normal and Industrial Institute, at the invitation of Booker T. Washington, he saw nothing but sand and bare yellow clay —

everything was deep in dust. A few pathetic shacks were visible, and just one brick building. There was no sewage system. "Your department exists only on paper," he was told by Washington, "and your laboratory will have to be in your head." He set his students to collecting old bottles, discarded pots and pans, fruit-jars, odd bits of metal, broken cups and saucers — anything that the school dump and the refuse collection system of the nearby town could provide. Out of this rubbish he then made his mortars and pestles, his beakers and retorts; a Bunsen burner was made out of an ink bottle, a piece of string stuck through the cork serving as the wick. Strainers were made by punching holes into tins with nails. This was Carver's equipment, to be used in huts and shacks which he and his students had first to build themselves. And for their farming experiments (which were supposed to make the whole venture self-supporting!) they had available "the worst soil in Alabama" and no fertilizer at all. Contrast this with the modern student, who is given wonderful accommodation; large libraries (Tuskegee, of course, had no books or journals at all in the fields which Carver was interested in — and no building to house them had they existed); all the apparatus needed; suitable areas of land comprising samples of all the soils his experiments require; fertilizer, skilled help and the financial resources of a large university. Some modern students have been known to complain when they found that they did not, each one of them, have access to a separate computer terminal!

The argument is sure to be raised that it is precisely the adversity which George Carver encountered which was responsible for his outstanding success: it is this which put steel into his soul. "All the modern youngsters have had it too easy; what they need is a period of fending for themselves." Does this amount to a suggestion that our educational system should return to single-teacher shacks? that all children should be made to earn their living while attending school?

that children are better separated from their parents at an early age and made to fend for themselves? Unless it means that — as well as making sure that every child is persecuted because of its color — the hypothesis in question means very little. And in any case it does not account for George's brother, Jim; he too encountered the same degree of deprivation and adversity, but he never learned to read and write, and became a witless shepherd, never showing any signs of even average intelligence. The fire that melts the wax tempers the steel — sure enough. But does not this saying carry with it the admission that wax and steel are constitutionally different?

I said before that individual examples are essentially anecdotal. However true the details, they cannot provide wide-ranging scientific conclusions. But they can illustrate points established otherwise by scientific evidence, and they can provide examples on which protagonists of different theories can try the value of their weapons. Whole-hogging environmentalists will find this a hard nut to crack — and of course this is not the only example which could have been chosen. The biographical history of science, of painting, of music, of literature, of war leaders contains many well-known examples of children from the most unpromising homes, untutored, uncared for, and quite unexpectedly blossoming out and reaching heights of genius which leave us to stand and stare in silent admiration. There is nothing in the environment of these children which has ever been suggested by environmentalists as having been causal in this development, nor are there any obvious similarities which could give one a cue.

But to return to a more serious theme. If environmentalists were right in their exhaustive claims for the priority and over-riding importance of environmental factors, then they have a very easy method of proof in their hands. Let them specify the precise details of the environment which are required to produce a man of George Washington Carver's calibre; let these be provided for a random sample of, say, one hundred children. Let another environment, judged to be unfavorable, be provided for another one hundred children. (To make sure that we could not be accused of heartless cruelty, let us make sure that all 200 children are chosen from among those whose natural expectations would be below the kind of environment to be provided for the disfavored 100; in this way every child would gain, but some disproportionately.) Follow up these children over a period of seventy years, and discover how many in the former group achieved anything like what Carver achieved; and how many in the latter group did. Is there any reader who can doubt that the outcome of the experiment would be a complete failure — no genius, in fact, in either group, probably not even a third-rate scientist of limited local acclaim!

The truth, as every honest teacher knows, is that we have not discovered those aspects of environmental control which might confer crucial and significant advantages on those children whom we wish to make stand out from the common herd. We know to some extent a few of the conditions which on the whole produce a mild disadvantage, but even there we may often go wrong — as in the case of George Washington Carver. Environmentalism is a religion, not a scientific theory based on incontrovertible facts. Its adherents believe that environment is all-important, but cannot provide the only acceptable evidence — actual control leading to better results. Until they can do that, their arguments cannot command respect among scientists.

WE HAVE GONE A LONG WAY from the beginning of our discussion, but the relevance of what we have been dealing with will be clear. Men are created unequal in abilities, in temperament, in personality. Society depends for its survival and advancement on those with the greatest abilities, in many different directions. There are not many so gifted, and we cannot afford to be prodigal with scarce resources. Society would be well repaid if it went out of its way to discover at an early age those whose abilities, personalities and attitudes fitted them for intellectual leadership; if it gave unstinting support to them on their way to the top, and tried at all times to smooth their way. This would not in any way redound to the disadvantage of other children; their schooling would not be disrupted or influenced in any way. The "talent-spotting" competitions which are such an interesting feature of the American scene are an example of what I have in mind; tens of thousands of bright youngsters enter, and the most successful are chosen for continued support — those so chosen have been almost uniformly outstanding, though it is a little too early to say whether any potential genius has been caught in the net.

Why not leave them to the buffeting of fate — it did not prevent Carver from succeeding? This is to over-generalize from a rather unusual story. It is *not* suggested that environmental forces cannot *help* or *hinder* the development of the child in any way. Any such suggestion would, of course, be nonsense. Even the average figure of 20 per cent or 25 per cent which we have allocated to environmental forces in the causation of individual differences in intelligence argues for the vital importance of environmental conditions — a 25 per cent handicap is something which few people would be able to overcome! The very notions of *genotype* and *phenotype* point to a balanced view which recognizes the inevitable interplay of both these sets of forces.

Nor should our strictures with respect to the lack of specific information on just how to organize the environment in our efforts to produce scientific or other genius be understood to result in some form of educational nihilism. We have organized our society in such a way that there is a clearly marked way from the bottom to the top; on this way we have placed successive hurdles. These hurdles are relevant to the purpose of the race in some instances. Children must learn to read and write before they can be admitted to secondary school, and they must learn some calculus before entering a university department of mathematics. But there is also a good deal of irrelevant contamination. Members of the middle class are preferred, in many instances, by middle-class teachers, and environmental pressures and facilities make it easier for certain children to surmount these hurdles, thus getting an unfair advantage in the race. Those who wish to abolish the notion of a meritocracy wish to abolish the race; this seems Utopian, and is certainly not practicable at the present time. Those who wish to afford a maximum of justice to all suggest that at the moment measures of intellectual ability can be used with some effect to redress the unfair balance, and cancel out advantages given to certain boys and girls because of their parents' wealth, social influence, and other irrelevant considerations. A mediocracy ultimately leads to stagnation, and a national preoccupation with "Buggins' turn." A meritocracy ensures that "from everyone according to his ability" should not remain an empty catchword. Experience suggests that intelligence tests help in leading towards a world closer to the ideals of natural justice; they cannot of course take us all the way, but then that has never been claimed by anyone.

What is the outcome of this rather involved discussion? Those who criticize the notion of a meritocracy have never really spelled out in detail what they regard as a desirable alternative. This is only natural because what they would really like suffers from the usual disability of all Utopias — it requires a race of human beings radically different from those actually existent. If all people were really created equal with respect to abilities, temperament, attitudes and other personal qualities, then it would be sensible to treat them all alike, and positions of leadership could be allocated by lot, or in some other random way. But reality being different, it seems difficult to get away from the need for an elite, and if this elite is not chosen on the basis of relevant grounds, such as ability, educability, and qualities of personality like persistence and integrity, then it will be chosen on irrelevant grounds, like aristocratic birth, family connections, and the general principle of "whom you know." We do not choose our Davis Cup teams by casually picking up a few players in the park, in a purely random manner; nor was any championship team ever chosen by vaguely drawing lots. We carefully choose youngsters who show promise. We give them special training to bring them on, discarding those whose ability or temperament does not come up to scratch. Among the survivors we then pick those who distinguish themselves in tournaments up and down the country, until finally a small meritocracy is left, with a clearly defined rank order. From these we then choose the team. Who would want to watch a championship final in which both opposing teams were strictly average in ability, or an Olympic Games in which competitors did not represent the best their country had to send? Is government, science and art less important than sport? Should we really allow rare talent go to waste in order that the rule of "Buggins' turn" could be implemented? Is this really in line with our national interests, and is it fair to those who happen to have inherited unusual talent or ability?

It is difficult not to feel sorry for and saddened by those who have inherited poor intelligence, who are born with little talent for anything, and whose personalities are weak and uninteresting. Within the limits of our national ability, we should certainly do what we can to bring such people up to the top of what their limited intellect can tolerate — without *forcing* on unwilling souls what *we* think would be *good for them*. But we must refuse to be stampeded into providing an education less than adequate for those most able to benefit from it, on the grounds that others are born less fortunate. We are not responsible for nature's genetic games, but we go counter to her dictates at our peril. The conscious cultivation of a mediocracy, in which the bright, the original, the innovators, the geniuses are held back in order to spare the mediocre the spectacle of outstanding success is to me an abomination. It is an abomonation which goes counter to the desideratum stated at the beginning of this chapter, which stresses the desirability of a policy "to secure the adult citizen's right to have been educated to the limit of his natural capacities." This right extends to the bright as well as to the dull. We have no business to adjust our bed of Procrustes in such a way as to hamstring our fastest runner. Compassion for the halt and the lame, bodily and mentally, is right and good; it is the hallmark of an advanced civilization. But we must take care that it does not exceed what is right and proper, and lead to the supression of high intellect and great merit. Even the able have their inalienable right, and a society disregards these at its peril. There is nothing wrong with a meritocracy, as long as the merits in question are relevant to the job in hand. The alternative is not Utopia, but a land of the dull, governed by the dull, for the dull; a country where the term "Art" refers to television programs made by the untalented for the Philistine; a country where science means nothing but the unimaginative churning out of small technological advances in aid of the principle of built-in obsolescence. Perhaps this Utopia of the mediocrats is not so far off. Perhaps it is time for the meritocracy to assert itself. It is later than you think!

⑤

The PARAdox of Socialism: Social Attitude and Social CLAss

ATTITUDES are interesting aspects of personality. We tend to believe that we have worked out our attitudes on a rational basis, but we often get extremely emotional when someone is attacking them. We tend to feel so emotional about attitudes (religious, social, political) that we are often unable to recognize the very meaning of the objections and arguments put forward, so blinded are we by our prejudices and biases.

I received a rather forceful introduction to this emotional side of what should be a purely rational, unimpassioned type of inquiry when I presented some empirical results of attitude measurement at a meeting of the British Association for the Advancement of Science, which was being held in Brighton, just after the War. I had carried out some work on anti-Semitism, and in the course of my talk gave detailed figures showing that people who were more conservative (more accurately, who voted Conservative) answered my question in the anti-Semitic direction more frequently than did those who were less conservative (more accurately, who voted Labour). In the discussion which followed, an eminent Jewish scientist got up and asked if the fact that such an unusually large number of Nobel Prize winners were Jewish did not prove that Jews were innately superior in intelligence to other groups.* I replied that there were two points to be considered. The first was that achievement of this kind had many roots and sources. Innate superiority could be one of them, but there were many alternative possibilities, such as the traditional Jewish love of learning; anti-Semitism, which forced Jews to work harder in order to be considered for academic jobs; and other such purely environmental causes. In other words, the facts were interesting, but in the absence of any more specific proof (*e.g.* Jewish children do not score higher on intelligence tests than do gentile children) I did not think this was a very likely hypothesis. The second point was that the Jews were a religious (and later a national) group; it was Hitler and other anti-Semites who advanced the theory that they were a "race" in the biological sense. Now only a race can be meaningfully said to have a gene pool different from other races, not a religious group living in the midst of and largely interbreeding with another religious group, or groups. Hence his argument assumed that Hitler was right in his absurd biological speculations and that the Jews were indeed a biologically separate race. This no modern biologist would agree with.

The consequences of this talk and discussion, duly reported in the papers, were rather astonishing. I received a shoal of letters, half from Brighton Conservatives telling me that it was a pity that Hitler had not succeeded in eliminating me before I could throw such slanders at their party, the other half from Brighton Jews telling me that I should never have left Hitlerite Germany, my spiritual home. Note that I was only concerned with the facts. My own opinions did not enter into my talk at all. Yet this mere mention of some innocent facts set up a buzz which lasted quite a long time. Attitudes to the psychologist

---

*The same point has recently been made by Lord Snow (the novelist, C.P. Snow), in a public lecture in America; he also suggested that the Jews had a superior gene pool.

are mental habits, just as the way you slice your tee shot at golf is a habit, or the manner in which you slink off every Saturday to cheer your favorite football or baseball team. Habits are very resistant to change, and attempts to produce such a change often encounter strong emotional resistances. Perhaps a psychologist should not have been too surprised at this curious reaction.

Undaunted, I continued research on social attitudes, and finally published the results in *The Psychology of Politics,* a book which I innocently thought would have a wide sale and become reasonably popular, in view of the rather interesting and novel findings I recounted there. I started out with the hypothesis that the widely held view that social and political attitudes were organized around a single right-left axis was mistaken, and that one or more further dimensions were required to give a more balanced view of what people actually thought. When I tested several different samples with inventories of attitudes ranging from religious to political, from ethical to sexual, I discovered indeed that in all these samples there emerged, in addition to the right-left, conservative-radical axis, also a second axis which I decided to call tough-minded versus tender-minded (following William James's playful distinction of philosophical viewpoints). I conceived this second dimension as a kind of projection of personality on to the social field, with introverts holding tender-minded views, and extroverts tough-minded ones.

Social and political attitudes thus fit into four quadrants. Radical views can be tough-minded (anti-religious, permissive), or tender-minded (pacifist, tolerant); and, similarly, conservative views can be tough-minded (xenophobic, repressive) or tender-minded (religious, traditional). Some attitudes are "pure" radical or conservative, *e.g.* "abolish private property" or "nationalization is inefficient." There are no purely tender-minded or tough-minded social attitudes, because these projections of personality qualities on to the political field must be polarized along the right-left axis. I did, in fact, discover some evidence in favor of the notion that tender-mindedness and tough-mindedness were correlated with personality as hypothesized. Extroverts tended to hold tough, introverts tender attitudes. Indeed, some additional evidence is contained in the second chapter of this book. It will be remembered that permissive sexual attitudes (tough-minded) are characteristic of extroverts, traditional sexual and religious attitudes of introverts. On the whole, therefore, the general picture (although of course grossly oversimplified) seemed to be very much along correct lines.

I went one step farther, and tried to fit existing political parties into this general picture. Instead of seeing them lined up along a single continuum, from the communist left, through labor to liberal, and then right to conservative and finally racist, I saw them located rather in the shape of a horseshoe—with the communist in the radical tough-minded quadrant and the fascists in the conservative tough-minded quadrant forming the two ends of the horseshoe. At the bend of the horseshoe, i.e. in the tender-minded position intermediate between right and left, were the liberals; labor and conservative were left and right respectively, but neither tough-minded nor tender-minded.

To test this view, I investigated the social attitudes of large samples of followers of these various parties, i.e. of people who either belonged to them or at least voted for them in the last election. In some cases considerable trouble was caused by attempts to track down adherents particularly of the Communist and Fascist parties. Thelma Coulter, a collaborator of mine who was later tragically killed in a street accident, actually had to join both parties in order to be able to approach and test reasonable numbers of their members! (It was fortunate that neither party knew of her membership in the other — this might have caused a lot of trouble.) In any case, the data finally collected did support the hypothesis, and personality data specially collected from the Communist and Fascist groups also seemed to suggest that these groups were characterized by a specially high degree of aggression — overt in the case of the Fascists, covert in the case of the Communists.

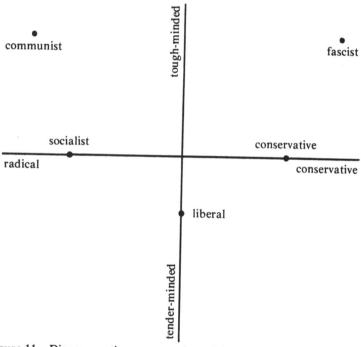

Figure 11   Diagrammatic representation of three hypotheses regarding the structure of attitudes as mirrored in the relative positions of different political parties.

THE FACTS were so clear-cut that interpretation was almost unnecessary. This is very satisfying in scientific work as it minimizes the dangers of over-interpretation and, worse still, misinterpretation. I therefore anticipated with some degree of confidence that critics would find little to object to in the book when it finally appeared. But I was mistaken.

Perhaps my previous experiences in falling foul of Freud should have been a warning guide to me. Any such criticism, however justified, and any experimental work seemingly contradicting the master's *obiter dicta,* however carefully done, are immediately subjected to a barrage of hostile and immoderate criticism, usually directed against the man, not the argument. In *The Psychology of Politics* I had inadvertently fallen foul of another great prophet of the nineteenth century, none other than the great Karl Marx himself, and his followers immediately set upon me to destroy any impact the book might have had.

The main objection seemed to be that I had classed Communists in some way with Fascists. This was a mortal offence, even though, as I was to point out again and again in rebuttal, this is precisely how the data came out. But facts are no defense in persecution of this kind, and sociologists and social psychologists almost to a man rose and condemned both book and author. They were joined by Russian psychologists who (naturally enough) considered the book subversive and "rightist" — although in relation to my work on behavior therapy and personality they considered this to be a "mechanistic left-wing deviationism"; they did not trouble themselves to explain the discrepancy.

The theory which I discussed in *The Psychology of Politics* is very widely held. It goes back to Rousseau and the notion of the "noble savage." Many people hold the view that primitive man was in some way more natural (which is no doubt true in the most trivial sense of that term). Equating what is natural with what is noble and generous in our nature, they conclude that civilization acts in such a way as to defile this primitive nobility and produce decadence and other symptoms of an unnatural life. Acquaintance with primitive groups of people does not on the whole support such a view. Some are nice, others are nasty, according to our preconceptions — there is no universal nobility apparent which transcends the individual peculiarities of a given tribe or group. But this myth has given rise to another belief which has been popularized by Marx, and has become the undoubted credo of many of his followers — as well as of many others who hold left-wing opinions, although not themselves Marxists in the technical sense of that term, nor members of the Communist Party. This belief may be called the Myth of the Underdog, or, more particularly, the Myth of the Wisdom of the Working Class. In its widest form this myth says, very briefly, that those who are oppressed (slaves, Negroes, working-class people generally) have a special kind of sagacity which enables them to hold socially valuable opinions. In this they contrast with the oppressors, who almost by definition hold views and attitudes which are opposed to those held by the exploited class, and are consequently reactionary and possibly "fascist." This view has become quite widely accepted, and is now characteristic of many left-wing and even vaguely "progressive" people. Is it true?

At first sight, the evidence is certainly not impressive. It was working-class members of the Second International who voted War credits in 1914, and destroyed the much-vaunted "international solidarity of the working class." Members of the working class have never seemed to be less chauvinistic, in any country I know, than members of other classes. The English notion that "wogs begin at Calais" is certainly not held less passionately by working-class people than by others — possibly more so. Objections to colored immigration into England, or to Negro equality in the U.S.A., do not come any less from working-class people than from other groups. It will be remembered that the dockers (who could hardly be accused of not being working-class) marched to Parliament in order to support Enoch Powell's anti-immigrant speeches. And those who protested on grounds of anti-apartheid against the visits of the South African rugby and cricket teams to England were not on the whole working-class people, but students and middle-class intellectuals. All this of course is not "hard" evidence. Nevertheless one may feel some doubt whether the communist and Marxist position is not in need of some factual support if it is to be defended.

The usual communist argument, and the usual communist practice, seem to cede the point; according to them the working class is dumb, and needs someone to speak for it. The chosen speakers are of course, the communists; they express the secret will of the working class (just as President Nixon finds it useful to express the will of the "silent majority"). It is always easy to express the "true" views of a group which is silent. There being no known method of discovering what this "true" view really is, the communist is very much in the same position as the Freudian — interpretation is necessary, and who else can give this interpretation but the Marxist, or the Freudian? Objective criteria are not recognized, and indeed are frowned upon by both groups. Just as Freud said that he did not need experimental proof for his discoveries, as such proof was to be found on the couch, so Marxists also do not require proof in independent investigations of social attitudes. Their proof lies in the leadership of the working-class movement which they have often seized, or aspired to. And when they have succeeded in seizing leadership, they have usually taken great care to muzzle the working class once and for all — just in case they might not agree with the interpretations put into their mouths. But this does not answer the doubter's question: What in fact *do* working-class men and women think about various social problems? The question does not seem to be meaningless, and although not too much should be made of the answers which might emerge, it is an interesting problem which seems not to have been put very often, or researched into with any diligence. This is the problem which the present chapter is written to investigate, using some recent studies carried out in our laboratories.

These studies are not purely inductive. They may be said to

have been carried out in order to support or invalidate a specific hypothesis. This hypothesis may be stated quite simply, because it is the obverse of the traditional hypothesis so widely accepted by left-wing writers. One way of stating it might be the following: progressive opinions which are not directly linked with the possession and disposal of private property are more likely to be held by middle-class people than by working-class people. And as a secondary hypothesis we might state that progressive opinions which are directly linked with the possession and disposal of private property are more likely to be held by working-class people than by middle-class people. Thus our hypothesis suggests a break between two kinds of progressive opinions, those dealing with socialism versus capitalism, and those dealing with all other matters. It suggests that within a given class there will be congruence between progressive views on all issues, but between classes there will be a split — working-class people progressive in the socialist sense, but reactionary in all other senses; and middle-class people reactionary in the socialist sense, but progressive in all other senses.

This hypothesis gives rise to an interesting paradox. Left-wing parties, such as the Labour party in Britain, or the Democrats in the U.S.A. (using the term "left-wing" in a purely relative way here, of course), have the reputation of being "progressive" not only in the sense of attacking privilege and property, but also in the sense of being more "liberal" or radical in other issues as well. Similarly, Conservatives and Republicans have the opposite reputation. They are considered reactionary not only in the sense of defending privilege and property, but also in all other senses of the term as well. Thus the Labour party in Britain tends to speak up for such issues as equality of women, dislike of apartheid, permissiveness, arms control, internationalism, abolition of hanging, racial equality, and other similar issues. In votes taken on the floor of the House of Commons, it is usually

Labour members, with a sprinkling of Conservatives, and often with the support of the Liberals, who vote in favor of such issues; and the Conservatives, with a sprinkling of Labour members and the occasional Liberal, who vote against.

The paradox now becomes apparent when it is realized that the majority of Labour voters (and Democrat voters) are working-class, while the majority of Conservative voters (and Republican voters) are middle-class. In other words, if our hypothesis is correct, then on a large number of important social issues each of the two major voting groups is represented in Parliament by members who oppose, on the whole, the attitudes taken by their own supporters! Working-class people hold conservative attitudes on many social issues, but vote into power M.P.s who hold progressive opinions on these self-same issues. Conversely, middle-class people hold progressive attitudes on many social issues, but vote into power M.P.s who hold reactionary opinions on these self-same issues. The issues, then, on which voters and the M.P.s they have elected agree would be those concerned with taxation, nationalization and economic power generally. On all other issues there is a clear-cut chiasma, where "cross-voting" takes place, with electors and elected pulling their different ways. No wonder the dockers support Enoch Powell. There are many interesting consequences which follow from this paradox, and we will discuss these later on in this chapter. For the moment let us consider whether the hypothesis is in fact supported by the evidence.

Let us first consider what is sometimes called "economic conservatism," *i.e.* that set of attitudes directly bearing on the capitalist-socialist controversy, and hence of direct and paramount self-interest to working and middle classes alike. In his *Psychology of Social Classes,* Richard Centers carried out one of the most competent studies in the field. He questioned a random sample of over a thousand American voters, using a battery of questions as follows.

(*1*) Do you agree or disagree that America is truly a land of opportunity and that people get pretty much what's coming to them in this country?

(*2*) Would you agree that everybody would be happier, more secure and more prosperous if the working people were given more power and influence in government, or would you say that we would all be better off if the working people had no more power than they have now?

(*3*) As you know, during this war [the research was done during the Second World War] many private businesses and industries have been taken over by the government. Do you think wages and salaries would be fairer, jobs more steady, and that we would have fewer people out of work if the government took over and ran our mines, factories and industries in the future, or do you think things would be better under private ownership?

(*4*) Which one of these statements do you most agree with? (*a*) The most important job for the government is to make it certain that there are good opportunities for each person to get ahead on his own. (*b*) The most important job for the government is to guarantee every person a decent and steady job and standard of living.

(*5*) In strikes and disputes between working people and employers do you usually side with the workers or with the employers?

(*6*) Do you think working people are usually fairly and squarely treated by their employers, or that employers sometimes take advantage of them?

These questions were found to correlate well together (except for the first one, which did not fit in too well), and they also correlated well with voting intentions; Democrats tended to vote for economic radicalism, Republicans for economic conservatism. Centers made up a single-scale score ranging from ultra-conservative, through conservative, indeterminate and radical, to ultra-radical, by suitably combining answers to these questions. Of the ultra-conservatives, 55 per cent voted Republican, of the ultra-radicals, only 5 per cent. This scale of economic conservatism correlated .59 with social class, showing clearly that working-class people (even in what was then thought by many to be a classless society) tended to favor economic radicalism, middle-class people economic conservatism. Centers interpreted his results as favoring what is sometimes known as the interest theory of social classes. He formulates this as follows:

> This theory implies that a person's status and role with respect to the economic processes of society impose upon him certain attitudes, values and interests relating to his role and status in the political and economic sphere. It holds, further, that the status and role of the individual in relation to the means of production and exchange of goods and services give rise in him to a consciousness of membership in some social class which shares those attitudes, values and interests.

Is it true that people identify themselves correctly with certain social classes? When given the opportunity of saying to which social class they thought they belonged, nearly three quarters of all business, professional and white collar workers identified themselves with the middle or upper classes, while an even larger proportion of all manual workers (79 per cent) identified with the working and lower classes. There is thus good evidence for the "interest theory" of social classes, particularly as far as economic radicalism is concerned.

Is it feasible to extend the meaning of the term "conservatism-radicalism" to issues other than the economic? This has often been doubted. American authors in particular have argued that there is no generality inherent in the conception of radicalism or conservatism spanning a wide variety of different and logically unrelated issues. This does not seem to be true, however. In *The Psychology of Politics* I showed that many different issues do in fact show marked patterns of interconnections when put to the vote. A very clear-cut demonstration of this fact has recently been given by Glenn Wilson, who constructed a simple type of attitude inventory which by his permission is reproduced below.

WHICH OF THE FOLLOWING DO YOU FAVOR OR BELIEVE IN?
(Circle "Yes" or "No." If absolutely uncertain, circle "?". There are no right or wrong answers. Do not discuss; just give your first reaction. Answer all items.)

1 death penalty	Yes	?	No	27 chastity	Yes	?	No
2 evolution theory	Yes	?	No	28 fluoridation	Yes	?	No
3 school uniforms	Yes	?	No	29 royalty	Yes	?	No
4 striptease shows	Yes	?	No	30 women judges	Yes	?	No
5 Sabbath observance	Yes	?	No	31 conventional			
6 beatniks	Yes	?	No	clothing	Yes	?	No
7 patriotism	Yes	?	No	32 teenage drivers	Yes	?	No
8 modern art	Yes	?	No	33 apartheid	Yes	?	No
9 self-denial	Yes	?	No	34 nudist camps	Yes	?	No
10 working mothers	Yes	?	No	35 church authority	Yes	?	No
11 horoscopes	Yes	?	No	36 disarmament	Yes	?	No
12 birth control	Yes	?	No	37 censorship	Yes	?	No
13 military drill	Yes	?	No	38 white lies	Yes	?	No
14 coeducation	Yes	?	No	39 birching	Yes	?	No
15 Divine law	Yes	?	No	40 mixed marriage	Yes	?	No
16 socialism	Yes	?	No	41 strict rules	Yes	?	No
17 white superiority	Yes	?	No	42 jazz	Yes	?	No
18 cousin marriage	Yes	?	No	43 straitjackets	Yes	?	No
19 moral training	Yes	?	No	44 casual living	Yes	?	No
20 suicide	Yes	?	No	45 learning Latin	Yes	?	No
21 chaperones	Yes	?	No	46 divorce	Yes	?	No
22 legalized abortion	Yes	?	No	47 inborn conscience	Yes	?	No
23 empire-building	Yes	?	No	48 colored			
24 student pranks	Yes	?	No	immigration	Yes	?	No
25 licensing laws	Yes	?	No	49 Bible truth	Yes	?	No
26 computer music	Yes	?	No	50 pyjama parties	Yes	?	No

Table 4

As can be seen, there is a great variety of issues included in Wilson's list. In spite of this variety, the reliability of the score was very high, amounting to a correlation of .94. This shows that a person endorsing one "radical" item would, on the whole, tend very strongly to endorse other "radical" items also. Where high scores are the mark of "conservatism," Wilson found that businessmen and housewives had the highest scores (58 and 61, respectively); unskilled workers had a score of 47. University students had the lowest score (33), and adult professional people also scored rather low (44). Wilson showed that his scale correlated quite well with known political opinions and voting patterns. A sample of Left Book Club members scored a mean of 17, members of a right-wing party 56. It is particularly interesting that the items which have high predictive accuracy for this radicalism-conservatism scale are clearly related to important areas of current controversy (beatniks, death penalty, colored immigration, chastity, mixed marriage, royalty, divine law, disarmament, modern art), while non-controversial topics correlate little with the rest (learning Latin, white lies, self-denial, student pranks, fluoridation). It does seem that we are entitled to extend the meaning of "conservatism" and "radicalism" beyond the confines of economic issues.

This more general conservatism-radicalism factor, which includes economic radicalism as one of its components, should differentiate between middle-class and working-class people. But the direction of this difference would be one way on the old hypothesis of the "radical working class," and the other on the hypothesis I have put forward in this chapter, that progressive opinions not directly linked with possession and disposal of private property are more likely to be held by middle-class people. I applied a 35-item questionnaire to over one thousand middle-class and working-class subjects, and scored their inventories for both the R factor (radicalism-conservatism) and the T factor (tough-mindedness versus tender-mindedness). Each of the two class groups was broken down according to their political allegiance, forming subgroups of conservatives, liberals, socialists, and communists. For each of these sub-groups the middle-class members were found to have higher radicalism scores; they also had higher tender-mindedness scores.

The actual figures are set out below in the form of a table. It will be seen that within all party groupings middle-class people are on the whole tender-minded radicals, working-class people tough-minded conservatives. This is very much in line with our hypothesis. The working class favor the death penalty and flogging, harsh treatment of criminals and a "spare the rod, spoil the child" philosophy generally. They are anti-Semitic, anti-miscegenation, and opposed to colored people. Furthermore, they are more patriotic, opposed to giving up national sovereignty for the sake of peace, and against conscientious objectors. All this is vehemently opposed to the progressive, humane, enlightened policies advocated by the Labour Party. It is more akin to the legendary Conservative women in their flowered hats screaming for the restoration in Britain of the death penalty! Our data are perhaps a more secure guide to the realities of social life than the newspaper reports, usually somewhat angled, of these highly selective and unrepresentative meetings.

	Radicalism		Tender-mindedness	
	Middle Class	Working Class	Middle Class	Working Class
Conservatives	4.6	2.8	7.6	6.3
Liberals	6.3	3.7	7.9	7.4
Socialists	9.4	6.4	8.0	6.2
Communists	12.4	10.7	6.8	6.0

Table 5

The subdivision of the social class groups by voting might be thought to distort the picture. Let me therefore quote some figures obtained on random samples of the population by the Gallup Poll, and reproduced here with their kind permission. In April 1968, *i.e.* when the Race Relations Bill was in the news, questions were being asked by the poll about whether Great Britain had been benefited or harmed by immigrants. Of the middle-class respondents, 24 per cent thought benefit had been derived from immigrants, a view shared by only half that proportion of working-class respondents. Of the latter, 64 per cent thought that harm had come from immigration, a view shared by only 54 per cent of middle-class subjects. Similarly, on the question of whether dependants of immigrants should be allowed to enter Great Britain, 49 per cent of middle-class respondents, but 59 per cent of working-class respondents, thought not. Clearly, working-class respondents are less liberal in respect to colored immigration. Other issues on which middle-class people were found to be more liberal were: the opening of the bars in public houses on Sundays; professional sport on the British Sunday; whether divorce should not be made more difficult; whether nudes in magazines were objectionable; and many others, both in this country and in the U.S.A., which it would be wearisome to print in detail. However, there is a sharp turn-around when we come to economic radicalism. To the question of whether more nationalization would be desirable, 5 per cent of the middle class said *Yes,* as compared with 9 per cent and 13 per cent respectively of the skilled and unskilled working class. Denationalization was favored by 54 per cent, as opposed to 38 per cent and 37 per cent. These figures seem to favor the generalization that middle-class, and not working-class, people tend to have progressive views on non-economic questions.

Let me now turn to a special study in which some 2,000 respondents, forming a reasonable sample of the population, were given an inventory of social attitude questions to answer. These questions were mostly taken from the larger inventory printed in *The Psychology of Politics*. The actual questions used are given below; after each question the respondent was to write a ++ if he agreed strongly, a + if he agreed, a *O* if he didn't know or couldn't be sure, a — if he disagreed, and a — — — if he disagreed strongly. These symbols were then scored from 1 (for ++) to 5 (for — —), and statistical calculations carried out on these figures. Interest centered of course on the differences which might emerge between social classes, but attention was also paid to sex differences, and differences between young and old.

INVENTORY OF SOCIAL AND POLITICAL ATTITUDES

1. People should realize that their greatest obligation is to their family.
2. Production and trade should be free from government interference.
3. An occupation by a foreign power is better than war.
4. Men and women have the right to find out whether they are sexually suited before marriage (*e.g.* by trial marriage).
5. Nowadays, more and more people are prying into matters which do not concern them.
6. Jews are as valuable citizens as any other group.
7. The death penalty is barbaric, and it was right to abolish it.
8. Most religious people are hypocrites.
9. Our treatment of criminals is too harsh: we should try to cure them, not punish them.
10. Sex relations except in marriage are always wrong.
11. It would be best to keep colored people in their own districts and schools, in order to prevent too much contact with whites.
12. Compulsory military training in peacetime is essential for the survival of this country.
13. Sex crimes, such as rape and attacks on children, deserve more than mere imprisonment; such criminals ought to be flogged or worse.
14. Persons with serious hereditary defects and diseases should be compulsorily sterilized.
15. It would be a mistake to have colored people as foremen over whites.

16. "My country right or wrong" is a saying which expresses a fundamentally desirable attitude.
17. The idea of God is an invention of the human mind.
18. A person should be free to take his own life, if he wishes to do so, without any interference from society.
19. Free love between men and women should be encouraged as a means towards mental and physical health.
20. A white lie is often a good thing.
21. The so-called underdog deserves little sympathy or help from successful people.
22. The church should attempt to increase its influence on the life of the nation.
23. Colored people are innately inferior to white people.
24. The dropping of the first atom bomb on a Japanese city, killing thousands of innocent women and children, was morally wrong and incompatible with our kind of civilization.
25. All forms of discrimination against the colored races, the Jews, etc., should be made illegal, and subject to heavy penalties.
26. Capitalism is immoral because it exploits the worker by failing to give him full value for his productive labor.
27. Christ was divine, wholly or partly in a sense different from other men.
28. The maintenance of internal order within the nation is more important than ensuring that there is complete freedom for all.

In the analysis social class groups (of which there were ten) were collapsed into three main ones: middle class (professional, administrative, technical and executive), skilled working class, and unskilled working class. Age, too, was collapsed into three groups—young, middle aged, and old. Together with the sex variable this gives us eighteen groups in all for which scores were computed for each of the twenty-eight questions. In comparing the social class groups, only those questions are considered to differentiate between classes which do so regardless of age and sex; similarly, in comparing men and women, only those questions are considered which furnish us with differences regardless of class and age. What, then, do we find with respect to social class?

HERE ARE THE ITEMS on which working-class people differ from middle-class ones—there is, in nearly every case, a progression from middle class, through skilled working class, to unskilled working class, so that although the analysis was done with three social class groups, the summary is still quite adequate in dealing with general differences between middle-class and working-class opinion.

Middle-class people favor trial marriages,* do not think that more and more people are prying into their affairs, believe that Jews are valuable citizens, that the death penalty is barbaric, and that our treatment of criminals is too harsh. They do not think that most religious people are hypocrites, or that extra-marital sex is wrong. They do not want to keep colored people separate, do not favor compulsory military training, flogging for sex crimes, or compulsory sterilization for those with serious hereditary diseases or defects. They are not opposed to colored foremen, and do not believe in the saying "my country right or wrong." They believe that underdogs deserve sympathy, that the church should increase its influence, but not that colored people are inferior, or that capitalism is immoral. They do consider order more important than complete freedom.

Working-class people hold the opposite views on these matters. In other words, they emerge on most issues as conservative and tough-minded (except on the one question dealing with economic radicalism—the immorality of capitalism). Thus working-class people, in summary, are more nationalistic, even jingoistic, xenophobic, anti-Semitic, racialist, inhumane, narrowly moralistic in sexual matters, and unconcerned with ethical or religious issues. The results bear out in considerable detail the hypothesis outlined before

* All the statements made are relative. The statement "middle-class people favor. . ." simply means that they hold this view more strongly than working-class people, etc. Even among them, however, it might still be a minority view.

that working-class people are conservative in all their beliefs except with respect to economic conservatism. This generalization holds as much for men as for women, as much for young as for middle-aged and old people. Taken together with the previous studies already discussed, this seems rather convincing evidence for the "socialist paradox" which gives this chapter its title.

There are, of course, also sex differences, independent of social class. Some of these may be of interest. Women think that occupation would be better than war, that the death penalty is barbaric, but not that religious people are hypocrites. They consider extra-marital sex wrong, do not agree that God is an invention of the human mind, or that free love is a good thing. They would like to see the church increase its influence, and consider the dropping of the atomic bomb immoral. They are against racial discrimination, and do not consider colored people inferior. They also consider Christ divine. In other words, as previous research had also shown, women are more tender-minded than men. This agrees well with the fact that they are also more introverted on the whole.

Age seems to make people both more conservative and more tough-minded. When we compare the older with the younger respondents, we find that more of the older believe in one's obligation to the family, resent government interference, do not believe in trial marriage, do not consider religious people hypocrites, think that extra-marital sex is wrong, want to keep colored people separate, believe in compulsory sterilization, flogging, and the inferiority of colored people; they also do not approve of colored foremen. They do not hold with free love, want the church to increase its influence, consider order more important than freedom, and do not feel that capitalism is immoral. These comparisons are probably very much what one would have expected. It should be noted that this is not a follow-up study, so that the old people whose opinions were canvassed were, in fact, born in quite a different intellectual climate. It is possible, but not necessarily true, that as the young people in this sample grow older, their opinions will change in the same direction. Only a longitudinal study could throw light on this problem.

This is not, of course, the only study to find such differences between social classes. Similar conclusions emerge from some work done by I. Pletka in an unpublished experiment. She found very clear indications of differential class attitudes on a large number of social attitude statements; some of these are duplications of the items already quoted. Further results obtained by her show that working-class people are in favor of not letting so many colored people into the country, letting the people of Asia fend for themselves, returning to the glorious and forgotten past in order that real social progress can be made, and imposing a heavy tax on large incomes. They do believe less in survival after death, more that Jews have too much power and influence, and "have a lot of faith in the common sense of the ordinary man, even though the masses behave pretty stupidly at times." According to them, most of the so-called aid to poorer nations usually ends up in the pockets of profiteers in those countries. Life is so short that a man is justified in enjoying himself as much as he can. The so-called underdog deserves little help or sympathy from successful people (a curious belief to be held by those who must be considered underdogs!). Working-class subjects, further, believe that if censorship were completely abolished, pornography would flourish and the morality of the nation would be undermined; that in taking part in any form of world organization, the country should make sure that none of its independence and power was lost; that while there may be a few exceptions, yet in general Jews are pretty much alike; that national minorities do not have the right to govern themselves; and that the rise of new Nazi-type parties in Germany shows that some people never learn anything from history.

On the other side, middle-class people (apart from believing the opposite of each of these statements) want all forms of discrimination against colored people to be made illegal, oppose apartheid in South Africa in every possible way, consider our treatment of criminals too harsh, and feel that we should cure them, not punish them. They also believe that it is the moral duty of strong nations to protect and develop weaker and poorer nations. Again, therefore, middle-class subjects appear very much more liberal than working-class subjects. All the progressive beliefs of our generation (such as might be found advocated in the pages of the *New Statesman,* or the *Weltbühne,* or the *Nation* and *New Republic*) are supported by them rather than by those whose political and social interests are so dear to the hearts of these journals' editors and contributors.

What has been said does not only apply in Britain, of course, but also in the United States, and probably in European countries as well. Only in the U.S.A. has sufficient empirical work been done to be certain of this conclusion. An excellent survey of such studies as have been published (and several which never saw the light of day) has been put out by J. Robinson, J. Rusk and K. Head, under the title of *Measures of Political Attitudes.* I shall paraphrase some of their conclusions, without quoting the numerous studies in detail.*

They point out that education and middle-class status are so closely related that they are almost impossible to disentangle. What is true of the better educated as compared with the less well educated is usually equally true of middle-class as compared with working-class subjects. This also means, on the whole, that intelligence is involved—well-educated, middle-class subjects will on the average be some 20 to 30 points of I.Q. higher than poorly educated, working-

* The particular chapter from which I quote was written by Alfred Hero of the World Peace Foundation; his data were derived from various polls conducted over the years in the U.S.A.

class subjects. The break is not of course absolute, and there is much overlap. What has been said is true only on the average, and with plenty of exceptions. What, then, are the attitudes of our well-educated subjects in the U.S.A.?

In the first place, Hero points out that "some types of issues, such as those which concern tolerance of ideas and groups different from oneself, have received considerably more liberal responses from the better educated." He adds that in some cases

. . . a proposal for a particular liberal program has initially had only minority approval, but then gradually received majority support after it became law. In such instances the better educated have tended to be in the vanguard of the supporters, while an increasing number of the less educated came to approve of it after it went into effect and prestigious national figures and institutions have spoken out in its favor.

These conclusions are based on long-continued studies extending over many years, in which certain issues were studied with the aid of successive samples. There is little such work done on such issues in Britain, unfortunately, but there is no doubt, judging from such public opinion poll figures as are available, that similar conclusions would be true for Britain, too.

Leaving this particular area, we find that

. . . with some exceptions, education has been more closely related in the post-war era to support for international cooperation than to opinions on most liberal domestic programs other than civil rights and civil liberties . . . Support for "utopian" proposals, such as world government, has been especially limited to those with college experience.

Altogether,

. . . the higher the level of education, the greater has been the willingness to engage in negotiation, conciliation, compromise, economic and cultural relations, and other non-military efforts to lower tensions with communist states (as well as with other countries). In general, the search for other than military solutions—through arms control, economic aid or otherwise—has been more characteristic of the better educated. Particularly has this been so with the lessening of cold war tensions during the last decade.

This decline in "hard-line thinking" among the better educated has been evident in attitudes towards the U.S.S.R., and also towards China. In March 1967, 38 per cent of the least educated versus 57 per cent of the most educated believed that a war between the U.S.A. and China was not very likely.

College-educated Americans have also been clearly more favorably disposed toward Chinese Communist membership in the U.N. and toward establishment of normal diplomatic relations with that country. Approval of the idea of so-called preventive war against either Communist China, the U.S.S.R., or other communist countries has likewise been largely concentrated among poorly educated citizens. Those who would expand or escalate local conventional military operations into broader conflicts, as in Korea or Vietnam, have likewise been disproportionately numerous among the less educated.

Aid to other countries is favored more by the middle-class groups. Support "for non-military aid at prevailing or increasing magnitudes has been much less widespread among the lower educational categories." Support for freer trade has been less dependent on education. "Nevertheless, majorities of grade schoolers with views have more or less consistently felt that U.S. tariffs and other trade barriers should be either kept at prevailing levels or increased, and that imports into this country should be held at current levels or reduced, whereas majorities of college-educated people have supported lower tariffs and expanded imports." At the other end, however, "grade-school educated citizens have sometimes been somewhat more supportive of a strengthened defense establishment, including conscription, than have their college-experienced compatriots." Last in the long list of "liberal" causes in which well-educated middle-class people make a better score than poorly educated working-class people is freedom of expression.

Endorsement of civil liberties, freedom of speech, and the like for such unpopular ideological groups as fascists, socialists, communists, atheists and "beatniks" has been closely associated with education.

Results on attitudes towards Negroes are somewhat confused by the fact that among the poorly educated, working-class subjects in these studies there is a marked preponderance of Negroes—who presumably would not show the same degree of ethnocentrism directed against their own group as would white working-class people. Even so, "the college-educated are twice as likely as those not reaching high school to have viewed inter-racial marriage as acceptable and to have said they would vote for a well qualified Negro for President"—although whether they would in fact have so voted is, of course, another question. The distribution of views on the Ku Klux Klan, lynchings, poll taxes, open housing, and biological inequality of Negroes and whites has not been closely correlated with education or social class, presumably largely because of the solid opposition to these views and policies of working-class, poorly educated Negroes.

WHEN WE TURN FROM these non-economic issues on which the middle-class groups are more liberal to more specifically economic issues, we find that Americans also follow the British pattern of middle-class conservatism.

On most questions involving social welfare, domestic expenditures, and transfers of wealth from more to less prosperous citizens, better educated Americans have been clearly more conservative, or less liberal, than the educationally underprivileged. . . . Thus, the higher the level of education, the more inclined has the citizenry

been to oppose "Federal spending" and deficit financing and to advocate reduction in the overall budget. College-educated Americans have been as much as three or more times as opposed as grade schoolers to such concepts as "the welfare state," "socialized medicine," and even Medicare and other less "radical" programs. Similarly, the former have been only approximately one half as ready as the latter to increase federal expenditure for veterans' benefits, farm subsidies, low-cost housing, old age pensions, and social welfare, health and social security. For three decades substantial majorities of college educated people have opposed, while equally substantial majorities of grade schoolers have favored, successive increases in the minimum wage. Over all, the former were almost twice as inclined as the latter to hold unfavorable opinions of the New Deal in the late thirties and of the Great Society thirty years later. The higher the level of education, the more likely have Americans been to side with business against labor, to feel union rather than industrial leaders have too much influence in Washington, and to approve of open shops, right-to-work laws, and other concepts opposed by unions.
As already pointed out,
income, standards of living, and particularly occupation have been so closely linked with education that it is difficult to determine their impacts—separate from those of differential education—on attitudes toward Federal policy. It is not surprising, therefore, that correlations of income with interest, knowledge, attitudes, and other behavior toward public affairs have been for the most part in the same direction as those of education. . . . In the domestic field, the more affluent elements, like the better educated, have voiced substantially more support for civil liberties, freedom of speech, and the like than have their less well-off

compatriots. Nonetheless, socio-economic status among the U.S. population in general has had but slight connection with feelings about Negroes and race relations. The disproportionate number of Negroes in the lower socio-economic orders has tended to reduce the average level of racism there. However, lower-class whites have been more racist than more privileged whites. . . . However, the reverse has been the case with respect to most internal welfare and economic issues, other than aid to education. Income has been more closely connected with preferred domestic policy alternatives than occupation, community size, or even education. Perceived economic self-interest seems a powerful determinant in such matters. The higher the income, the clearly more conservative the attitudes, even when such factors as education are held constant.

Differences between the most and least well-off of the population on most New Deal measures were very wide, with proportions in favor often two to three times as great among the latter. These differences have on the whole declined in recent years, "but even in the 1960s the well-off have been between one and a half and two times as apt to oppose expansion of welfare legislation and to advocate budget-cutting as their relatively poor compatriots. Moreover, whereas educational groups have differed relatively little in their general approval of trade unions in recent years, the more affluent have remained distinctly more hostile to them than have the lower economic orders."

In relation to *international issues,* "education has been a more important factor in determining most choices than has either income or occupation. In very few instances have differences in information levels or attitudes on international relations been larger between the more and less affluent, or even between the professional-business and manual labor groups, than those between the college-educated and grade schoolers. In fact, seldom have they been as large. When education has been held constant, income has had little bearing on most thinking about these matters. However, when income has been held constant, the better educated still have tended to be at least somewhat more liberal on world affairs."

THUS, WE SEE THAT in the U.S.A. the same paradox has become apparent as in the U.K. Working-class groups are radical with respect to economic and welfare issues, but conservative with respect to freedom of speech, tolerance, world government, reduction in arms, civil liberties, ethnocentrism, aid to foreign countries, and peaceful relations with communist countries.

Middle-class groups show exactly the opposite pattern, being conservative with respect to economic and welfare issues, and liberal with respect to civil liberties and all the other issues mentioned above. Parties are aligned with their supporters largely on the basis of class interests (*i.e.* with respect to economic and welfare issues), and are opposed to them with respect to all other issues.

This general statement is a generalization which must be qualified in numerous ways, and does not cover every member of either the working class or the middle class. Many middle-class members presumably vote for the Labour Party (or the Democratic Party) because that party, although opposed to their economic self-interests, advocates policies which in all other ways are in line with middle-class thinking. Similarly, many working-class people presumably vote for the Conservative Party (or the Republican Party) because that party, although opposed to their economic self-interests, advocates policies which in all other ways are nearer to working-class thinking.

Again, presumably, there are many other reasons for such 'cross-voting" behavior. "Uncle Tom" attitudes of British working-class people towards their "natural" leaders have been suggested as playing a part, and in the U.S.A. there are many local problems which may be more important in a particular election than national and general questions such as those discussed here. Nevertheless, the hypothesis that "cross-voting" may be linked with the crossing over of liberal and conservative attitudes where economic and liberal policies are concerned may still be worthy of serious consideration.

It is curious that the paradox to which we have drawn attention has gone rather unremarked hitherto, even by middle-class persons who in its terms would be excluded from this source of all wisdom and goodness. One might raise the question of whether it might be possible to accommodate this paradox within the confines of the "social class interest" theory. If not, then the facts would require some other, alternative form of interpretation. I believe that to some extent this theory can be adapted to perform this service. All we need to do is to look closely at the differences in self-interest between the social classes.

Consider attitudes to colored people. As far as middle-class persons are concerned, they are hardly incommoded by Negroes, Pakistanis, Indians and other colored groups. These do not compete with them for jobs, for housing, or in any other way. Consequently, for them, tolerance is a virtue only too easily practiced; we would all be virtuous if it cost us nothing. But for working-class people the position is quite different. They are (or believe they are) in direct competition with coloreds for jobs, for housing, even for girls. Every colored on the housing list means so much longer to wait for the white person below him. Cheap colored labor may make it impossible to raise the pay level of certain jobs in conformity with rises in other occupations; bus drivers and conductors, perhaps nurses too, are good examples of this economic fact of life. Thus the social class interest theory would predict precisely what we do in fact observe. Working-class people are more strongly opposed to immigration, to coloreds in general, and to other minority groups who might provide competition for scarce resources. Schooling, too, must be considered in this category. It is largely working-class people who feel the standards of education threatened by the influx of large contingents of colored and other immigrant children, many of them unable to speak English.

To say, therefore, that working-class people are not as liberal in their attitudes to colored people is not to contradict our general theory of social attitudes. Such a reaction to the realities of working-class life could have been predicted, and should certainly have been foreseen by politicians. The dockers' march in support of Enoch Powell is thus seen not as an isolated and rather "odd" and unforeseen event but as a perfectly logical and predictable happening which gives expression to the frustrations of working-class life.

Consider next the treatment of criminals. Here too middle-class and working-class people are in quite different positions. The middle-class person is most likely to encounter crime in the sense of robbery, and he will in the majority of instances be insured, and thus not suffer too much from the consequences of this criminal activity. Working-class people are more likely to be victims of aggression, to be beaten up and injured, than are middle-class people. If they are robbed they are far less able to stand the loss than are middle-class people—and they are much less likely to be insured. Thus, the activities of criminals weigh much more heavily on working-class people than they do on members of the middle class, and again the social interest theory would predict that the latter would have less motivation to feel strongly the force of the Talonic law, which takes an eye for an eye and a tooth for a tooth.

In sexual matters the middle-class person is more enlightened, more liberal, and more inclined to grant freedom and easy divorce to people. Here, too, however, the actual position of working-class people and middle-class people is by no means the same. There are considerable differences between them in respect to the constraints which their mode of life imposes upon them. The husband who breaks up the middle-class home in order to live with another woman is likely to earn sufficient money to make it possible for his wife to live without experiencing the extremes of deprivation. The working-class wife who is left is likely to have no money at all, and to be completely helpless in the face of sudden catastrophe. Similarly, the unmarried middle-class girl who is pregnant can more easily find medical and other help in her troubles. The working-class girl faces much greater difficulties. The family as a social institution is more clearly needed by working-class people. Middle-class people can often buy their way out of trouble, and hence again their tolerance and progressive opinions may be merely the mirror of their privileged financial position.

Or take the greater concern of middle-class people with religious and moral issues. Karl Marx had already remarked that religion was the opium of the working classes—long before Oscar Wilde added that work was the curse of the drinking classes.Working-class people live too near to the edge of poverty and destitution to be able to afford the degree of ethical and religious sophistication which is characteristic of middle-class morality. To deny or neglect these objective differences in favor of name-calling is not likely to convert working-class "racists" to better ways. Ultimately all education, all art, all sport and all morality is the product of a standard of living above the barest minimum. Men and women all of whose energies are absorbed by the needs of making ends meet are not likely to indulge in any of these non-utilitarian activities. Religious salvation as an alternative to here-and-now satisfaction of reasonable needs is another aspect of the "interest" theory of beliefs and attitudes. It is this aspect of religion which Marx had in mind. But the ethical content of religion is another matter. This is not covered by the "interest" theory, and hence working-class people are less likely to embrace views which are ethically desirable, but which contradict their individual or class interests.

What has been said here about English conditions applies with even greater force to American conditions. The white "backlash" in the Northern States should not have been as unexpected as apparently it was by many social scientists. The interest theory of attitudes clearly predicts precisely such a reaction on the part of the white working-class groups mainly implicated. To say this is not of course to agree with "racist" arguments, or to consider the political and social remedies suggested by such people as justified. All that the interest theory has to say is that the growth of such attitudes is neither capricious nor inexplicable. It also suggests that the liberal habit of calling such attitudes "stereotyped" and irrational does less than justice to the objective causes which give rise to them. Nor is it suggested that, according to the interest theory of attitude formation, people who form these attitudes are necessarily correct in their appreciation of reality. Consider the British race problem. It is true that colored immigrants cause problems to white working-class people; thus far the reactions of these people are "rational." There is also another side to this medal; colored people also perform positive services which are of considerable use and help to the white members of the community. Colored nurses and doctors are indispensable to the maintenance of Britain's national health service; colored bus-drivers and conductors are equally indispensable to the maintenance of Britain's transport services. Many other examples come to mind. From the psychological point of view, however, the positive contributions of immigrants are somewhat remote (in obvious everyday benefits) from the typical working-class man or woman; while the negative aspects of their presence, as manifested in overcrowding and the use of scarce resources (*i.e.* those aspects for which, as scapegoats, colored people are held responsible), are only too obvious (even though what seems obvious is not necessarily true, there being all sorts of other factors involved). Even though, therefore, the positive contribution on balance outweighs the negative, this is not fatal to the interest theory. The formation of attitudes which it predicts takes place in the complex context of everyday living, where purely rational weighing up of evidence is difficult, and not in the laboratory, or the statistician's study. This point may require some elaboration.

What we are suggesting in formulating the interest theory of attitudes is this. Attitudes are mental habits, as already pointed out; that means that they develop according to much the same laws as do other habits. Now habits and their growth follow the general laws of reinforcement discussed in the chapter on behaviorist technologies; actions which are positively reinforced ("rewarded") tend to be repeated until they become habitual. The effect of such reinforcement is dependant on many factors; among these are the number of reinforcements, and their strength and immediacy. Negative reinforcements for habits of racial tolerance and understanding are frequent and immediate for many white, working-class people who are in immediate competition with coloreds for jobs, housing, and other necessities of life. Similarly immediate and frequent are negative feedbacks from school and other educational institutions. Positive feedback is less immediate and less frequent. We know that there are many colored doctors and nurses in our hospitals, but this is cognitive knowledge—it does not serve the purpose of reinforcement of actual physical habits of responding, except in a few people who actually come into contact with hospitals. Thus the dice are loaded against the reinforcement of tolerant and friendly attitudes, and in favor of hostile and intolerant ones. The interest theory of attitudes does not seek to excuse racist and other illiberal attitudes, nor should it be understood to countenance them in any way. It merely seeks to understand them, and to present a rational theory of their growth and development.

SUCH A THEORY must, of course, have something to say about ways and means of controlling prejudice, and indeed the deductions from our theory are fairly obvious. If objective conditions affecting the personal interests of (mostly working-class) people are in part responsible for the growth of anti-colored prejudice, then what seems required is of course a change in these objective conditions. Great Britain and the U.S.A. have adopted what amounts to a simple *laissez-faire* approach to these problems. Very little in the way of special arrangements were made; there was no effort to anticipate difficulties in housing and education; and there was finally indignant surprise that problems should arise as a consequence of this dilatory and uninterested attitude.

Contrast this with the much less troublesome introduction of colored workers into the Netherlands. Special attention was paid to possible sources of friction, much planning was undertaken ahead of time, and housing and education received priority. As a consequence, few of the difficulties which plague us have arisen and there is an absence of prejudice in Holland which puts Britain and America to shame. Prejudice may be irrational, but that does not mean that it does not follow a regular course. It must be possible to understand the causes and to control them. It is unfortunate that such control is much easier to exercise before than after the event; prevention, here as always, is better than cure. Even now there is little attempt at scientific understanding leading to rational ways of dealing with the problem. What we get instead is political wrangling and jockeying for party advantage. Granted the importance and size of the problem, it is perhaps characteristic of our non-scientific approach that there is practically no money being spent on the much-needed research without which all action must be relatively blind. Action in the absence of knowledge must inevitably be less efficient than action taken on the basis of proper scientific understanding.

The interest theory of attitudes covers some, but not all, of the questions raised by the paradox of cross-voting. Clearly, personality factors also play an important part, as we have seen in Chapters 1 and 2. It is impossible to understand individual differences in attitudes to sex, for instance, without looking at extroversion and introversion. The interest theory as stated is too broad and general to predict with any accuracy individual attitudes, which are shaped by a given person's temperament, and by accidental events in his life history, as well as by the contingencies of his class membership. The (vaguely Marxian) interest theory is clearly along the right lines, but it is too limited on its own to give us all the information we need. Economic and other causes can only determine behavior by acting on the individual person. This seems so axiomatic that I find it difficult to see how anyone can seriously doubt it. A person's class membership clearly affects his behavior in many ways, but these effects are modified by his innate temperamental peculiarities, his equally innate abilities, and what Skinner calls his "reinforcement history," *i.e.* the more or less accidental events of his life which determine which actions, attitudes, and habits are positively or negatively reinforced.

The interest theory, as discussed thus far, has carried the implication that the interests which are being made responsible for the growth of attitudes are real ones. The positive or negative reinforcements which are received by the holders of such attitudes are objective properties of the situations producing them. A person may, of course, be mistaken about his real interests, but by and large there is an element of rationality about the theory which may be misleading. This element is not necessary, and indeed many beliefs and attitudes are purely superstitious. Consider the following excerpt from the *Indian Express*:

> Three goats were sacrificed yesterday in a ritual to ensure the safety of an Avro aircraft, newly acquired by the Nepal Airlines. The airline officials here feel that the

recent crash of one of its aircraft at New Delhi was the result of their failure to hold a similar ceremony at Dushera. At the time of that traditional Hindu ceremony, the ill-fated Fokker Friendship was undergoing repairs at Bombay.

How do superstitions of this kind—often religious in character—originate? I have already quoted Skinner's famous "superstitious" experiment in an earlier chapter; it applies with equal force to superstitious religious and "racist" beliefs as to Freudian motives.

There is an analogy to the growth of superstitions in pigeons in a well-known story of an obsessional-compulsive patient who kept constantly snapping his fingers. When the psychiatrist asked him why he did this he said: "To keep the lions away." The psychiatrist said: "But there are no lions around here." To which the patient replied: "See how successful finger-snapping is!" Reinforcement can be administered on a realistic basis, in which case the attitudes produced are in line with reality and useful. But reinforcement can also be administered on an accidental basis, as in the case of the pigeons, in which case the result is superstition. The basis of such superstitious attitudes is no different as far as the law of their genesis is concerned, but they are not adapted to reality and will not be useful to the holder. Nevertheless they may be very difficult to eradicate, because reinforcement may still be forthcoming on an accidental basis. The pigeons indulging in their superstitious behavior would be fed whether they did or did not hop or trail their wings. They do not know this, however, and hence they misinterpret the contingencies relating to their being fed. Human beings are not pigeons, but the irrationality of so many of their attitudes suggests that these are acquired, not through a lengthy process of rational investigation and scientific understanding, but through an accidental or random process of reinforcement. We tend to smile at such attitudes as those revealed in the sacrifice of the goats, but we should realize that while often superstitions are harmless and amusing, at other occasions they can be deadly in their effects.

Consider, for instance, the position of the African Sotho tribe which lives near the sea. The tribe is suffering from grave malnutrition, due to the fact that its numbers have been increasing. The introduction of modern medicine has cut infant mortality to a fraction, but there has been no corresponding increase in the provision of food. There is danger of famine, and many of the infants saved from infectious and other diseases are now likely to die an even more painful death from hunger. There is ample food available in the sea. Fish are plentiful, and the men of the tribe are excellent sailors. But they will not eat fish. They have acquired superstitious attitudes and beliefs regarding fish which rule out of order any attempt to solve their problem in this manner. As is well known, a similar position exists in India, where famine threatens, and is almost endemic in certain parts, while religious superstitions make impossible the obvious way out, namely the killing and eating of the "holy cows" which are at present untouchable. Clearly, if it were possible to change these attitudes many lives could be saved. The truth of this statement is even more obvious when we consider Hitler's attitude towards the Jews, or the attitudes of the Holy Inquisition towards those (even Christians) who did not share their specific beliefs.

In these cases the source of reinforcement clearly is different from that which nourishes anti-colored beliefs in British and American working-class families. The most likely source would seem to be social approval. Certain beliefs are positively reinforced, others negatively, by teachers, parents and peer groups. This is, obviously, a very potent form of brain-washing. One learns to take for axiomatic the attitudes which are so uniformly lauded and reinforced. Religious and nationalistic attitudes come particularly to mind here. These are obviously irrational, yet they are very strongly held, and hence one suspects have been frequently and strongly reinforced.* Indeed, it is odd, and perhaps paradoxical, that anti-Negro prejudice, which is often regarded as almost the prototype of irrational and biased attitudes, should have a considerable amount of realistic, rational background in the reinforcing conditions of the environment, while religious beliefs, such as those exemplified in the story of the three goats, come out as purely superstitious in the Skinnerian sense.

There are, of course, psychological methods of combating prejudiced attitudes, and much experimental work has been done along the lines of trying to undo the evil which previous accidental (or not so accidental) reinforcement of "wrong" attitudes has produced. This is not the place to discuss these methods; it seems peculiar that those most concerned with the practical problems posed by prejudice often know the least about this store-house of knowledge and practical suggestions. But in this the field of attitude research does not differ all that much from other fields of psychology. As I shall be arguing in the last chapter, practical people often resent the introduction of scientific methods of reasoning and experimenting into their fields, and prefer to muddle haphazardly along the good old ways, rather than take new knowledge into account. This anti-scientific attitude itself, is, of course, of some interest to the research worker, and might repay much more

---

* It is perhaps not necessary to go into detail as to why these beliefs are irrational. Few Christians have made their choice of religion on the basis of an impartial examination of the 300 or so religions available. Children of Muslims become Muslims; children of Hindus become Hindus; children of Christians become Christians—if only of a kind. Even within these religions, children adopt the beliefs of their parents with respect to the particular sectarian aspects favored by their parents; they become Christadelphians, or Protestants, or Jehovah's Witnesses, or whatever specific belief father or mother may favor. This does not argue rational choice, but irrational determination through positive reinforcement.

careful study than it has received so far. Of all the many superstitions which afflict humankind, this is one of the most pernicious.

THE GENERAL PARADOX from which this chapter has taken its title must of course have many political implications, and we may end by considering some of these. It has often been pointed out, sometimes as criticism of the class interest theory of attitude formation, that many British working-class people vote Conservative, possibly as many as one in three, while many middle-class people vote Labour, possibly as many as one in four. Thus it is argued that quite a high proportion of people vote against the party which represents their economic interests, and the explanation sometimes given is that such an action is "irrational." This clearly is not necessarily so. Economic radicalism is only one aspect of the more general factor of radicalism, and a working-class person may feel more at home with the generally conservative policies of the Conservative party, which serves his interests in many ways, even though disapproving of its economic policies. Similarly, a middle-class person may feel more at home with the generally progressive policy of the Labour party, even though disapproving of its economic radicalism. There is a conflict built into the two-party system, and this conflict permits of several different types of solution. None of these is necessarily irrational, although voting against one's economic class interests might seem so to a confirmed Marxist.

It seems possible that the economic argument is gradually losing in importance. Nationalization is no longer the source of such impassioned European debate it once was. Few socialists now wish to extend nationalization much farther; not many conservatives wish to dismantle the whole edifice of the nationalized industries. According to Gallup, only one in five Labour voters wishes for more nationalization in Britain, but equally one in five Labour voters wishes for more denationalization; clearly Labour cannot be regarded as a party committed to wholesale nationalization. If this were true, then there might occur a gradual re-alignment of classes and parties; more middle-class people would tend to vote for the (non-economic) radicalism which is the stock-in-trade of the Labour party, and more working-class people would tend to vote for the (non-economic) conservatism of the Tory party. It should not be impossible to document such changes if they were to occur; they would provide an interesting support for the theory here advocated.

The paradox discussed in this chapter can be traced right through modern English history, from Cromwell's day to the present, and seems likely to play an equally prominent part in other industrialized countries as well.

Cromwell had struggled to overthrow the power of the king, but he could not trust the common people to vote into power a Parliament that would not promptly restore royal rule. Hence his final concession of failure, the "Barebones" parliament, made up of "diverse persons fearing God and of approved fidelity and honesty" who were "nominated by myself with the advice of my council of officers." When even Barebones failed, there was no alternative to personal rule. The Lord Protector took over. The first dictator had found to his cost that the common people in whose interests he thought he acted, had very different ideas about what these interests were. Like others later on, he decided to "interpret" their "true" interests for them. Somewhat more familiar are the events of the 1970 election when Labour was narrowly beaten, in spite of being predicted likely winners by the opinion polls. Investigation of what went wrong showed that working-class support for Enoch Powell and his anti-colored attitude was a major reason for the Tory victory; a widely publicized speech by Anthony Wedgwood Benn, strongly criticizing Powell, was singled out as "the biggest single blunder of the campaign." Thus wisdom after the event suggests that Labour lost, and the Tories won, because the former neglected to pay attention to the precarious position into which the class-attitude paradox puts them. Enoch Powell, of course, has been disowned by the leader of the Tory party, but to the man in the street his widely reported speeches counted for much more than the disclaimers by Mr. Heath and others, tucked away in the middle pages. It will be interesting to see how the parties play the game when next an election is in the offing.

⑥

The Uses and ABuses of Pornography

MORE jokes are probably made about sexual activities than about all other things combined, and no wonder—looked at without the rose-colored glasses of romance, the sexual act must surely rank among the most comic performances of all time. My own introduction to the mysteries of sex took place rather early. My father had remarried when I was nine, and I went down to Munich to be introduced to his wife. Unfortunately there were some festivities going on at the time, and the hotel was full; the owner kindly allowed me to sleep on a sofa in his study. I was even then a compulsive reader, reading anything I could lay my hands on; looking for something to read after I had gone to bed I found nothing but a copy of Van der Velde's book on sex. This was one of the first of the many modern successors to the *Kama Sutra,* giving detailed descriptions of the many different positions of sexual intercourse; it became the Bible of every *Backfisch* (teenage girl) in Germany. Like most bright youngsters, I had already concluded from observation that grown-ups were a fraud and a delusion; that their precepts and their actions were miles apart; and that it was a toss-up whether they were more vicious or more ridiculous in their behavior.

Van der Velde brought the scales down on the side of funniness; when I read about the kinds of things adult men and women did together, I was so convulsed with laughter that

I fell out of bed, and rolled helplessly around the floor. I imagined my form-master, fat old Dr. P., doing the "tree" with his tall, thin wife, and was so shaken with uncontrollable amusement that my sides began to ache. Finally my father came in to find out what the racket was all about, and promptly confiscated the book, but it was too late. From then on, whenever a teacher or some other grown-up in a position of authority annoyed me, I relaxed and imagined him in one of the positions so graphically described by the good Dr. Van der Velde. This immediately restored my good humor, and enabled me to sit quietly through any number of lectures about my sins and venality. Even nowadays Van der Velde is my standby when I have to attend committees; the boredom would be unbearable without allowing imagination to commit slander on the sexual proclivities of the participants. Van der Velde was of course labelled "pornographic" in his time, and my imagination has since been powerfully assisted by *Fanny Hill, Candy* and other flowers out of the same garden. But first loves do not die, and I still remember his book best.

Second to the amusement I have received from a consideration of sexual behavior itself has been the amusement of reading about pornography. Not "reading pornography"; while I would say nothing against pornography as such, it does not provide much amusement. Whatever its functions may be (and I will come to those presently) amusement is not normally one of them—unless it be quite accidental and unintentional. No, it is the discussions about what is and what is not pornographic; the long and endless arguments about whether literary merit or scientific importance should be allowed to offset the pornographic content; the legal hair-splitting about whether pornography is obscene or not, and whether it tends to deprave and corrupt. These I have loved, and shameful as it is to admit it, I have always much preferred to read about pornography than to read pornography—rather like the psychologist who at burlesque shows is supposed to be the one man who looks at the audience rather than at the stage.

I would not like to suggest that I am insensible to the fact that sex can be tragic. One cannot work in a mental hospital and remain ignorant on this point. And sex can of course be beautiful, too, when set in a proper love relationship. But neither tragedy nor beauty is the common coin of everyday sex, and thus laughter is the only antidote to tears. Why is sex funny? I think that Bergson's theory of humor finds here one of the few places where it can be applied with impunity.

Bergson, it will be remembered, thought that humor arose from the contradiction between our conception of human dignity, and the mechanical nature of our bodies, and certain aspects of our behavior. The classic example of humor, the man slipping on the banana skin, brings this incongruity out well. The person involved has a mind, a social position, financial problems and an unfaithful wife, but as far as the banana skin is concerned he is merely one further proof of the applicability of Newton's law of universal gravitation. The reason, of course, is that the sexual act, and the events leading up to it, contain a great deal of "mechanical" activity; this has not been lost on those who look for symbolisms of sexual activity. Driving in a nail, "screwing," aiming and firing a pistol, inserting the gasoline pump nozzle in the car's tank— these are only some examples, and others covering the male and female genitals are of course legion.

Some people still believe that the use of these symbols was discovered by Freud, and that prior to his writing blissful ignorance reigned; but this is not so. Take but one of many possible examples, the book *A Discourse on the Worship of Priapus*, written in 1786 by the antiquarian Richard Payne Knight (with the help of Sir William Hamilton, husband of Nelson's "dearest Emma"). Having argued that the round towers of Ireland and the English maypole were phallic symbols, Knight went on to argue that "even the spires of our churches are now shown to be nothing more nor less than existing symbols of this pagan and strange worship." It is this contradiction between the romantic ideal of love and the mechanical nature of the sexual act, this incongruity between the humanistic values put on the other person and their physical function as receptacle or stimulant, which account for the humor inevitably involved in sex. In addition there is also of course the incongruity between the covert allusion to things sexual, and the overt refusal to talk openly about these matters. But the main cause of the amusement is the contrast between the mechanics of the act and the spiritual gloss cast over it by poets, writers and moralists.

THIS INCONGRUITY, of course, applies equally to such things as behavior therapy. There is an obvious incongruity between the divine essence of humanity (if any) and the mechanics of giving homosexuals electric shocks while they are looking at pictures of naked men. This may cure them of homosexuality, but it is either funny or tragic, whichever way you like to think of it. It certainly creates a conflict of values which is as obvious to behavior therapists as it is to critics. Critics are usually more vocal because they are less concerned with the patient's side of it; they do not see the immense pressure on the therapist to cure the patient because they do not see the suffering of the patient. Thus, to critics the "inhuman" or mechanistic side of the treatment predominates and they fulminate against it. These criticisms would of course be more acceptable if they had something better to put in the place of aversion therapy. Until such a method is found, we will have to learn to live with the incongruity, and laugh or weep as we feel inclined.

Link sex and behavior therapy, and you get situations like the one created for me one day when I was visited by an emissary from a group of Arabian sheikhs. I had been writing on the treatment of sexual disorders by behavior therapy, and it appeared that these immensely rich refugees from the Arabian Nights had clubbed together to try and get me to go out to Arabia and cure them of impotence. I found it difficult to preserve a straight face; in my imagination I saw a picture of a dozen or so Rudolph Valentinos, in rich Arabian dress, lining up for me to inspect their limp organs of procreation, while in the background their numerous wives were praying in their rich tents to Allah to restore their manly vigor to their husbands. Callous? Perhaps, but surely such scenes have a comic flavor, however sad the underlying facts might be to the proud and fierce warriors in question. Life is a comedy for those who think and a tragedy for those who feel; laughter may act as a protection which enables us to keep our sanity. And sanity is not one of those commodities often found in relation to discussions of sex, pornography and "obscene publications."

WHAT IS PORNOGRAPHY? The dictionary tells us that the term derives from the Greek: *porne*=harlot and *graphos*=writing about. According to its derivation it would seem to denote writings about harlots. But of course the term is used in a more general fashion to denote "obscene writings or pictures"; this adjective does not seem to have any recognized semantic history, but refers to things which offend modesty or decency.

Now thoroughly aroused, we inquire about the meaning of these nouns. Modest, we find, means decent, which does not help much. Decency is defined as "a proper regard for modesty"; this seems somewhat circular. Decent also means "conforming to the standard of good taste"; does this mean that all badly written, offensive books are pornographic? As usual, the seven veils of language hide rather than reveal what we seek to uncover. Perhaps the *Oxford English Dictionary* comes nearest to an intelligible definition when it says that pornography means "the expression or suggestion of obscene or unchaste subjects in literature or art." And for "obscene" it suggests "offensive to modesty or decency; expressing or suggesting lewd thoughts." And what is "lewd"? Why, that which is indecent or obscene; also that which is lustful or lascivious. And as lascivious is defined in terms of lust, we are finally driven back to this term, which means "desire for indulgence of sex." At long last our search through all these euphemisms has brought us to a simple word which most people can understand without having to go to the dictionary: pornography is lustful writing about sex.

Most arguments about pornographic writings get off to a bad start by phrasing their questions in terms of what is and what is not pornographic. These arguments have been well rehearsed in such books as H. Montgomery Hyde's *History of Pornography* (1964). I would suggest that we could clarify the whole situation by abandoning this notion that there are two groups of writings, pornographic and non-pornographic, and recognize the fact that we are dealing with a dimension ranging from 0 (no mention of sex) to 100 (entirely concerned with sexual matters). Every book can be graded somewhere on this scale. The scale—shall we call it the P scale, and the score obtained by a book its P score?—does not concern itself with artistic merit, or scientific value, or historical interest—these considerations are of course not unimportant, and may be vital from a legal point of view, but they are independent of the P score (the number of *pips*, or Pornographic Index Points) of a book.

A book may have a high P score or a low one, irrespective of its artistic, scientific or historical value; the evaluative content of the term "pornography" obscures this fact. When I worked my way through Goethe's *Collected Works* as a schoolboy, I came finally to the famous Volume 53, in which were collected all his pornographic writings; these have a high artistic and historical interest, but are nevertheless concerned with sexual matters and would be considered "obscene" and "lascivious" by most people. They are no less so than the stories in *Girlie*

Mag, although few people would suggest that the latter rivalled Goethe's writings and poems in respect to literary quality. It is of course common in everyday parlance to neglect the vital measurement properties of a given topic and employ instead a rough-and-ready classification—like tall and short, bright and dull, fat and thin. But for most practical purposes some more refined measurement is desirable, and the "either-or" type of categorization may induce quite erroneous ways of thinking about the subject. We conclude therefore that it may be useful to give a simple, one-dimensional definition of pornography; that this one dimension is probably capable of being measured, at least in a rough-and-ready manner; and that where other considerations enter into our evaluation, they should be separately measured and determined.

MEASUREMENT, to be useful and effective, must make certain assumptions, and it is the business of the scientist to check whether these assumptions are justified or not. If we want to grade pornographic writings in order from most to least, then there are three and only three relations which must be discovered to hold between the units to be so graded. Like all modern notions of measurement, these are ultimately derived from Cantor's theory of classes (*Mengenlehre*). They have become known mainly through the writings of Bertrand Russell, whose *Introduction to Mathematical Philosophy* may cast a mantle of respectability over some very common sense notions. What we are required to do is to find a relation that is (*a*) connexive, (*b*) asymmetrical and (*c*) transitive, and to show that the units involved in our analysis actually obey these rules.

Let us exemplify these somewhat arid statements by an example: let x stand for the act of kissing, y for the act of intercourse, and z for some complex act of "perversion" like *soixante-neuf, i.e.* the combination of cunnilingus and fellatio. Let the sign $>$ stand for greater than, on the intended scale, while the sign $\langle$ stands for lesser than; what the three postulates assert is:

(a) Connexive Postulate: If x and y both $\rangle$ z, or both $\langle$ z, then either $x \langle y$, $y \langle x$, or $x = y$;

(b) Postulate of Asymmetry: If $x \langle y$, then neither $y \langle x$ nor $y = x$;

(c) Postulate of Transitivity: If $x \langle y$ and $y \langle z$, then $x \langle z$.

In other words, if kissing and intercourse are both lower on the scale than perversion, then either kissing and intercourse are equal on the scale, or one is higher than the other. If kissing is lower than intercourse, then intercourse is not lower than kissing, nor are the two equal. And if kissing is lower than intercourse, and intercourse is lower than perversion, then kissing is lower than perversion. Readers may not feel that this poses much of a restriction, but essentially this is the basis of measurement as modern mathematics and physics regard it. Does it work for *P?*

In a previous chapter I have given a Table listing nineteen forms of sexual conduct which respondents were asked to tick, indicating whether they had or had not indulged in each. Taking the percentages of "yes" answers for each item tells us how frequently each was indulged in compared to each of the others, but no reasonable scale can be derived from these figures because percentages require transformation in terms of the normal curve of distribution before they give a scale the distances along which then are equal. When this is done, we get the following scale, which will strike most people as intuitively reasonable and acceptable. I have arbitrarily multiplied the actual figures by a constant, and added another constant, in order to have a scale ranging from zero to fifteen; this does not affect the issue, but merely makes for easier reading.

Scale of Sexual Activity	Points:
1. Social talking.	0
2. One minute continuous lip kissing.	3
3. Manual manipulation of female breast, over clothes	4.5
4. Manual manipulation of female breast, under clothes.	5.3
5. Kissing nipples of female breast.	6.3
6. Manual manipulation of female genitals.	6.5
7. Manual manipulation of male genitals.	7.2
8. Mutual manual manipulation of genitals.	7.3
9. Sexual intercourse, face to face.	8.3
10. Manual manipulation of male genitals to ejaculation.	8.6
11. Oral manipulation of female genitals.	10.3
12. Oral manipulation of male genitals.	10.8
13. Sexual intercourse, man behind woman.	12.2
14. Mutual oral-genital manipulation.	12.5
15. Oral manipulation of male genitals to ejaculation.	12.8
16. Mutual oral manipulation of genitals to mutual orgasm.	15.0

In this scale a few items have been dropped because they duplicated positions already occupied; in addition, male and female reactions have been averaged, no doubt with some loss of accuracy. But in all the scale is clearly a meaningful one, and provides us with a convenient starting-point. The three postulates of measurement have been tested in connection with the replies received, and there is no doubt that to all intents and purposes responses can be treated as constituting a scale—provided we are willing to accept a certain very limited amount of error.

This scale is, of course, meaningful only in a relative sense. It would not necessarily apply to other cultural groups—to the Japanese, for instance, kissing on the lips would constitute a perversion, and have a rating up around 12. For the Romans, the "missionary position" in intercourse would not have seemed the right and proper one, and they would have given it more points. This cultural relativity does not affect the value of the scale as far as use in our particular culture is concerned: it merely reminds us that we must not extrapolate beyond the evidence. But for our system of sexual mores, we can use this scale to construct a rating table which makes it possible to measure with objectivity and reasonable accuracy the amount of P (pornography) contained in a given passage of prose. This table is reproduced below; its use is simplicity itself. Any pornographic book contains descriptions of people (particularly their primary and secondary sexual parts) and of acts (particularly acts having sexual significance). We give points for the mention of bodily parts involved in these descriptions of persons and activities, according to the Table—1 point for lips, or shoulders, 4 points for breasts, 8 points for the sexual parts proper, and so on. To these points given for descriptive nouns we add points for favorable adjectives (1 for each, up to a maximum of 2 for one noun) or subtract points for unfavorable adjectives (—2 points for each, up to a maximum of 2). Let us try this out on a magnificent prose effort from *Naughty Ladies* which goes like this:

"His eyes devoured her magnificent body. Her firm, uppointing breasts seemed to burst their confines, and her luscious red lips lured him on to his downfall. He dropped his gaze to take in her long, well-shaped legs, her beautifully muscled buttocks, and his breathing became heavy. Slowly she began to unbutton her blouse, revealing the swell of her bosom, until the transparent material fell away, showing her nipples in all their glory."

The points gained by this inspiring adventure in English composition have been written above the words which are responsible; it will be seen that these two sentences aggregate 32 pips. This is of course a simple descriptive paragraph;

when the action begins far more points can be gained in equal space, as will be demonstrated presently. (Adjectival phrases count as adjectives.)

P (PORNOGRAPHY) INDEX				
Nouns	*Points*	*Adjectives*		
lips, mouth	1	favorable	+1 ⎱	up to two adjectives
shoulders	1	unfavorable	—2 ⎰	for one noun
body	2	*Verbs*		
back, stomach	2	signifying manual	2 ⎱	
legs	2	manipulation	⎰ multiple appropriate	
breasts	4	signifying oral	4 ⎰	nouns
nipples	5	manipulation		
buttocks	5	*Adverbs*		
thighs	5	favorable	1 ⎱	up to two adverbs
sexual parts	8	unfavorable	—2 ⎰	for one verb

Table 6

When actions are being reported the nouns in the sentence are multiplied by 2 if the action is manual, *i.e.* when bodily parts are being grasped, fondled, handled, stroked, caressed, or otherwise manipulated. Nouns are multiplied by 4 if the action is oral, *i.e.* when bodily parts are being kissed, licked, sucked, bitten, or otherwise orally manipulated. This multiplication is of the noun alone, not of the noun + adjective. Thus, "he fondled her cool, firm breasts, and then bent down to kiss her nipples with hot lips" would rate 4 for breasts, multiplied by 2 (for fondling), making 8; to this would be added 2 points for "cool" and "firm," making 10 for that part of the sentence. Similarly, 5 points for nipples are multiplied by 4 (for kissing), making 20; to this would be added 1 point for the adverbial phrase "with hot lips." Thus the whole sentence rates 31 points. (Favorable adverbs rate 1 point, up to a maximum of 2 for one verb; unfavorable adverbs rate —2, also up to a total of 2 at most.)

The reason for not counting more than two adjectives or adverbs is, of course, that a noun or verb should not be qualified too much as otherwise it loses its force. It would be more than slightly ridiculous to say: "he gazed at her magnificent, warm, pulsating, upstanding, red-tipped, large, well-shaped breasts." To give additional points to reward such sloppy writing would be a crime against the English language! The reason for discriminating between favorable and unfavorable adjectives and adverbs will also be clear. Pornographically speaking, "firm, large breasts" provoke lascivious and lustful thoughts, but "pendulous, sagging breasts" have the opposite effect. Similarly, "he made love madly" has a more marked pornographic effect than "he made love listlessly." Pornographic writers seldom use unfavorable terms, but when these are being used, the formula is ready to deal with all eventualities.

THERE ARE SOME COMPLICATIONS to be considered. Bodily contact is scored like manual manipulation, *i.e.* in the sentence: "He lay down on his back, and she sat down on his stomach." The sitting down is rated as if she had touched him manually. Euphemisms which are quite unequivocal are rated as if the proper term had been used, *e.g.* "honeypot" for vagina. The same is done with colloquial terms, like "quim" for vagina. Latin terms present a difficulty; they probably do not deserve points at all. The reason is a simple one. What produces pornographic effects is detailed description of sexual acts, and terms like "intromission," "fellation," or "cunnilingus," even when they are understood by the reader, do not provide such description. The point here made is similar to the well-known tendency of people to react far more strongly to the detailed description of one single child dying of starvation than to the factual statement in a newspaper that "one million Indians have died of starvation." The same argument applies to the famous four-letter words; unless they are part of a detailed descriptive account they do not really qualify as pornographic—although they may qualify as obscene, as we shall see in a moment.

So far we have dealt with what one might call love-play. Preceding this there is the stage of disrobing. Garments do not score anything, unless they are tight, revealing, transparent, or in some other way suggestive; if they are, they score one point. Panties and bras score two if they are mentioned, and 4 if they are removed. Altogether not many points can thus be scored with the act of disrobing, unless of course points are gained by mentioning parts of the body scored as in our table.

When we come to intercourse itself, which is defined as beginning with intromission and ending with ejaculation, scoring is changed. Each word in the passage describing the sexual act itself is given 3 points. No extra points are given for mention of particular parts of the body. We thus have three parts of our pornographic masterpiece, all scored somewhat differently. First, there is the disrobing scene (*1*), followed by love-play (*2*), followed by intercourse (*3*); all three are summed to give a total number of points. The major source of points will usually be the third part, with the first part contributing relatively little; however, in more reputable journals and books the proportions may be reversed. In fact, the relative contributions of these three parts to the total are of interest in themselves; the ratio 1 + 2, divided by 3, is high in relatively non-obscene writing, and low in what might be legally objected to.

WE HAVE SO FAR concentrated on the allocation of points. However, for measurement we require more than that. Two books might have the same number of points, but one might be completely unobjectionable, accumulating a pip here and another pip there throughout the narrative by simply describing some innocent kissing and cuddling, while the other scored no pips at all for 99 per cent of its length, and accumulated all its points through the highly pornographic and indeed obscene description of a torrid love scene. Many romantic library novels resemble the first of these, while such a book as Frank Harris's autobiography resembles the second. The average number of pips per page of these very different types of books is about the same, but Harris intersperses his pornographic passages with many pages not even mentioning women, or sex. Henry Miller, similarly, intersperses his well-known pornographic passages with much pseudo-philosophizing; his overall average would not be as high as that of many books which are not considered at all pornographic. It follows that we cannot average points over a whole book; we must adopt a different principle.

It is suggested that we regard as the pornographic unit (P.U.) a coherent descriptive account of a sexual encounter which is separated from what went before, and what follows, by at least 100 words totalling less than 10 points. Such a passage, in order to qualify, must contain an average of at least three points per 10-word section. Having located all such passages in a book, we can next average the number of points for each by dividing the number of words in each passage by the number of points. A book can now be described with some accuracy by stating (a) the number of P.U.s and (b) the average number of points of each P.U.; (c) it might also be useful to state the average length of each P.U., or perhaps give as a ratio the number of lines in the whole book divided by the number of lines in all P.U.s. Additional information which might be of interest would be (d) the highest mean score for any consecutive 100 words; this indicates with some accuracy the highest level of lewdness reached in the book. It might also be possible to draw a profile of the pornographic content of a book by plotting consecutive 100-word passages on the horizontal axis, and their P score on the vertical axis. I have done this for various books dealing with sexual matters, but never considered as very pornographic, books considered pornographic by some, but legally permitted to be read by citizens of this country, and books considered pornographic and banned. The typical outlines for such publications are shown in Figure 12, below.

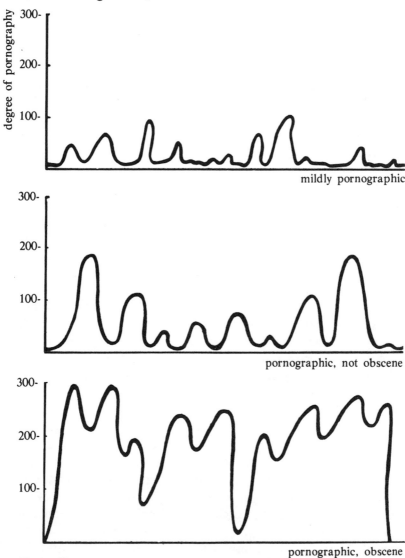

Figure 12   Successive paragraphs

There are a number of points on which doubt remains. What are we to do with homosexual practices, with voyeurism, with transvestism, with sadism, and with masochism? All these are related to the concept of obscenity rather than pornography as defined; they give sexual thrills to some people, but not the majority. This means that they do not belong to the same universe of scoring and measuring as do the activities mentioned in our scales. The same is true of anal and scatological items or descriptions. These are certainly obscene, but they tend to have a non-pornographic effect on most normal people, in the sense that they reduce the lascivious feelings aroused by the remainder of the text; if anything, they should be scored minus. For any straightforward scoring system, therefore, these odd perversions must be considered out of court; they do not have the same effect as those descriptions which score positively for our *P* index. Legal considerations of obscenity are irrelevant in this context; these are not restricted, as is our index, by the rules of homogeneity and other statistical desiderata.

Does this method of quantifying pornography actually work? The answer seems to be self-evident; if the reader will score for himself relevant passages in Henry Miller, Frank Harris, and other *soi-disant* pornographers, as well as less obviously pornographic passages in other authors, he will find that his subjective judgments of the degree of pornography shown by these passages will agree very closely with the *P* score. This experiment has been done a number of times, and agreement exceeding 90% has usually been found. At one time I had considered the possibility of reproducing here passages increasing in pornographic content in equal steps, from 0 to 100, but as the law might not permit the reproduction of the top passages, and as the inclusion of such passages would in any case give the book the wrong kind of reputation, I have not done so; the reader may if he wishes do so for himself. In this way he will obtain a rough-and-ready pornographic thermometer against which to evaluate any new book or article he may encounter. Alternatively, readers may like to write such passages themselves. Our formula may be useful in demonstrating the desiderata of pornographic writing, and in instructing neophytes! These are, of course, incidental benefits to be derived from this invaluable measuring instrument; its main purpose is *not* to train every man to be his own pornographer.

THE TERM "OBSCENE," while sometimes used as equivalent to pornographic by laymen and dictionary-makers alike, has a different legal connotation. To write pornography is not actionable, to write obscenities is, or at least may be. Some pornography is obscene, but not all. A slight case of the pornographics is not offensive, while even a slight case of the obscenities is—by definition.

The definition of what was regarded as obscene used to be related to certain assumed behavioral effects, *i.e.* whether
the tendency of the matter charged as obscenity is to deprave and corrupt those whose minds are open to corruption, and into whose hands a publication of this sort may fall.

This judgment used to be absolute, *i.e.* there was no refuge in the literary or scientific quality of the writing; neither was the whole book taken into account, but judgment could be made on the strength that one or two passages were obscene. These matters have since been changed, although whether the law is in fact working reasonably is, of course, another matter. Here I wish rather to discuss the psychological meaning of this "tendency to deprave and corrupt." Volumes have been written on this, but usually by lawyers, writers, politicians, journalists, sociologists, and others without much knowledge of the psychological literature. This seems odd, as this clearly is a purely psychological question; yet I cannot recollect any psychologist ever being asked his opinion. (Psychiatrists and psychoanalysts occasionally get a look in, not because they are supposed to know anything about psychology, but because they are medically qualified; why their medical knowledge should qualify them to speak on such a technical subject has never been clear to me.)

First of all let us try and get clear what is meant by the terms "depravity" and "corruption." If we consult the dictionary we see that depravity is wickedness, corruption; corruption is evil conduct. In the context, we must understand the adjective "sexual" added, so that obscene literature is said to incite people to indulge in sexual conduct which is evil and wicked. Oddly enough this conduct has never been described in detail by the lawyers concerned with these pronouncements. When D. H. Lawrence says "What is pornography to one man is the laughter of genius to another," we might add that one man's wicked conduct is another's fun. The law presumably assumes that there is considerable, even if not universal, agreement about what constitutes evil and wicked conduct in the sexual field, and that consequently no clear-cut definition is needed. This seems unlikely. Most other terms used in jurisprudence are defined very carefully, and it is not intuitively obvious for what legal reasons an exception should be made here. But of course an actual demonstration is more impressive than a mere argument, and for the purpose of illustration I carried out a little experiment which demonstrates more clearly than words what I have in mind.

In this experiment several hundred intelligent and cooperative students were asked which of a number of activities they considered "depraved and corrupt." Such activities only make sense in relation to a particular type of person—having intercourse with an innocent young girl is one thing, having it with a mature widow may be quite another—and consequently types of persons involved have been indicated in each case. The questionnaire is reproduced in Table 7. The respondents were simply asked to mark each action, as performed with or on each particular type of person, with a tick if they thought that such conduct was "depraved and corrupt." If law-makers are justified in their refusal to give proper definitions of the acts which constitute such conduct, then we would have to have substantial agreement among our respondents. If my criticism is right, then such agreement would be conspicuously missing. What are the facts?

Below are listed a number of activities of adult males towards different types of females. For each female type please place tick in the appropriate box if you consider that the activity towards that particular female is either depraved or corrupt.

N.B. There are *five* female types to be rated for each activity. Do not make any mark if you do not consider the activity to be depraved or corrupt.

ACTIVITY (of adult male) towards FEMALE TYPE

	A	B	C	D	E
	A 15-year-old virgin	*A 25-year-old virgin*	*An unmarried non-virgin*	*[Husband] to married woman*	*[Man other than husband] to married woman*
1. Kiss on the mouth					
2. Seduce					
3. Have intercourse, normal fashion					
4. Lend pornographic books					
5. Touch and kiss sexual parts					

ACTIVITY (of adult male) towards FEMALE TYPE

		A	B	C	D	E
6.	Initiate into prostitution and live on immoral earnings	A	B	C	D	E
7.	Take to strip-tease show					
8.	Take to watch couple having intercourse					
9.	Take to see "blue" films					
10.	Vigorous petting					
11.	Take to theater in which male actors simulate intercourse					
12.	Exhibit sexual parts to female					
13.	Make female dress up in clothes					
14.	Take to an orgiastic party					
15.	Use four-letter words					
16.	Rape; force to have intercourse					

Table 7

Some people—mostly introverts—sprinkled ticks liberally over the surface of the inventory; apparently they disapproved of all sexual activities outside the marital union. Even within that union, anything going beyond the "missionary position" was condemned. Others—mostly extroverts—had only a few crosses, indicating that as far as they were concerned "anything goes," provided it is within the law. Rape and the seduction of a minor tended to be frowned upon even by the most "enlightened." Most respondents tended to come in between these two extremes, but their notions of depravity were clearly not identical either. Indeed, the spectrum of opinion goes right across the board, from one extreme of permissiveness to the other extreme of puritanism, without a break anywhere. There is no evidence here of that substratum of reasonable agreement on which the law seems to rely. The only degree of agreement is upon those behaviors which are indeed frowned upon by the law, and made the explicit target of its wrath.

Thus we might argue that our task of finding empirical support for the fundamental basis of the existence of the laws of obscenity should be relatively easy. Is it true that the unlimited freedom of writers, painters, film-makers and all others to produce and publish without let or hindrance pornographic wares of one kind or another leads to an increase in the number of sex crimes? For the answer to this question, we may turn to Denmark, where, as is well known, the abolition of the laws relating to obscene publication and the burgeoning of all sorts of pornographic writings, pictures, films, etc., have led to an alleged decrease in sex crimes amounting to some 22 per cent. This figure cannot, of course, be taken too seriously. All official statistics must be viewed with great suspicion, and statistics relating to crime (and particularly to sex crimes) more so than any others. Criminal statistics can only deal with what becomes known to the police, and in the case of sex crimes this is often only the tip of the iceberg. It would only need a relatively small change in the attitude of girls towards the issuing of a formal complaint to the police about a sexual attack to find a marked change in the number of "rapes" notified. However, further detailed study of the Danish experiment is, of course, extremely important and relevant; it seems to indicate at least that those who feared a great upsurge of sexual viciousness and lawlessness as a consequence of great permissiveness in this field have been disappointed. Whether such permissiveness actually produces a reduction in crimes cannot yet be asserted.

CAN WE CLAIM, THEN, that greater permissiveness in the publication of pornographic writings, pictures and films (using the term in the sense in which we have defined it previously) has no effect on the sexual mores of society, and leaves everything exactly where it was before? Can we assert that the tendency to permit more and more to be shown, and written about, is a consequence, rather than a cause, of the general relaxation of moral rules? I think the evidence shows fairly conclusively that this notion is not very realistic, and that pornographic writings and pictures do have a definite effect in shifting the average person's behavior in the direction of greater P—again, as defined in our Table. If we regard such a tendency as depraved and corrupt, or as depraving and corrupting, then it seems only too likely that the changes that have taken place have indeed increased sexual depravity. Adherents of the abolition of censorship would be well advised to base their case on the harmlessness of sexual behaviors which are not actually subject themselves to criminal proceedings. If they argue in terms of lack of proof for the "tendency to deprave and corrupt," as many have done in the past, then it is to be feared that their arguments receive very little support from experimental psychology. I shall deal with this evidence presently; let me say here that I am neither arguing for nor against proposed changes in the rules governing censorship of books, plays, films or pictures. My concern is merely to set down the known facts; what conclusion these lead to depends on many factors regarding which the psychologist is not necessarily a better judge than anyone else. But in so far as the facts themselves are concerned, it seems that the psychologist does have a contribution to make. Ethical discussions and moral conclusions are more securely founded if they are based on ascertained facts, rather than on assumed ones. It is an unfortunate fact of human nature that those who, for one reason or another, advocate a course of action, tend to make assumptions regarding the facts related to their proposals which are in line with their proposals; thus they indulge in some form of self-justifying argumentation from assumed premises to predetermined conclusions. This vicious circle provides a sort of logical feedback system from which few people ever escape. Scientists are not being presumptuous when they attempt to get away from this practice and suggest a more factual approach. *

What kind of evidence is available to indicate that pornography has any effect on people's behavior? One might take the line here of Mr. Milton Shulman, the British television critic, and point out that directors of television companies who argue that sex and violence on the screen have no effect on people also argue (although usually in another place) that advertisements showing certain types of cars, or drinks, or chocolates have a tremendous effect in making people use that type of car, or drink, or chocolate. Why the difference? If television advertising is effective (and there is little doubt that it is), then why should television be less

---

* Part of this Chapter was written before the Report of the Presidential Commission into these matters appeared in the U.S. Superficially their conclusions may seem to contradict some of the things said here. Unfortunately the empirical part of the report has been summarized somewhat tendentiously from the ten volumes reporting the original work. Readers will find a well argued criticism in the minority conclusions of the report, prepared by a widely respected psychologist whose strictures on the authors of the majority report are unfortunately only too well taken. (See pp. 305-323.) Anyone interested in these matters ought to read both sides (and the original ten volumes as well, if patience permits); they provide a wonderful example of one-sided reporting, biased selection of evidence, and failure to maintain concentration on the evidence.

effective when it advertises lax morals, cruelty and violence, and permissive behavior generally? The attitude of television company directors is disingenuous, dishonest and absurd. It is clearly presented only to make it possible for the television companies to continue to coin money with the least effort. But although one may recognize the force of the argument, more experimental evidence is still clearly desirable. It is interesting that the British Postmaster General, who is responsible to Parliament for the activities of television in the widest sense, has publicly stated that if he knew of any such evidence, he would feel obliged to take action; his position hardly excuses his ignorance. One might have imagined that before publicly declaring his absence of knowledge in a field in which the public might rightly expect him to show some rudiments of acquaintance with the facts, he would have taken care to be briefed by his experts. Unfortunately there is no reason to expect that his "experts" would have any greater knowledge either. In the game of politics facts do not score party points, and can be safely disregarded. Even if there had not been any facts, one might have expected, in such an important field, that the government would have set up a research organization to investigate rather closely what its policies were doing to the moral fibre of the nation; ignorance and avoidance of action are the perennial twin sins of politicians.

The Postmaster General, and his American equivalents who also have claimed to hear no evil, speak no evil and see no evil with respect to the effects of television and film obscenity, are not alone in respect of this ignorance. They are joined by a whole group of people who are actively concerned with the problem. Consider as an example a recent *Report on the Obscenity Laws by the Working Party set up by a Conference Convened by the Chairman of the Arts Council of Great Britain* (this is the full title of the publication). Does obscenity corrupt? they ask, and answer that "verifiable fact is virtually non-existent." They quote as their authority a Professor R. M.

Jackson, who is the Downing Professor of the Laws of England in the University of Cambridge. He writes that

the supposed depravity and corruption produced by obscene articles is a matter of conjecture. No hard evidence can be put forward, for nobody can demonstrate that anybody has ever been depraved or corrupted by a particular obscene article. A decision that an article would have such a tendency is based entirely upon opinion unsupported by verifiable facts.

Even if the syntax of the last sentence were better than it is, the reasoning would still be suspect. A jurist is not necessarily expert in the interpretation of scientific evidence, and may be entirely in error when discussing the kind of experiment required to prove a particular statement. What he calls "hard evidence" is in the nature of the case unobtainable, but even in law there is such a thing as circumstantial evidence, and this is at times sufficient to hang a murderer; can the Downing Professor of the Laws of England not envisage the possibility that even in science there may be many different ways of skinning a cat? The working party go on to quote a number of persons, none of them familiar with the literature of experimental psychology. All acknowledge their ignorance, and the working party take this to signify the absence of available information, rather than evidence for the professional ignorance of its informants. No doubt others will now quote the confession of ignorance of the working party as proof for the non-existence of evidence, and so the merry game continues. We must, however, follow a scientific line of inquiry; and in science only the views of recognized scientists are considered, and a declaration that no evidence exists in a given field is only accepted from persons intimately concerned with that field. Such an attitude of skepticism might have helped the working party to arrive at a more sensible conclusion.

What kind of information would we regard as relevant to

our question of whether pornography affects behavior? People often think of some form of direct experimental evidence, but such is of course impossible in the nature of the case. We cannot take 10,000 virgins, expose half of them to television, or to pornographic books, while keeping the others away from any such infectious material, and then follow them up over a period of twenty years to find out which group produced more illegitimate babies—or whatever we might choose to be our criterion of "conduct unbecoming a gentlewoman." This sort of thing is impossible for ethical and practical reasons. Ethically speaking it is simply not permissible to furnish our subjects with pornographic material if the hypothesis to be tested is that this would do them some kind of harm; it will not need much of an argument to establish this point. Practically we cannot in the nature of the case protect our non-pornographic virgins from coming across this type of material in the course of their lives, and in any case they live in a permissive society partly produced by the effects of television, pornographic literature and the other forces which we are trying to investigate. Their response to a small added dose of pornography is hardly likely to be measurable under the circumstances. Efforts have been made to establish such direct consequences of television viewing, but they have not been very successful; the problem of self-selection must defeat most such research schemes. (We want to contrast viewers and non-viewers, but the personality of those who view is *ab initio* different from that of those who do not; this self-selection vitiates any comparison. We would like to allocate people at random to the viewing and the non-viewing groups, but of course that is impossible. Even to compare people living in districts which receive and which do not receive television is not an answer; these people are self-selected in terms of their decision to live, or not to live, in the main centers of conurbation.)

If the answer is not in terms of direct experiments, then it must be in terms of the much more usual indirect type of proof. If we want to investigate lightning, we create a duplicate of more manageable proportions in our laboratory, by having small sparks travel from one electrode to another. If we want to test hypotheses about the mass of the neutrino, which is a very elusive particle indeed, we must have recourse to indirect tests, such as the measurement of electron spectra from nuclear beta decay using tritium. If we want to measure the speed with which remote stars recede from our galaxy, we must have recourse to the indirect measurement of the Doppler effect. In physics, indirect tests in which deductions are made from theories, and then tested in the laboratory, far outweigh direct tests. If we can establish a strong theory which is relevant to the question we are posing, then we can use that theory to answer our question directly. There are, of course, always provisos in this type of hypothetical and deductive procedure; but it is well in line with orthodox scientific methods.

Let me return for a moment to the approach-avoidance conflict theory mentioned in an earlier chapter. Look at Figure 13, which shows on the horizontal axis our P scale, with sexual behavior ranging from 0 to 15, as in our Table. The solid lines indicating approach and avoidance gradients are for some hypothetical introvert; their point of intersection indicates the type of sexual behavior he is most likely to indulge in. Types of behaviors to the right are unlikely because of the supremacy of avoidance feelings over approach feelings. Types of behavior to the left are of course indulged in up to and including the point marked A. Now consider a hypothetical extrovert, B, whose approach gradient has been raised, and whose avoidance gradient has been lowered, for reasons already explained in earlier chapters (broken lines). He too will indulge in sexual activities up to and including the point of intersection, which in his case is displaced towards the right; in other words, as we found in Chapter 2, he will indulge

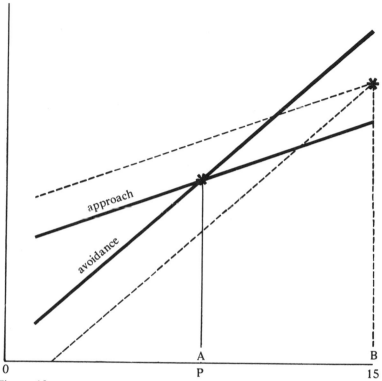

Figure 13

in more "perverted" conduct than *A*. If we could show that the reading of pornographic literature had the effect of either raising the gradient of approach, or lowering that of avoidance, or both (or else making the approach gradient steeper, or the avoidance gradient less steep), then it would automatically follow that sexual behavior was indeed influenced by the reading of pornographic literature.

The avoidance gradient is clearly determined by social factors which for the sake of convenience we might group together under the heading of "conscience." This includes ethical, religious and moral scruples, together with aesthetic ones (of the *intra urinam et faecem nascimur* kind), as well as practical considerations, such as the likelihood of begetting unwanted babies. As already explained in Chapter 2, these considerations of "conscience" are most likely to have been acquired through a process of Pavlovian conditioning. Sexual activities (either all or some types only) are presented as bad, naughty, wicked and forbidden, and through punishment, either symbolic or real, now become conditioned stimuli which arouse conditioned responses like fear, anxiety, and so forth. These reactions can be exceedingly strong. In my book on *Crime and Personality* I have mentioned an experiment on puppies in which they were conditioned not to eat horse meat by being rather playfully slapped over the rump with a folded-up piece of newspaper whenever they approached the meat. The conditioned response was so strong that when the dogs were allowed alone in the room with the meat, with the experimenter absent, they would rather starve than touch the meat! (They were of course not allowed to starve, but fed outside the room before this happened.) These conditioned avoidance responses are clearly observable in humans, particularly young ones. Women, who are exposed to a much stronger regime of conditioning, and who seem to condition better in any case (is this why they tend to be in less trouble with the law generally?) show them much more clearly than men.

Approach gradients are presumably determined in part by the "sensation-seeking" component of the extrovert personality. Having higher sensory thresholds, as explained in Chapter 2, such people need stronger, more varied stimuli to avoid the actual pains of boredom and monotony. Sexual activities seem pre-eminently suited to serve this function, and hence extroverts tend to have raised approach gradients. The outcome of this combination is as shown in Figure 12, and the general truth of the picture there given has been indicated by our experiments recounted in Chapter 2. What would be the effect of reading pornographic literature, or seeing pornographic films and plays, on these gradients? The answer can be given with some confidence, because of the considerable body of evidence which has been built up in relation to behavior therapy, particularly that part of it which is usually referred to as desensitization therapy. I have described this in some detail in *Fact and Fiction in Psychology*, and quite briefly alluded to it in other chapters of this book. Here I will just recapitulate the main points.

A PERSON SUFFERING from a strong anxiety or fear reaction to a particular object or situation (snakes, or confronting a superior) is considered to have acquired a conditioned sympathetic reaction to the object or situation in question. The sympathetic branch of the autonomic system is concerned with the mediation of strong emotional experiences of anger and fear. It is antagonistic to the parasympathetic branch, which mediates peaceful, relaxed emotional experiences. The essence of desensitization is the building up of conditioned parasympathetic responses to the objects or situations which produce fears. This is done by getting the subject to relax very deeply (or administering relaxing drugs), and then presenting him with minimally disturbing images of the objects or situations he fears. Thus he might be asked to imagine that he heard snakes mentioned on the wireless, or that his boss was walking along the street, and that he could just see him out of his window. The combination of an object or situation provoking mild anxiety, and the parasympathetic-produced relaxation, results in a small increment in parasympathetic conditioning, which subtracts from the original sympathetic conditioning. Hence the next time a stimulus provoking stronger anxiety can be presented to the deeply relaxed patient, and so on until the top of the hierarchy has been reached, and he can imagine the most feared object or situation without undue upset. This conditioned calm and relaxation have been found to transfer to experiences in the outer world, and complete cures can be thus achieved.

The disorders so treated are commonly referred to as neuroses, but this only means that they are maladaptive. In England a fear of snakes is absurd, and hence neurotic, but in Australia it might be useful, and save a person's life. Sexual anxieties and fears may be considered neurotic by the free-and-easy extrovert, and morally and ethically advantageous by the introvert. There is no absolute scale on which we can measure social adaptivity. When it comes to "conscience" in relation to criminal activities, most people would probably agree that this was not neurotic, but desirable; yet the mechanism of acquisition is much the same in all these cases. The fate of such conditioned fear and anxiety responses is much the same under similar conditions of treatment; hence fairly firm generalizations can be made in this field.

Consider now the likely effects of reading pornographic literature, or viewing sexually arousing plays or films on television. The subject-matter produces a certain amount of anxiety (this has been experimentally verified in a number of studies carried out in the U.S.A.). However, viewing takes place under conditions which are the most relaxing, *i.e.* in the viewer's own home, sitting in his armchair, surrounded by his cherished possessions, etc. Hence conditions are arranged in such a way that maximal deconditioning (or desensitization) of the fears and anxieties which are normally aroused by the presentation of such material is produced. As a consequence the avoidance gradient is lowered, or made less steep. Next time the viewer or reader is able to tolerate even more outspoken material, until finally he is in a position to go the whole hog and view (or read about) activities of a sexual nature which originally would have shocked him so much that he would have turned off the television, or thrown away his book.

What has been said here of sex is equally true and applicable when applied to violence. Our negative feelings when confronted with violence, the shedding of blood, and suffering are partly innate, partly acquired through a process of conditioning. Monkeys will without any form of suggestion carry out various activities to cherish and rescue another monkey (unknown to them previously) who is in pain (getting electric shocks); this seems to be an innate characteristic. Positive feelings are equally obvious. Getting one's own way, hitting other people, or in other ways getting the better of them, is immediately rewarding to the ego, and hence positively reinforced. The negative feelings are essential for civilized society to survive; no police force could cope with a population which was not constrained in their aggression by some form of conscience. But, of course, films, television viewing and modern books glorifying violence and aggression are in fact (if not by choice) breaking down this carefully built up set of conditioned responses. By showing these activities, which would normally be frightening and so aversive, in a slightly reduced form, and in the comfort of the reader's or viewer's own home, desensitization must inevitably take place, and hence these conditioned responses are constantly reduced until they finally disappear altogether. If I were asked by some Martian invader how one could best destroy the human race without overt show of arms, I would have to say that the destruction of the moral and ethical standards which alone maintain a society would be the best method; and in order to achieve this aim I would have to say that the unrestrained and continued showing of violence on television and film screens throughout the country, day in and day out, was by far the easiest and cheapest way. People ask wonderingly why there has been such a terrible outbreak of violence in the U.S.A., where television programs of this kind have of course been showing for much longer than anywhere else, and where saturation has been much more complete. I would answer that this is precisely what one would have predicted on psychological principles. But of course nobody asks psychologists about these things.

One of the most satisfactory methods of desensitization is that of modelling, and it is here that we receive the strongest support for our thesis. Consider a person who is afraid of snakes, and cannot tolerate being in the same room with one. Sit him at a safe distance, then bring in a snake in your arms, showing no fear, and start to fondle the snake, curl it around your neck, and generally demonstrate that there is nothing to be feared. Gradually you will be able to bring the snake nearer, until finally the patient's fear is completely overcome, and he will start to fondle the snake himself. Many fears and anxieties have been overcome in this way, and control experiments have shown that this method works particularly well with children—although even with adults it tends to be better than most others. Alternatively the modelling can be done symbolically, *i.e.* the snake handling can be done on film which is shown to the patient. It seems to make little difference whether the snake is actually introduced or not; films seem to be very potent media in reducing fears of this kind.

In the same way it has been shown that violence can be induced by film modelling. Test children before showing the film in situations where conflict arises over the possession of some toys; then show a film involving one child hitting the other, taking the toy and getting away with it to some of the children, and a film in which the child is punished for doing this to the rest. Then put the children back into the same sort of situation. What will they do? The answer, of course, is that they will imitate the modelled behavior; those who saw film 1 (where the child got away with it) will now be much more aggressive than before, while those who saw film 2 (where the child was punished) will now be less aggressive. Imitation used to be considered an instinct, and this notion was not very useful—you can clearly label any type of behavior "instinctive" without appreciably adding to the total sum of knowledge available on this type of conduct, and without making it clear how you could control behavior of this kind. Experimental studies of modelling have added greatly to our knowledge in this field, and we know now with some precision what the effects of modelling are, and what kinds of factors influence "imitation." There seems no doubt that films showing certain types of behavior have a very strong influence on what children and adults do. Imitation, to use this somewhat outdated term, is clearly a very powerful factor.

Direct sexual films have not so far been experimented with, for obvious reasons. But there is no doubt that the principles which govern other activities, such as aggressive and violent behavior, are not likely to be different from those which govern sexual behavior. Show a film in which people indulge in certain forms of sexual activity, without punishment, and with obvious enjoyment, and the avoidance gradient will be lowered, and the approach gradient raised. The only proviso of course, is that the exposure to these films has to be gradual. As in all desensitization forms of treatment, sudden exposure to extreme forms of feared conducts, whether in real life or on the screen, provokes too strong an anxiety reaction to be brought under control by the relaxed atmosphere of the home, or the cinema, and the effect is aversive, rather than the opposite. In the absence of a psychologist carefully planning gradually increasing exposure to such stimuli, many people will make occasional mistakes. This is particularly likely on television where little choice is actually involved on the part of most people who just passively view whatever is put before them. Hence the sudden storms of complaints when something daring is shown—the presentation went beyond the point where the anxiety aroused was reduced to minor proportions by the parasympathetic stimulation involved in the total setting. There is the further point that often the activities suggested in the film or book are out of reach of the viewer or reader, because of age, or for other reasons; this would of course influence his reaction profoundly. But for most young people the course of events is very much as I have described above—a continuous process of desensitization, leading on to ever more daring and intimate sexual activities.

SO FAR WE HAVE BEEN concerned with the avoidance gradient; we must next turn to the approach gradient. Here, too, modern research has provided a much needed corrective to the rather primitve views held even a few years ago. Sex used to be considered a biological instinct, rather like hunger and thirst; its aim was orgasm, and everything preceding this was only a preliminary. This single-act philosophy, held strongly by the Freudians, is so over-simplified as to be completely misleading. Of course there is a biological underpinning to our sexual needs and expressions; for instance, stimulation of certain parts of the brain in monkeys can produce erection of the penis and ejaculation. But sexual arousal depends much more on external stimuli than does hunger or thirst—although even there external stimuli cannot be neglected. A hen will tend to eat a certain portion of the grain given it; increase the total amount, and the hen will eat more *in toto*. Many animals will eat more when put with another animal which is also engaged in eating. Thus even the most clearly "instinctive" activities, in very primitive animals, are subject to social influences; how much more so the sexual "instinct" in higher animals! Harlow has shown that when monkeys were brought up in isolation they virtually lacked sexual activity when on becoming adult they were put with other monkeys—the instinct just failed to materialize because of an upbringing which failed to produce the social stimuli essential to its fruition, despite the physical, physiological substratum being perfectly intact. Sexual appetite is certainly in large part acquired; when Schofield studied the sexual behavior of young adolescents he found that of those who had had sexual intercourse, most had not enjoyed it much—less than half of the boys, and less than a third of the girls had thought it much fun! Clearly social factors were paramount in producing and perpetuating a form of conduct which had little intrinsic satisfaction.

F.A. Beach, whose work on sex in man and amimal is well known, has made this point very clearly:

No genuine tissue or biological needs are generated by sexual abstinence. It used to be believed that prolonged inactivity in adulthood resulted in the progressive accumulation of secretions within the accessory glands, and that nerve impulses from these distended receptacles gave rise to sexual urges. Modern evidence negates this hypothesis. . . . What is commonly confused with a primary drive associated with sexual need is in actuality sexual appetite, and this has little or no relation to biological or physiological needs.

This sexual appetite, he makes clear, is

. . . a product of experience, actual or vicarious. The adolescent boy's periodic preoccupation with sexual matters is traceable to psychological stimuli, external and phantasied, and is not dependent upon his recently matured reproductive glands. His erotic urges stem more from socio-cultural factors than from those of a strictly physiological nature.

This is in line with modern attempts to differentiate between the sexual arousal mechanism and the orgasmic mechanism.

THE SEXUAL AROUSAL MECHANISM is based upon the fact that touching the genitals produces pleasurable arousal. This mechanism is very changeable in human beings, and subject to conditioning; touches on other parts of the body, and even imagination and other thought processes, can produce the pleasure which originally was produced only by the touching of the genitals. It is then the context in which sexual stimulation occurs which determines the other emotional responses which become associated with it. Youngsters who had a childhood involving conflict with their parents were found to associate sexual arousal with aggressive feelings; other youngsters associate it with tender feelings instead. It is this social context in which sexual arousal is seen which is particularly susceptible to the influence of films, books and television. How else could the growing boy or girl find a context which traditionally is not provided by parents themselves, anxious to avoid mentioning sex, or discussing it with their children? The peer culture is of course important, but where do the peers get their values and ideas from, if not the self-same television, films and books?

Frequency and kind of sexual arousal are very strongly determined by conditioned stimuli, then, a fact which is obvious when we look at the preference and customs of different nations and races. We consider breasts sexually stimulating, whereas the Polynesians do not. We like thin women, the Chinese used to prefer them inordinately fat. We consider the kiss an innocent form of sexual arousal, the Japanese consider it extremely obscene. These are not innate forms of conduct, nor are they reasoned actions. They are the outcome of accidental variations perpetuated through conditioning.

The extreme plasticity of the sexual arousal mechanism can be shown even in the experimental laboratory. In one experiment a penis plethysmograph was used, *i.e.* an instrument to measure the volume of the penis, in order to measure sexual arousal. Slides of shoes were shown to male subjects; these produced no reaction. Then slides of nude women were shown; these produced strong reactions. Now the conditioning procedure was begun. Slides of shoes preceded, by a second or two, slides of nude women. After a while, the slides of shoes produced penis arousal even when not followed by the unconditioned stimuli. What is more, the conditioned stimuli showed generalization, in that slides showing boots and other types of footwear also produced sexual responses, although they had never been paired with the nude slides. This, then, is the experimental analog of the development of a fetishist. No actual fetishism is produced, of course, because the experiment is stopped long before such a development can take place, and also because the unconditioned stimulus (the nude slides) is not powerful enough to produce very strong sexual reactions.

As sexual arousal gets more intense, it inevitably leads to the second mechanism, the "intromissive and ejaculatory" orgasm mechanism; this is of course relatively stereotyped and involuntary, and as such resistant to conditioning. But as it always follows the easily conditioned sexual arousal mechanism in time, and is closely associated with it, this is not very important. It is the conditionability of the primary mechanism which determines the marked social determination of sexual behavior. D. H. Lawrence kept cursing "sex in the head," by which he meant the socially conditioned determinants of sexual arousal. He was more concerned with orgasmic mechanisms. But if we abolished "sex in the head" we would abolish nearly all sex; this despised component is a vital one, and slighted at our peril. For us, whether we like it or not, sex is aroused, sustained and directed much more by conditioned stimuli which the individual has learned to perceive as arousing, sustaining and directing, and by imaginary acts and ideas taking place in his head, than by simple physiological mechanisms. It seems a pity that the popular view of sexual activity has just caught up with the "instinct-libido" theory of sexual behavior when serious psychologists have dismissed it as a figment of the imagination. It is to be hoped that more realistic notions will prevail in time to avoid the excesses which the older, more primitive ideas seem to support.

These excesses are based on the view that if sex is a biological need pure and simple, rather like hunger and thirst, then it must be satisfied regardless of social and other consequences; to try and avoid such satisfaction is in fact impossible! Hence pornographic films and books do no harm; people have sexual instincts anyway, and no added fuel is provided by these films and books. It might even be argued that such books and films have a positive contribution to make. Some people are "repressed" and try to suppress their sexual activities, thus endangering their health. Pornography triumphantly sets them free to follow a healthier and more beneficial course, by encouraging a maximum indulgence in sexual activity. Many a virgin has succumbed to arguments of this kind, provided by her swain—motivated of course entirely by his concern for her mental and physical health! That such arguments are still being advanced in this day and age by "responsible" leaders of opinion shows merely that scientific information does not infiltrate literary circles very quickly. Freud's notion of a given quantity of sexual energy or "libido" inhering in a given person, and demanding an outlet, was never taken seriously by scientists. That it is still trotted out as an argument to justify complete freedom to publish any kind of pornography does little honor to those making use of this argument.

The appetite theory leads to rather different conclusions. Modern society is extending ever farther the field of the sex-conditioned stimuli, thus creating more and more stimuli and conditions which are conducive to sexual arousal. This increase in provisions for sexual arousal is accompanied by other provisions for sustaining such arousal through the use of sexual imagery continuously presented in books, films and television programs. Within our biological limits, we have as a society chosen to maximize sexual arousal. This may or may not be a wise choice, but let us not deceive ourselves about this matter. There is a choice, and this choice is not pre-empted by biological necessity. It may not be open to the individual to make such a choice; it may be made for him by those who are in command of the mass media, particularly television. But this makes it all the more important that the decision should be made in the full consciousness of what is involved. At the moment it goes by default—there is no informed argument, and hence rational decisions are impossible to arrive at. To say this is not to agree with those who would wish to increase censorship; this may or may not be a desirable method of dealing with the matter. I am concerned with the facts; the decisions which are made on the basis of these facts obviously depend also on values, ethical and moral and other considerations.

The actual amount of sexual activity encouraged by modern permissiveness is not the only, nor is it necessarily the most important, aspect of this whole problem. We cannot separate sex from those emotions which are inevitably conditioned to accompany its arousal. Novels, films, television programs, advertising and many other influences tend to isolate sexual experiences from the rest of personality, and to depersonalize sex. They also associate a great variety of emotions with sex, not all of which are desirable. Aggression, hostility and cruelty have already been mentioned. Desire for social status, curiosity, fear, anxiety, contempt—all these and many more are mixed up in the unholy brew which is being peddled to our children under the guise of entertainment. At least some of these are likely to increase the separation of sexual activity from affection, tenderness and love; to link it rather with selfish seeking after maximum stimulation, or with cruelty and aggression. Marriage is not always the home of love either—too frequently it is a transaction undertaken for the mutual advantage of the contracting parties, with many irrelevant aims and aspirations unspoken in the minds of the man and woman so joined in holy matrimony. Clearly the whole position is a difficult one, but it is not eased by the frequent misunderstanding of the true biological and psychological basis of the argument, or the exploitation of certain aspects by commercial interests.

THE POSITION of the "approach gradient" of our Figure

12, to which we must now return is very much determined by those conditioned stimuli which, through their association with the simple biological pleasures derived from genital stimulation, have acquired the status of secondary reinforcing drives. Reading pornographic literature has the obvious effect of providing this much reinforcement, and therefore of raising the approach gradient—very much in the same way as reading a motoring magazine raises the approach gradient for the purchase of a new car. The motoring magazine gives you information about new types of cars, new accessories, new engines, and generally concentrates your interest in this area. Similarly, a pornographic book gives you information (sometimes true, often false, but the reader does not know this!) about the many ways in which intercourse can be undertaken, how sexual appetite can be aroused and satiated in different ways, and what sorts of consequences can be expected. Better sources of information can, of course, be imagined, but as long as these are not available, or if available do not carry with them the same amount of reinforcement as do pornographic novels, many people will continue to derive their knowledge of patterns of sexual behavior and mores, and the appropriate emotional accompaniments of sex, from such novels.

The factual information provided (or believed to be provided) by pornographic literature can be very important. It is not often realized how misleading is the information on which many people have to rely in this field. I remember well my first "patient," whom I encountered during World War II when I was doing research as psychologist to the Mill Hill Emergency Hospital in London. Our patients were neurotic or psychotic soldiers and airmen, and while testing them for various purposes I used to talk to them—not so much because I wanted to talk, but because they insisted on telling someone about their symptoms. One of the patients told me that the main reason for his breakdown was his incapacity to have intercourse; he had tried many times, but never succeeded. Not knowing what to say I asked him how he had in fact attempted this difficult feat, and it turned out that he had tried it standing up! I pointed out to him that it might be easier lying down, and as he did not seem to know much about it I lent him a copy of *Fanny Hill.* He devoured it within a day or two, and on his day off I saw him racing off to the bus (he lived in London, fortunately). When he came back he was glowing with happiness, and told me all about his brilliant success. He emerged from treatment as a complete cure; in the statistics this will no doubt go down as a "+" for his psychoanalytically inclined psychiatrist, who had never shown any interest in his actual performance, but was much more concerned with his Oedipus complex. If only pornographic literature were more factual in its accounts, how useful could it not be for the purpose of providing information alone! As it is, it is likely to have the opposite effect. Many men, finding that they are unable to achieve the countless bouts per night which the heroes of these books seem to find so easy, fall prey to ideas of unworthiness and inferiority. Thus closely are uses and abuses of pornography allied! It is certain that many other false beliefs are promulgated and endorsed by pornographic books, and the same is true of sex manuals, where a higher standard of accuracy might have been expected. A good example is clitoral stimulation in the female.

Masters and Johnson, in their well-documented book on *Human Sexual Response,* which is based entirely on their own extensive experimental investigations, state that

> . . . most marriage manuals advocate the technique of finding the clitoris and remaining in direct manual contact with it during attempts to stimulate female sexual tensions. In direct manipulation of the clitoris there is a narrow margin between stimulation and irritation. If the unsuspecting male partner adheres strictly to marriage manual dictum, he is placed in a

most disadvantageous position. He is attempting proficiency with a technique that most women reject during their own automanipulative experiences.

This rather waspish comment is followed by their own recommendation:

As stated previously, no two women practice automanipulation in similar fashion. Rather than following any preconceived plan for stimulating his sexual partner, the male will be infinitely more effective if he encourages vocalization on her part. The individual woman knows best the areas of her strongest sexual focus and the rapidity and intensity of manipulative technique that provides her with the greatest degree of sexual stimulation.

This is good sense. People differ, and it is a mistake to generalize too freely about patterns of sexual conduct which are supposed to produce satisfaction, orgasm and heavenly delights. It is indeed disconcerting to find the blind leading the blind. Most writers of marriage manuals seem to rely more on hearsay, gossip and "experience" than on scientifically ascertained fact—often necessarily so, because good facts are hard to come by. And where textbooks go wrong, pornographic books make even grosser mistakes. The insufferable Walter, whose secret life we have already encountered in an earlier chapter, is full of good advice to others who might wish to emulate his conquest of 2,000 vaginal barrels (to use Masters and Johnson's beautiful phrase—who could treat a vaginal barrel seriously?). Clearly conscious of his superiority over Solomon, who after all only had a thousand wives (which would make Walter twice the man, on this particular scale of values), he advises would-be seducers to pull out their sexual organs as early in the game as possible and wag them in front of their girl. This, he assures us, acts as an invariable aphrodisiac, and leads them on to bigger and better things. Having achieved this necessary first step, the man must apparently snatch at the female's sexual parts, helped, it is true, by the Victorian habits women had of not wearing any panties. He curses away at one or two girls who had got into the new-fangled habit of wearing these "kill-joys." And having reached this target, the man must work away at the clitoris, if necessary for hours, until the fair damsel swoons with delight, and is ready to receive his "copious libations." It is interesting to speculate what would happen to a male who followed this advice, tirelessly repeated many times—Walter was very keen that others should emulate his own successful conduct. (He tends to soft-pedal at times the fact that he was dealing with harlots, or with female servants held in such subjection that they could hardly refuse the master's approaches without losing their position, and all possibility of gaining another one because they would not be given a favorable testimonial. He does add, but *sotto voce,* that it is extraordinarily effective in relation to your sexual advances if you offer the girl in question a golden sovereign or two, *i.e.* an amount of money which they would have to work for several weeks to earn in the ordinary way.)

Walter, like Frank Harris, Henry Miller, Casanova and many other libertines, is a father figure of the permissive society; his sense of values (or non-values) is being peddled around as the modern morality. It is difficult to think of these rather comic and often sad figures as prophets of the new enlightenment, but there is no doubt that many voices are raised in support of their type of sexual behavior. The Kronhausens, for instance, an influential couple of American psychoanalysts, have published an annotated and abbreviated set of Walter's writings. They make clear in this their admiration for his intrepidly modern attitude to sex, and chide those of us who do not feel that we would like to go all the way with Walter for our "repressions." What, they seem to suggest, are a few rapes, a few dozen abortions, and a hundred or so lives ruined—a mere bagatelle in comparison to the importance of Walter's ability to express his individuality and his sexual athleticism! Adultery—pshaw; such scruples are unbecoming to modern man (and woman). Of course one must forgive psychoanalysts such pronouncements; truly, they know not of what they speak. But that such tirades should find willing ears, that serious people should actually read and approve such sentiments, is a sad comment on the divorce between sexuality and tenderness, between love and lust, which seems to characterize our modern attitude to sex, and which is almost certainly abetted, if not created, by pornographic writing.

HOW DO OUR FINDINGS agree with the results of the widely publicized Presidential Commission in the U.S.A.? It will be recalled that in 1967, the U.S. Congress created a Commission to investigate the effects of pornography and obscenity; each member of the Commission was appointed by President Lyndon Johnson, but of course when the report appeared it was President Nixon to whom it was submitted. When the report was published, it produced a storm of controversy. The fact that the report was not unanimous but contained critical comments on the majority opinion by a minority of members served to fan the fires of discontent. Critical attention was particularly directed towards the main legal recommendation of the report, namely that "the Commission recommends that federal, state, and local legislation should not seek to interfere with the right of adults who wish to do so to read, obtain, or view explicit sexual materials." Two of the minority Commissioners stated in their reply that "the Commission's majority report is a Magna Carta for the pornographer." The majority feel that "public opinion in America does not support the imposition of legal prohibitions upon the rights of adults to read or see explicit sexual materials," to which the minority Commissioners reply: "Credit the American public with enough common sense to know that one who wallows in filth is going to get dirty. This is intuitive knowledge. Those who spend millions of dollars to tell us otherwise must be malicious or misguided, or both."

The *New York Times* has published the report in book form; it runs to 700 pages many of which are of purely legal interest. The only part of the report with which I shall be concerned is that entitled: "The Impact of Erotica." This describes in some detail psychological researches undertaken at the request of the Commission. Actually these researches have been published in some ten volumes separately from the report, and the report merely summarizes the main findings. It is important to read the material contained in the ten volumes before forming much of an opinion, because in the minority section of the report Dr. Victor Cline, a well-known psychologist from the University of Utah, has seriously criticized the majority report's summary of the empirical studies on the grounds that important findings were *repressed* or *misquoted*. He presents a lengthy and well-argued case, suggesting that the findings of the various researchers on whose work the Commission based their recommendations were far less clear-cut than might have been wished, and that no far-reaching recommendations can reasonably be based on these findings. I shall first of all discuss the findings, as presented in the report, and then go on to discuss Cline's criticisms. Having done that, I shall tentatively suggest what I believe are the main conclusions to be derived from all this work.

Some of the most interesting experiments done in response to the Commission's request concern themselves with behavior responses to erotica. As the report puts it:

there are two elementary, but fundamental, questions about erotic materials upon which nearly all concerns with the subject are based. First, does exposure to erotic stimuli sexually excite and arouse the viewer? Second, does such exposure affect the subsequent sexual behavior of the user?

The first question is of course much easier to answer; the second presents daunting problems of design and execution. Sexual arousal can be measured along two quite different lines. We can ask our subjects to view (or read) pornographic material, and then ask them to rate the degree of their arousal on a 10-point scale. Or we can actually attach electrodes and other devices to their persons and measure the amount of physiological arousal present. Let us first of all look at the results given by the first method. There is little doubt about the arousing nature of pornographic material; between 60% and 85% of both male and female subjects experienced varying degrees of sexual arousal when presented with visual or printed material containing explicit reference to sexual behavior. Males more often reported arousal from visual stimulation than from reading; females showed the opposite tendency. Females also reported "disgust" more frequently than males. "Blue films" are more potent than are stills, as far as visual stimulation is concerned. These results are borne out by psychophysiological studies, although these are rather complex and difficult to summarize.

Measurement of physical reactions can be direct or indirect. Direct measures can be taken, *e.g.* from the penis; attach a strain gauge to it, or a simple plethysmograph (a device for measuring changes in volume), and you get a direct measure of the degree of erection consequent upon the exposure to the stimulus. This technique can be adapted to female subjects, but only with difficulty; one can measure, after a fashion, the increase in lubricity of what Masters and Johnson call the "vaginal barrel," or one can measure the slight increase in temperature which accompanies sexual excitement in the same area, or one can measure the slight change in color as the vagina becomes suffused with blood. Several such studies have left no doubt about the effectiveness of pornographic material, for both sexes. Another direct measure which has sometimes been used is the excretion of urinary acid phosphatase; this has been found to be greater after stimulation by erotic films than after stimulation by other erotic media.

Indirect measures are of a more general nature, *e.g.* heart rate, sweating, or breathing. These have been found rather less suitable on the whole, particularly because they are so undifferentiated. You may react emotionally because you are disgusted, or annoyed, with the presentation, rather than because you are sexually aroused. Indirect measures will not be able to differentiate between these different reactions. Ideally one would seek for verbal report, direct measures, and indirect measures also, in assessing the effects of erotic stimulation. However, it is possible to overload the subject with electrodes, plethysmographs, and other bits of apparatus, to an extent that he cannot attend to the erotic stimuli themselves!

Sexual arousal depends to some extent on the sex of the viewer, and on the scenes viewed. Males are more aroused than females by scenes depicting oral sex, for instance, while coitus produces equal degrees of arousal. (It is interesting that quite generally oral sex appears to be more appealing to men than women.) Sexual experience is relevant; more physiological reactions are reported by experienced than by inexperienced subjects. One finding which anyone with experience in art could have predicted, but which is woefully disregarded by makers of "blue" films, is that less explicitly sexual presentations may be more arousing than more explicit presentations; leaving something to the imagination apparently is actually more arousing than putting it all down in black and white (or glorious Technicolor). In one study subjects who were asked to think about some sexual themes without visual cues were twice as highly aroused as comparable subjects provided with literary stimuli. In another, subjects reported higher levels of arousal to films which had deleted a rape sequence, but implied its occurrence, as compared with films containing the scene. The same point is brought out by the fact that many subjects describe their reactions to explicit depiction of coitus scenes as "boredom"; there is too little variety to maintain interest.

What happens when normal subjects are given free access to all sorts of erotic material? The answer seems to be that satiation sets in quite quickly; subjects spend less time viewing "blue" films, looking at pornographic pictures, and generally amusing themselves along these lines. At the same time, their physiological and psychological level of arousal in response to such material drops, and they spend far more time looking at other types of material, and reading neutral books and magazines. This is a laboratory replication of events in Denmark after legalizing pornography, when it was also reported that very soon satiation set in, and sales fell off, rather than increasing, as had been expected by many. "Nine weeks after the daily exposure sessions ended, all subjects reported boredom and a number refused private opportunities to view erotica." Thus overexposure tends to lead to loss of interest in pornography. There is, however, a recovery after several months; loss of interest in not permanent. Probably most subjects would settle down to a low level of exposure if they had their own way.

There appears to be a connection between the amount of pornographic material viewed or read by a person, and his general amount of sexual activity. The more active he is, the more pornography he consumes. This may appear unexpected; one might have thought that pornography would be an alternative to more normal sexual outlets. The figures suggest otherwise. "Among American college students, frequency of exposure to erotic materials is associated with relatively high rates of sociosexual experimentation (hugging, kissing, light and heavy petting, coitus) during both high school and college years." Similar studies in Sweden showed similar results. Early experience of masturbation seems linked with the other two variables; early masturbators tend to use pornography, and also seek early and frequent sexual contacts with the other sex. This is less surprising when one considers my own findings linking personality with sexual behavior and attitudes. Extroverted people generally have more, and more diverse, sexual outlets, as well as smoking more, drinking more, and generally "living it up." If this is so, then one might expect that on the whole personality determines the whole "life pattern" of a person, and that viewing pornography would not produce much of a change in this pattern. This seems to be the conclusion come to by the various authors who studied this question and whose results are summarized in the President's report.

These studies show that established patterns of premarital, marital and extramarital coitus, petting, homosexual activity, and sexual fantasy are very stable and are not substantially altered by exposure to sexually explicit stimuli. Relatively high rates of sexual activity prior to exposure to sex stimuli are associated with similarly high rates after exposure, and relatively infrequent sexual activity prior to exposure is associated with similarly infrequent activity after exposure. In some circumstances, exposure to erotic stimuli temporarily activates sexual behavior. Such activation, when it occurs, follows established patterns and tends to be shortlived, diminishing markedly within 48 hours. The presence or availability of an established sexual partner appears to determine whether the activated behavior is masturbatory or coital.

How are such conclusions arrived at? The typical experiment establishes a base-line, *e.g.* by asking participants to keep a detailed diary in which they record all sexual activities (coitus, masturbation, etc.). They are then exposed to the film(s) which constitutes the experimental stimulus, usually a very explicit "blue" film depicting intercourse, oral sex, and/or some kind of perversion. Having viewed the film, subjects carry on keeping their diary, and entries preceding and following the film are then compared. The usual finding, as already mentioned, seems to be that there is very little change; a temporary increase may occur, but the pattern comes back to normal pretty quickly. There are several such studies, both American and European, and the findings are remarkably similar. The notion of the pure innocent, viewing a pornographic film and immediately rushing out to rape the nearest virgin, could hardly be more wrong.

Similarly small changes were observed in the attitudes of viewers of pornography. They did not become emotionally more "calloused" towards women, nor did they change their views about the need or otherwise of "love" and tender emotions generally in a sexual relationship. Attitudes towards pornography did change, particularly when the films shown were in ascending order of obscenity. Viewers tended to take a less serious view of their likely influence on people's behavior under these conditions. When the order was reversed, however, attitudes did not become more favorable, and might get less favorable. This is not unexpected. Extinction of emotional responses of a neurotic nature follows a similar course. On the whole, the results from studying attitudes and values are similar to those observed in the case of behavior; changes are small and relatively unimportant.

Inevitably, the report mentions in detail the results of the "Danish experiment," *i.e.* the 1967 vote by the Danish parliament to remove erotic literature from its obscenity statute, followed by the 1969 repeal of the statute *in toto,* thus allowing all forms of sexually explicit material to be sold without let or hindrance. The effects of this ruling had been expected to be disastrous in many circles; the actual result was hardly in line with expectation. There was a marked decrease in reported sex crimes, with the total falling from 783 (in 1966) to 591, 515 and 358 in subsequent years. These are substantial decrements, amounting to over 30% in 1969 alone. Such a decline would be welcome in the U.S. and the U.K., where nothing comparable has happened. All classes of sex crimes decreased, but some decreased more than others. Rape and attempted rape decreased less than did exhibitionism or "unlawful interference short of rape" with children, and these latter offenses decreased less than voyeurism and homosexual offenses which showed the most dramatic decreases. "Changes in the incidence of sex offenses could not be attributed to legislative change, alteration of law enforcement practices or modified police reporting and data collection procedures. A survey of Copenhagen residents found that neither public attitudes about sex crimes nor willingness to report such crimes had changed sufficiently to account for the substantial decrease in sex offenses between 1959 and 1969." (The decrease preceded the abolition of the statute; during these years there had been a constant liberalization of attitude by the law enforcement agencies, such that the eventual abolition was only the final stage in a long procession.)

A more direct study of any possible relationship between reading and viewing pornographic and obscene material, on the one hand, and sexual crimes on the other, has recently been completed. This is not contained in the material surveyed by the Commission. In this study, rapists and child molesters were interviewed and questioned in detail about their experiences with pornographic material; they were compared with non-criminal groups of similar social class, education and color. (The study was carried out in the U.S.A., and it is important to compare white with white, black with black.) The results were quite clear-cut. "Adolescent exposure to erotica was significantly less for all deviant and offender groups compared to the nondeviants. During adulthood, the sex offenders . . . continued to report less exposure to erotic stimuli than controls." In addition it was found that "less than a quarter of the respondents in any group imitated sexual behavior seen in the erotic material immediately or shortly after its viewing. The hypothesis that extent of exposure during adolescence to erotica is positively associated with the later emergence of sexual pathology is not borne out by this study." Such results may go counter to expectation, but they are not to be disregarded for that reason. Taken in conjunction with the Danish experience, they make the conclusion almost mandatory that pornography does not by or of itself have a causal influence on the major sex crimes, such as rape, sex molestation of children, etc.

Other studies have shown that, if anything, sex offenders respond less strongly to pornographic material. One writer concluded from his study that "about all that can be said is that strong response to pornography is associated with imaginativeness, ability to project, and sensitivity, all of which generally increase as education increases, and with youthfulness, and that these qualities account for the differences we have found between sex offenders, in general, and nonsex offenders. Since the majority of sex offenders are not well educated nor particularly youthful, their responsiveness to pornography is correspondingly less and cannot be a consequential factor in their sex offenses unless one is prepared to argue that the inability to respond to erotica in general precludes gaining some vicarious stimulation and satisfaction and thereby causes the individual to behave overtly which, in turn, renders him more liable to arrest and conviction."

This lesser responsiveness of sex offenders to erotica may account for their using them less; clearly they derive less satisfaction from pornography than do normal people. In fact, clinical studies of the early family history of sex offenders suggest that they tend to come from repressive homes where sexual matters are not discussed openly, where there is a low tolerance of nudity, and punitive or indifferent parental responses to children's sexual curiosity and interest. As children, these future offenders encounter less in the way of erotica than does the average child, and this tendency apparently continues into adolescence—pictures of coitus are seen by the average child at fourteen, by the future offender at eighteen! As the report says, "such literature . . . suggests that sex offenders' inexperience with erotic material is a reflection of their more generally deprived sexual environment. The relative absence of such experience probably constitutes another indicator of atypical and inadequate sexual socialization." We can now see why the abolition of pornographic censorship in Denmark may indeed have caused a lowering of the sex crime rate. If sex crimes are in part due to too puritanical an upbringing, then greater social permissiveness may indeed have a prophylactic effect on the youngsters involved. Looked at from this point of view, one might conclude that pornography plays an important educational role, a role which neither parents nor teachers at the moment are filling very adequately.

THE MAJORITY REPORT of the Commission thus presents a very strong case for the liberalization of pornographic and "obscene" legislation, but it should be borne in mind that they are concerned to "make a case," and that in doing so they may not always have been entirely scrupulous to weigh the evidence impartially. This is the main charge of the critics, spelled out in detail by Dr. Cline. He maintains that "a careful review and study of the Commission majority report, their conclusions and recommendations, and the empirical research studies on which they were based, reveal a great number of serious flaws, omissions and grave shortcomings which make parts of the report suspect and to some extent lacking in credibility. Readers of the majority report are at the 'mercy' of the writers of that report, and must assume that evidence is being presented fairly and in good faith on both sides of the issue . . . A number of the research studies upon which the report is based suggest significant statistical relationships between pornography, sexual deviancy and promiscuity. Yet, some vital data suggesting this linkage are omitted or 'concealed.' Findings from seriously flawed research studies or findings which do not follow from the data are sometimes presented as fact without mentioning their very serious limitations."

These are strong words; are they justified? In part, the answer must be in the affirmative. How seriously one must view these defects we will have to discuss later on.

Here let us note just one example of the kind of omission Cline refers to. This is a study by Davis and Braucht into the relationship between exposure to pornography and moral character. They found "exposure to pornography is the strongest predictor of sexual deviance among the early age of exposure subjects . . . In general, exposure to pornography in the 'early age of exposure' subgroup was related to a variety of precocious heterosexual and deviant sexual behaviors." They note that since exposure in this subgroup was not related to having deviant peers (bad associations and companions), it would be difficult to blame the sexual promiscuity and deviancy of these subjects on other factors such as being influenced by friends (rather than pornography) into these kinds of anti-social activities. This research was contracted and financed by the Commission, and is mentioned many times in the report—but "not a single mention is made of these negative findings."

It would be tedious to go in detail through Cline's allegations; I will instead try to summarize his main points, and then attempt to set these criticisms in a wider frame-work. His main point might be said to be this. The researches reported have shown that relatively short exposures to pornographic material of students and non-student adults have minimal effects on their sexual behavior and their sexual attitudes. This is interesting, but of limited value. These are all fairly experienced individuals, usually of good education, and mentally non-pathological. The crucial question is what exposure to these materials would do to youngsters of poor education, and with slightly pathological mental make-up. In short, the experiments answer some questions, but they do not answer precisely those questions which are of most concern. What short exposure to pornographic material does to well-integrated adults is one thing; what long-term exposure to such materials may do to not-so-well integrated youngsters is quite another. The writers of the majority report do not enter the necessary caveats in discussing these researches. They tend to generalize far too freely, from one group to other groups, quite dissimilar in age and character, and from short, often single exposures, to lengthy and multiple exposures. Such generalizations are not permissible, and although one may recognize the ethical difficulties involved in presenting such material to children, say, or of going beyond the limits of single or at most very limited presentations, nevertheless these limitations should be recognized and indeed emphasized. Failure to do so implies a deviation from scientific discussion to propaganda. The majority report tries to "make a case," and this is anathema to the scientist. This is bad enough; but in addition the majority report suppresses information which goes against its recommendations. One example has been given; Cline gives many more. It might be argued that all the information is in fact contained in the ten volumes of detailed research findings I alluded to at the beginning, but this is no real defense. Very few people would rush out to buy and read these highly technical monographs after having waded through 700 badly written pages of a jargon-filled report!

I think that there is no doubt that in part at least Cline is right. There is evidence of suppression of evidence, of failure to point out the limitations of the researches reported, and of jumping from limited evidence to whole-hogging conclusions and legal recommendations. The evidence presented is interesting and important, but it certainly does not justify the majority's opinions. If I were asked to state the conclusion which one can draw from the evidence, I would say that any conclusions must be very tentative, but that certain points do emerge. Whether these justify any social action, rather than suggesting the need for further research, I will leave to the reader. In formulating these conclusions, I have tried to integrate the research surveyed in the report with my own work, which was concerned with rather a different sort of approach, and one which unfortunately the Commission neglected completely, namely the area of individual differences, and of correlations between sexual attitudes and behaviors, on the one hand, and personality, on the other.

IN THE FIRST PLACE, THEN, it will be remembered that there seem to be important differences between individuals in their degree of sexual libido, general sexual motivation, or "randyness" if you like. Some people, generally extroverted in personality, have a much more active sex life than others, generally introverted in personality. They engage in petting earlier, have intercourse earlier, have intercourse with more different partners, in more different positions, indulge in "perversions" and deviant practices more actively, and generally behave in a manner which one might designate "libertine" or "permissive." Such people also tend to read and view pornographic material early in life, and the crucial question is one of causation. Does the strong libido of the extrovert make him read pornography at an early age, look at obscene photographs as a youngster, and to see blue films when he can afford it, or is it rather the other way about—does the exposure to pornography make him show all the varied traits of the "libertine"? Cline would presumably choose the latter alternative, the majority report writers the former. It must be admitted that there is no hard-and-fast evidence on which to base a decision. This is indeed admitted by the majority report writers, although perhaps not as prominently as might be desired; nevertheless, they do admit it. My own work would seem to suggest that the former alternative is more likely to be right than the latter; that pornography appeals, and is sought out, by those who have inherited extroverted proclivities, and who would in any case have a more active sex life, *i.e.* by the more extroverted type of person. Direct evidence would of course be needed to establish this conclusion. But as far as the evidence goes, and circumstantial as it is, it does nevertheless support, if only mildly, this general conclusion.

We also find, however, that in addition to a group of people (extroverts) who enjoy pornography and also lead a very "sexy" life, there is another group of people who are sex-starved and who also consume a great deal of pornography. These are people who score highly on the "neuroticism" scale of the personality inventory I used. In other words, people who are not in the pathological group of neurotics we find in our mental hospital outpatient departments, but who are "tending that way." Such people often have difficulties in their sexual lives—ejaculatio praecox, failure to achieve orgasm, frigidity, impotence—as well as mental symptoms, like mood swings, headaches, etc. For them, one might think, pornography is an alternative outlet for their sexual desires (which are very strong). Afraid to contact people of the other sex, they have recourse to erotic material which is pornographic or obscene. Here again we must ask the question about the chicken and the egg, and again we must admit that there is no direct evidence. As in the previous case, however, the indirect evidence (*e.g.* from twin studies) suggests fairly strongly that neurotic disabilities, however mild, are likely to have a genetic background; and that the anxiety/fear responses to members of the opposite sex, and the turning to pornography instead, are due to these genetic factors, and possibly to early childhood experiences not themselves involving pornography.

These are reasonable suppositions, but of course for the purpose of taking social action one would require much stronger evidence. Perhaps a combination of the Commission type of experiment with the "personality" approach might furnish us with such evidence; twin studies might also be of help. But whatever the outcome of these experiments, I feel that in the nature of things it will always be extremely difficult, if not impossible, to rig up authentic experimental replicas of the sort of every-day encounters with pornography which anti-pornography exponents really object to. Inevitably, the experimenter can only expose his subjects to a very limited, short-term set of pornographic materials. What may be doing the damage, in the opinion of many, may be the general penetration of pornographic material into every corner of our culture. More important than the furtive sale of obscene material in the Soho bookstore may be the blatant exposure of female thighs in mini-skirts in public places, the bra advertisement in the train, and the nude in the tabloid. It may be this constant insistence on sexual stimulation, even in quite irrelevant contexts (like the exhibition of new models at the Motor Show!) which produces a climate of opinion in which "obscene" pornography plays only a minor part, but which tends to "deprave and corrupt" many of those who come into contact with it. It is this climate of opinion which may be the crucial variable, with published hard-core pornography only the tip of the iceberg, which leads to general permissiveness, increases in illegitimate pregnancies, abortions and venereal disease. Again it would be difficult to establish which is the cause and which the effect. Quite likely all these different factors are interacting in complex ways which would be extremely hard to disentangle. But to hope that laboratory experiments can do more than suggest conclusions, or further lines of enquiry, is being overly optimistic at this stage of the game. The facts reported in the Commission's enquiries cannot readily be made into a "pornographer's Magna Carta," however our natural inclinations may be opposed to censorship in all its forms.

Even if this "general climate of opinion" view is correct, it is difficult to see what can be done about it—even assuming that we would wish to do something about it. Short of banning bra advertisements, forcing all women to wear maxis, and eliminating pictures of bare breasts from newspapers and journals alike we can hardly reverse the trend towards greater permissiveness; certainly the banning of really obscene material is likely to play only a very minor part in this process of changing the climate of opinion. It is here, I think, that battle is really joined—do we want to reverse present trends, or do we welcome them? Do we prefer an extroverted or an introverted society? Do we prefer libertinism or puritanism? Such large-scale opinion studies as have been done suggest that we want neither of these extremes. The vast majority prefer something in between—as indeed fits the majority of people's personalities which are intermediate between extreme extroversion and extreme introversion. In other words, most people look for a compromise. Such compromises are perhaps not terribly exciting, but they tend to be easier to live with than extremes. Writers, philosophers and other molders of public opinion tend rather to be carried away with their eloquence, and go to extremes; hence the view that people are embattled along rigorously drawn lines of pro and con. Nothing of the sort. Most people cry "a plague on both your houses," and firmly hold to the middle ground. The majority report tried to break away from this middle ground, and was firmly slapped into place; it is doubtful if it could have been more successful had its argumentation been less one-sided.

SO FAR OUR ARGUMENTS have dealt entirely with reasonably normal people, with a minimum of mental pathology. When we turn to sex criminals, however, the evidence is a good deal more clear-cut. It does seem that a greater freedom to publish obscene material may help the potential sex criminal to suppress or sublimate his libidinal impulses. Again, the evidence is not conclusive; even with respect to the Danish experience Cline adduces some salutary criticisms which should be borne in mind. But on the whole I doubt if many experts would hold that criminal activity in the sexual field is increased by the open sale of explicit sexual material, and it may very well be curtailed. This is an important conclusion, and should certainly be considered when making decisions in this complex field.

One further argument is often advanced by those who disagree with the conclusions of the President's Commission. They argue that permission to show publicly, and without let or hindrance, many different varieties of intercourse, oral sex, and various perversions soon make these lose their "spice," and that other, even more decadent forms of titillation will be put up for sale. This has certainly happened in Denmark, where torture scenes, intercourse with animals, and scenes involving small children are now openly for sale. Even the most determined opponent of censorship may doubt whether this escalation is in anyone's best interests, and in particular whether those taking part in the actual filming (*e.g.* the children) should not be offered some protection. Some connection between sex and cruelty has often been suggested by psychiatrists; this may be a very sensitive area in which to allow unfettered commercialism to ply its trade.

One last point should perhaps be made. Underlying all the discussions about pornography, obscenity, and our present perilous moral condition, is the assumption that we are indeed now a "swinging" civilization, with pre-marital sex, adultery, and all sorts of unspeakable vices and perversions everywhere. This assumption is assiduously fostered by the mass media, but I found little evidence for its accuracy in my own studies. There was much evidence for girls preserving their virginity until they met "Mr. Right"—or thought they had; for great interest in personal relationships, and against "sleeping around." Similar conclusions emerge from the most recent study of "Sex and Marriage in England Today" by Geoffrey Gorer; he too found little evidence for the assumed prevalence of "easy sex" and casual love-making. Instead, he discovered that the "great majority of the younger English married men and women still put a very high value on marital fidelity:"

A quarter of our male respondents and one thirtieth of our female respondents is the largest group to whom the journalistic phrase "permissive" can possibly be applied with any accuracy . . .

despite the impression given by contemporary mass communications with all the emphasis of the "permissive society," "swinging London," and the like in reporting, and the prevalence of erotic themes in much fiction (not to mention the disappearance of the taboo on printing a few common-speech words), England still appears to be a very chaste society, according to the replies of our informants.

These "informants" constituted a random sample of the population; of this random sample, "a quarter of our married male informants and nearly two-thirds of our married women said they were virgin at marriage; and a further 20% of the men and 25% of the women married the person with whom they first had intercourse." Taking these groups together, Gorer argues that "it would appear that just under half the men (46%) and nearly nine-tenths of the women (88%) reached the stage of marriage as technical virgins."

Figures like these put a rather different complexion on the state of modern morality; London is still somewhat remote from Sodom and Gonorrhea, in spite of all that advocates and opponents of pornography alike have to say on the subject. Similar figures are available for America, and there too, exaggeration of current trends seems to have been prevalent. As I pointed out in connection with my own findings, "when all is said and done, more is said than done." There is certainly less hesitation in talking about sexual themes, and even using the occasional four-lettered expletive in circumstances where this would have been unthinkable twenty years ago, but talking and doing are two different things. All the fine talk about liberation from ancient taboos has not led to the anticipated consequences; as Gorer makes clear, the song about "love and marriage" still attracts the overwhelming majority of our young people. Impersonal sex is probably no more widespread than it was when I was a student; the difference is simply that people talk about it more, and that the arts and the media in general are freer to exploit sexual themes and issues. Youngsters who grow up expecting the life of Riley when they become teenagers, or go to University, may have a rude shock! In this area, more than in most others, T.H. Huxley's words seem to have preserved their applicability, when he spoke of "the great tragedy of science—the slaying of a beautiful theory by an ugly fact."

Pornography clearly presents a problem; is there an answer? Probably not; the problem is not a factual one, nor a technological one. Indeed, it is very difficult to state the problem in any unequivocal fashion. In terms of the title of this chapter, you might ask if pornography is a good or bad thing, a use or an abuse of the media which are being employed to purvey it. But such questions only *seem* meaningful. They depend on the answer one gives to another question, namely: What do you mean by "good" in this context? Pornography does not have one set of consequences, but many; some of these might be considered good, others bad. Furthermore, what is good for one person may be bad for another; individuality is supreme in this field. It would be very foolish indeed to come down on one side or the other and say with conviction that pornography is or is not an abomination which should be banned from television, the screen, and the printed page. Some arguments, as we have seen, can be dismissed pretty well out of hand. We cannot agree with the abolitionists that pornography induces people to commit sex crimes. Unlimited permission to publish and show pornographic material of any kind may not seriously lower the sex crime-rate, but it does not seem to put it up. Nor does freedom to publish pornography turn society into pornographers. There is evidence from Denmark that when pornography is freely permitted to appear, then after a short period of increased interest sales drop disastrously, and the whole business is kept alive only by exports to other countries still maintaining the taboo on such productions. Both these arguments used to be advanced with some effect by the abolitionists; their disproof is pretty thorough, and it would need much strong evidence in their favor before we can ever reverse the judgment that these feared consequences of freedom simply do not follow complete abolition of censorship.

Similarly, on the other side, it cannot any longer be argued with any degree of conviction that pornography, or the potrayal of violence, have no effect on the behavior of the people who see these things on the screen, or read about them in books and magazines. Laboratory evidence shows quite clearly that effects of even quite short pieces of film modelling certain types of behavior have a very pronounced effect on the actual behavior of children and adults; so do verbal representations. Both behavior and emotional reactions are affected, and the effects are not transitory. The evidence is admittedly indirect, but that is not really a valid point of criticism; much scientific evidence in the "hard" sciences is of this kind, and is readily accepted on much the same level as direct evidence. Thus those who would wish to abolish censorship cannot reasonably go on arguing that pornography should be permitted because it has no effect on behavior or emotion. This argument never carried much weight, being seen to be unreasonable and counter to experience with other types of "advertising"—and much pornographic writing, from Walter to D. H. Lawrence, and from Henry Miller to Frank Harris, is similar in intent to advertising. These writers want desperately to convince the reader that their outlook on sexual matters is right and the orthodox outlook wrong. The argument thus shifts to rather a different ground, one where it should have been conducted from the beginning, free from all the red herrings which so many protagonists have dragged across the path. What the argument is about is simply the nature of the society in which we wish to live, and in which we wish our children to live—neither more nor less.

WE TEND TO THINK of people as being introverted or extroverted, but clearly we can extend this typology to societies. Puritan society was introverted: opposed to smoking and drinking, wenching and dancing, intent on moral and religious questions, on serious behavior and deep thought. The Permissive society is extroverted; fond of materialistic belongings, sensually appealing trappings, music, dancing, smoking and drinking, with an emphasis on sexual pleasure and no thought for the morrow. Advertising has taken the place of the Bible, pornography that of the Lives of the Saints, burlesque that of the religious meeting. If these comparisons are too pointed, they at least point in the right direction. If spokesmen for Puritanism and for Permissiveness were to fill in an extroversion-introversion questionnaire, indicating in each case whether his peers approved or did not approve of any given activity mentioned, there is no doubt that the results would resemble very closely a typical introverted and a typical extroverted form. It is, of course, not being suggested that in a given society everyone approves of the prevailing value system, or orders his life accordingly. It is merely being suggested that there are different value systems, and that these tend to emphasize types of behavior usually associated with introverts and extroverts respectively. It is further suggested that such societies propagate, as Plato saw all too clearly, their value system through the writings they encourage or tolerate, the poems they produce and publish, the pictures they paint, or the films shown in their cinemas. Societies engage in a gigantic process of brainwashing in order to ensure some degree of conformity: a process of brainwashing which makes use of the principles of conditioning. This process is more or less supple. It does not necessarily require force or torture— indeed, the use of force and torture is an acknowledgement that subtler methods have failed. The little American boy who is made to salute his flag at school every morning, and pledge allegiance to his country, is being brainwashed as surely as the Russian boy who is made to read about the divine intervention of Lenin in the power-struggle after the first World War, or the Chinese boy who is made to carry Mao's *Thoughts* around in his pocket. "Brainwashing" is an inevitable part of welding together a society out of recalcitrant, different, individualistic pieces. We may not like it, and prefer reasoned consent and intellectual discussion, but these presuppose some premises which are being taken for granted, and are never questioned. Without such premises, no argument; if you have no premises at all, then solipsism is the only possible conclusion to be drawn.

Arguments between censors and abolitionists of por- nography are therefore rather spurious, because they derive from different premises. Alleged facts are adduced, and logic (of a kind) is being chopped mercilessly, but it is all to no avail—the arguments used cannot in the nature of the case carry conviction for those who start from different assumptions. The same is true of religious, political and aesthetic arguments; they cannot be solved by the provision of facts, because they are not about facts. They are rather like arguments of the kind: "I like cheese"—"I don't like cheese." Both protagonists are clearly right (unless they are telling lies, of course), but there is no real disagreement between them, unless what they say carries the implication that every right- thinking person should (or should not) like cheese. This implication is clearly absurd, but is actually made by many people. To differ from their set of values, preferences, and likes and dislikes is to place yourself beyond the pale.

WHAT, THEN, DO THE PROTAGONISTS of the two opposing sides say—when we strip their views of irrelevant arguments, emotional outbursts and alleged facts?

First the adherent of traditional morality. He would say that he wishes to live in a society which places a high value on family life, lasting human relations, security of upbringing for children in a loving, permanent home. Sexual satisfaction, while important, comes definitely below the other requirements in his scale of demands. Sexual technique would be regarded as infinitely less important than affection, and he would particularly oppose the publication of books, or the showing of films, which would have the effect of conditioning young people (including his own children) to associate inappropriate emotions and attitudes with sexual arousal and satisfaction. He would not readily accept the retort that everyone would be free to read or not to read, to view or not to view. There are meretricious attractions and vicarious pleasures associated with pornographic presentations—even leaving out social pressures which young people are not always well equipped to resist. He would want to protect his value system by recourse to the law. Only by forbidding opposing ideas to corrupt and deprave the young (or even the not-so-young) can such a system be preserved. He might go on to say that by stressing physical aspects only, by separating love from lust, and by promoting wrong kinds of associations in the imaginations of children, adolescents and adults, por- nographers are trying to brainwash those vulnerable to their persuasions into accepting a sexual code which is destructive of happiness, of permanent relations, and ultimately of society itself. History has shown that the decline of a flourishing society is often preceded by a loosening of morals, a loss of ethical considerations, and the abandonment of the virtues which made the society great. Sexual promiscuity, the flourishing of perversions, and the easy toleration of homosexual practices are both symptoms of a wider abandonment of traditional values, and causes of a quicker decline into obscurity and chaos. Vigilance is the price of freedom, and such vigilance needs to be supported by the forces of the law in curtailing the activities of the pornographer.

It is difficult to fault this argument, provided that we accept the premises. If we want to live in a society which stresses permanent, secure and loving unions between a man and a woman, then pornography (and all the other forces which it stands for in this connection) certainly provides a threat, and a serious one at that.

What does the advocate of permissiveness have to say? He would point out that all too often the alleged values of traditional marriage are mere pretence; that many marriages are in fact hollow, loveless, and social forms without content. Marriage can be a prison, and children often suffer more in unhappy homes than they would if their parents were to separate and follow their own inclinations in sexual matters. He would go on to point to all the repressions involved in the old system, the unhappiness caused by lack of sexual information to youngsters, the evils of prostitution which apparently cannot easily be separated from monogamous marriage. He would protest against the implicit degradation of the sexual appetite in favor of other values, and insist on its restoration to what he considers to be its appropriate place. He would argue against censorship on grounds well known since John Milton's *Areopagitica* (although Milton might have been surprised by these new recruits to his banner). And he would protest on aesthetic grounds against any form of license or inspection for works of art. The artist must be completely free to follow his genius, regardless of consequences.

These arguments, too, are fine and incontrovertible. Given the existing value system of the advocate, the Permissive society is obviously preferable to Puritanism. In fact, both sides simply show the favorable consequences of their policies to the public, and try to hide the less acceptable ones; the opponent in each case turns the medal around, and exposes the other side. This does not help us to find a solution. In fact, both sides argue as if such a solution, uniquely satisfying to everybody, could in fact exist. It is here that I think both sides are vulnerable.

Let me remind the reader of an experiment described in Chapter 1, where subjects were seated in a dark, silent room and instructed to manipulate a lever. Strong manipulation produced three seconds of bright light and loud jazz from a juke-box. Extroverts, it will be remembered, pressed hard to get lights and music all the time. Introverts pressed very little, in order to keep the room silent and dark. This is fine, as long as the subject is alone in the room. Now consider a room full of introverts and extroverts. The former would want the room silent and dark, and would act accordingly, while the latter would pull hard, hoping to get light and music. Who is right? And is there an answer to the problem which would satisfy everyone? The answer is clearly: No. Different people want different proportions of light and dark, silence and noise; in any given society, no one can have everything he wants. A compromise is the only reasonable conclusion, and both the Puritan and the Permissive society depart from what would probably be regarded as a reasonable compromise by most people.

Victorian repressiveness almost certainly failed to have the desired effect of promoting happy family life, security of upbringing and permanence of emotional attachment. These are all difficult to legislate for. Our own society, by extending the boundaries of what is socially acceptable without destroying completely the legal and moral warp and woof that regulate the nature of more permanent unions is probably nearer a true compromise. To push liberalization much beyond the point reached might have the effect of reducing the total satisfaction experienced by the majority, by going too far towards the extroverted extreme. It is always difficult to say when a compromise is working most efficiently. But in the absence of further information one has the uneasy feeling that any extension of permissiveness would not only reduce general happiness and contentment, but create a strong impetus for the pendulum to start swinging back towards repressiveness. Both the original swing in the direction of greater permissiveness, and the beginnings of the swing back towards repressiveness, can be best studied in the U.S.A. If only these movements were routinely measured and documented by psychologists and sociologists permanently employed by governments to accumulate information for future research into these complex and extremely important problems!

For let us make no mistake—genuine information on most of the issues raised here is almost entirely lacking. We know practically nothing about the proportion of happy and unhappy marriages, the influence on children of the actions parents may take when their marriage is breaking down; or the changes that may be taking place in the number of extramarital and premarital affairs. Research into sexual matters is still in its infancy, and while a little is known, much more remains to be explored. It is a tragedy that such research is almost shunned by experimenters, grant-giving bodies and universities alike. The intrepid investigator is looked down upon as a dirty old man whose thoughts are entirely preoccupied with pornography of the most salacious kind. Society cannot give expression to reasoned policies when the factual basis for such policies does not exist; all must be surmise, theory and speculation. It is doubtful if from such a background of ignorance, spiced with bias and emotion, any sensible policy can spring. We need a great increase in the quantity, and a marked improvement in the quality, of research in the general area of sexual behavior, its antecedents and consequences, before we can say anything about these matters with much conviction. The reaction I received from

heads of colleges and other learned institutions when I wrote
to ask permission to approach their students in connection
with the sexual questionnaire discussed in Chapter 1 was
distinctly odd. Many seemed offended at being asked, refused
permission curtly and sometimes offensively, and some wrote
long letters beseeching me to consider the error of my ways
and return to the bosom of the mother church. Others pointed
out the uselessness of research in this area, implying that they
knew all there was to be known about these things—or at
least, all that was worth knowing. These were all eminent
literary or scientific men of high intelligence and of good
academic standing. Reactions from other sources were even
more absurd. The head of a modelling agency who had been
approached for permission wrote in high dudgeon to a variety
of newspapers complaining that her girls were being exposed
to unmentionable dangers. The London newspapers (from the
News of the World to the *Sunday Express*) gave vent to their
indignation, the former taking care to publish several of the
actual questions, thus affording the modelling girls a first
opportunity of actually seeing the material from which they
had been so carefully protected. (Also affording this
opportunity to several million other readers—all under the
guise of punishing vice and helping virtue!) No wonder
scientists shy away from a topic which guarantees a maximum
of unfavorable comment, which is so difficult to work on that
important discoveries are not easy to come by, and which is
not held in high esteem by their colleagues.

What I think is needed is for the television networks—in
Britain, the B.B.C. and the Independent Television
Authority—to finance an independent research organization,
or at least give generous research grants to independent
investigators, for research into the problems raised in this
chapter. Possibly the film industry should also be made to add
its mite—perhaps one per cent of all profits from "X"
certificate films might be a fair suggestion? Pornographic

books not actually banned might be more difficult to pull into this net; but the possibility should be investigated. In other words, modern government makes it a statutory duty for the chemical industry to carry out research on drugs, and furnish the results to an independent government-appointed committee, for the simple reason that some of the products are dangerous, and the public needs protection. In exactly the same way I would suggest that some of the products of the mass media are dangerous, and that the public is entitled to protection. It might be objected that our knowledge is so much greater in the pharmacological field, but this is simply not true. The panic measures taken when some pesticides, some oral birth control pills, and some sweeteners were banned did not originate in relevant, well controlled and properly executed research. The amount of knowledge in all these cases was minimal—so small that had nothing more substantial been available in the psychological field, I would certainly never have considered writing this chapter. We must avoid being carried away by the rightful prestige of the hard sciences into believing that everything in the field of physics and chemistry is part of a body of certain (or almost certain) knowledge, while everything in the social sciences is surmise and guesswork. As a rough-and-ready guide this is certainly more acceptable than the feverish claims of psychoanalysts to have achieved scientific knowledge in the field of psychology. But only too often do even the hard sciences produce results which are inconclusive, but which are easily over-interpreted by anxious politicians and made the excuse for hasty and unwarranted action. The products of the social research proposed would also have to be interpreted and judged by hard common sense, preferably reinforced by some more specialized knowledge. But there is no reason to fear that in due course these products would have so much lower a degree of validity than those of the hard sciences that no reasonable action at all could be taken as a consequence.

There has already been a small move in the right direction. In England, the I.T.A. has given a small sum of 50,000 pounds per annum for five years in aid of research in the general field of television. This amount is, of course, totally inadequate and it is not being spent on anything closely related to the topic of our discussion. However, the precedent is there; an extension of this principle, to take in the B.B.C. and the film companies, and a proper increase in the amount of money involved, might produce important results. It is curious that politicians, chairmen of television companies, the directors of the B.B.C. and the I.T.A., and others responsibly involved with the mass media should not realize that their responsibility extends to the investigation of possible injurious effects of the wares they peddle. Even if it were true, as such people constantly reiterate both in Britain and in the U.S.A., that there was no evidence for such injurious effects of their programs, this would simply show that they had failed to instigate the needed research; there certainly is no research to *clear* the programs from suspicion. The onus of proof is on the side of those who provide a suspect service. They must prove that it is safe, not wait for others to undertake the extremely difficult and expensive task of proving that it is dangerous. Drug firms are not given the benefit of the doubt; it is not obvious why television and motion picture companies should be treated differently. But in any case, as we have seen, there is a considerable body of evidence to show that in effect the position is not as it is represented by official spokesmen. Such evidence as there is, and there is a good deal, all tends to show that even short snippets, shown once, have a profound effect on the viewer. To argue that there is no evidence about long, carefully and professionally prepared and endlessly repeated films and television shows having any effect is no longer acceptable. It is the business of the purveyors of these shows to demonstrate the alleged lack of effect. Such demonstrations would of course be regarded with suspicion if they were made under the direct authority of the companies involved. This is why an independent organization should be set up, financed through a levy by the interests concerned, but controlled in its running by some scientific body like the Medical Research Council or the American Psychological Association.

THE READER MAY FEEL that I have been contradicting myself when I first pointed out that facts are not very relevant to the dispute between orthodoxy and permissiveness, between Puritan and anti-Puritan. This is true on the moral, ethical and religious plane, and with particular reference to sexual matters—although even here many people in what one might call the uncommitted or middle range might come to attention rather sharply if the soothing chorus of "it doesn't have any effect on anybody" were to be contradicted by specific evidence that their own children were in fact being changed in a direction they themselves would not approve of. But the position is quite different in regard to violence, aggressiveness and cruelty. Here even the most permissive would draw a line. Our whole social structure is based on the rule of law, and the freedom from random violence or directed aggression. If it could be shown that these values were being undermined seriously by the current types of television and film programs, and by certain types of writings, then I think even the most permissive and passive might decide that the time had come to take a hand and redress the balance.

I would argue that the evidence that already exists is pretty conclusive, but that bigger and better studies, more extensive in numbers, involving different types of children and adults, using different media, different criteria, studying the interaction with personality (are introverts or extroverts more easily changed in the direction of greater or lesser aggressiveness?) and making detailed physiological recordings of the visceral and emotional concomitants of viewing and post-viewing behavior, should be conducted with all speed so that more certain and more directly relevant knowledge could be procured. It would be easy to use actual films and television programs showing violent and aggressive behavior with children and adolescents, and note their pre- and post-demonstration behavior in situations which readily deteriorate into quarrelling and fighting. So much could be done; so little is being done. It is easy to blame sponsors, Senators, M.P.s, television authorities and film makers. Ultimately in a democracy it is the voter who bears the responsibility. It is rather late in the day for him to make his voice heard, but it may not be too late.

⑦

Don't Shoot THe Behaviorist: He is Doing His Best

NOBODY ever loves a behaviorist. That seems a trifle unjust, and one may inquire why this should be so. However hard we try, our image always seems to be slipping, and the most bloodcurdling accusations are slung at us—those of "brainwashing" and "torture" being among the more benign. Philosophers, literary intellectuals, artists, men of religion, politicians, educationalists, psychiatrists—all look sad and grave, as if one had just contracted some dreadful disease, and withdraw to some safe distance, so as to be reasonably immune from infection. This is very curious, because all we are trying to do is to study human (and animal) behavior in a scientific manner, in order to be able to offer help and advice based on sound and well-established fact, rather than on guesswork and surmise. We are concerned, most of us, about the sad state of humanity; we recognize the tremendously difficult problems which confront it; and we feel that some empirical information about *homo sapiens* might just occasionally be of some assistance in solving some of these problems. This does not seem an ignoble aim. Why, then, the universal dislike and disdain, sometimes amounting to active hatred and persecution?

Kathleen Nott, philosopher and poet, confesses in her book *A Soul in the Quad* (which is largely devoted to a determined and quietly ferocious assault on behaviorism in general and the writer of these lines in particular) that she finds behaviorists "annoying," a term which is very revealing in such a quiet and rational soul. Why are we annoying? A good beginning to this chapter might be a brief description of the three faces of behaviorism: metaphysical, methodological, and analytical. These distinctions were drawn by C. A. Mace, one of my teachers and later a friend, who combined the training of a philosopher with that of a psychologist, and who managed to cast a friendly but also critical eye on the activities of his more empirical colleagues. They form an essential background for any informed discussion of behaviorism, because without them arguments tend to go off at right angles to each other, each party attributing different meanings to the terms used.

METAPHYSICAL BEHAVIORISM is really little but a disguise for a very ancient philosophical belief, namely old-fashioned materialism. Descartes was responsible for our widely held modern belief in some form of dualism, *i.e.* the assertion that there exists a class of objects called "things" with physical dimensions as well as a class of objects called "minds" without measurable dimensions. Idealists deny the existence of the former (in spite of Dr. Johnson's kicking a boulder, saying of idealism "I disprove it thus"—he was as poor a philosopher as some modern behaviorists). Materialists deny the existence of the latter; this is also what metaphysical behaviorists do, without adding anything interesting to the age-old arguments. There are, to be sure, a number of positions on this mind-body problem which one can occupy, and which are neither idealist nor materialist; dualism is an example. But I do not want to rehearse these ancient philosophical quarrels. Not only is there no agreed answer, there is not even any agreement on the criteria on which an answer could be judged, and no agreement either on whether this is a factual and meaningful question at all, or on what kinds of facts would be relevant to it. In other words, like so many other metaphysical problems, this one seems pretty murky, insoluble and rather meaningless. Hence it is still a favorite old bone on which to try your argumentative metaphysical teeth. But that is for young philosophy students; experience teaches one that nothing important is likely to come out of all this argumentation. And while some behaviorists are materialists in this sense, the great majority yawn and leave the problem well alone; you would not find many behaviorists who showed any great interest in metaphysical questions. There is a temperamental affinity between behaviorism and naive realism, but this is not fundamental and thought out in any philosophical manner. Most behaviorists would tend to say rather impatiently: "Let's get on with the job of doing our experiments, and never mind about philosophy"—using that word in the most pejorative sense possible. Philosophy to the behaviorist is idle speculation about matters either unknowable or uninteresting, or both. In this he would find support in some of the more able modern philosophers themselves who have relegated metaphysics to an academic backwater, or legislated it out of existence altogether.

The natural affinity between behaviorism and materialism is brought out very clearly in the early history of the former, particularly in France which, although this is not always realized, provided the cradle out of which sprang many of the fundamental ideas which now go to make up modern behaviorism. Descartes was a complete materialist as far as animals were concerned; he likened animals to the moving statues in the royal gardens which move when someone steps on the hidden plate to which they are connected. Man, too, is an automaton as far as his body is concerned, but he is also the possessor of a soul which determines the actions of this automaton. Yet this dualistic conception was illogical and contradictory even in his writings, and the trend was inevitably towards monism. The soul was to be made just another piece of mechanistic furniture by La Mettrie, and finally dismissed altogether by Condillac.

Julien Offroy de La Mettrie was born in 1709. He studied theology and joined the Jansenists. This sect, following St. Augustine, believed in predestination; thus at an early age La Mettrie became convinced of determinism. He switched his studies to medicine, and at the age of fifteen received his doctor's degree and began to practice; later on he studied physiology in Leyden under Boerhave, whose works he translated. He also wrote books of his own, a youthful presumption which produced an angry outburst from the medical profession. Apparently even then being young was a crime which could only be expiated by keeping quiet. When La Mettrie fell very ill with a fever, he noted the loss of mental power paralleling that of his physical powers, and he became convinced that thought was nothing but the product and outcome of the action of the brain and the nervous system. This led him to a materialistic view of the soul, and he extended Descartes' mechanical view of animals to man himself—a view which did not commend itself to his colleagues, and he was forced to retreat to Leyden, where he published his most famous book, *L'homme machine*. This was too much even for the burghers of Holland, and he had to take refuge in Berlin, where Frederick the Great made him Court Reader. There he worked on the second part of his theoretical model, again anticipating rather curiously the most modern behavioristic theories of Thorndike and Skinner. He put forward the hedonistic view that conduct is governed entirely by positive and negative reinforcements—or, as he put it, that pleasure is the end of life. He died at the age of forty-one— perhaps the first truly behaviorist writer, execrated by all right-thinking persons.

Condillac combined La Mettrie's physiological materialism with English empiricism. He is best known perhaps by his parable of the sentient statue which learns, thus demonstrating the irrelevance of a soul for generating behavior. Condillac did not follow La Mettrie in mechanizing the soul, but dumped it overboard altogether—*"une hypothèse dont je n'ai pas besoin."* Condillac's stress on sensations and perceptions furnishes a third strand of modern behavioristic concern—his statue was the first exponent of a stimulus-response configuration.

Thus we have in these early writers a preview of modern behaviorism in philosophical and physiological guise—an exclusively mechanistic account of behavior, a motivational theory stressing reinforcement, and a stimulus-response theory of what Thorndike was to call "connectionism." But these anticipations did not issue in anything really important because they were entirely metaphysical. Recent knowledge in physiology was indeed incorporated, and used in argument, but the vital ingredient of modern behaviorism was lacking—a scientific methodology. Hence these early writers prepared the ground, and they certainly have affinities with later American behaviorists. Nevertheless, there is all the difference in the world between La Mettrie and Watson, Condillac and Skinner, Descartes and Thorndike. The former were philosophers and metaphysicians, primarily concerned about the mind-body problem. The latter did not care about this problem in the slightest, and never thought about it—they took it for granted that stimuli and their effects determine human conduct, and went on from there to elucidate the actual laws according to which this determination takes place. Such a program must stand or fall by its empirical success. The truth or falsity of its philosophical underpinnings is irrelevant. Materialism might be "true" (I insert the quotation marks because I doubt if the term here has any meaning), and yet the behavioristic program might fail. Conversely, materialism might be "untrue," and yet the behavioristic program might succeed very well. Metaphysics is just not relevant to experimental work, and so the private or non-existent metaphysical ideas of behaviorists are neither here nor there. Some have admittedly ventured out into the battlefield of metaphysics, but their mangled corpses attest the foolishness of such temerity.

Metaphysical behaviorism, then, is of no interest to anyone. It does not say anything new, and it does not say anything sensible, and it is not specifically behavioristic. Indeed, one might say that there is a *contradictio in adjecto*, because the term "metaphysical" implies the possibility of arguing on *a priori* grounds about what the world is like, and behaviorism implies a completely empirical attitude, *i.e.* a denial that such *a priori* arguments can have any sense whatever. You cannot at one and the same time hold such contradictory beliefs (or if you can, you should not), and consequently metaphysical behaviorism need not bother us any further. Behaviorists can, of course, have philosophical views, but *qua* philosophers, not *qua* behaviorists. If I had to come down in favor of one of the many body-mind theories (which I fortunately do not), I think I would favor evolutionary epiphenomenalism—it makes just a little more sense than any alternative view that in the course of evolution, matter acquired the properties of life and living matter the properties of consciousness. Am I ceasing to be a behaviorist by admitting to possessing conscious thoughts and feelings? I hope not. It seems foolish to deny something so obviously true. Whether the existence of such conscious thoughts, feelings, and desires contradicts anything asserted by behaviorism we must consider presently.

METHODOLOGICAL BEHAVIORISM is quite another thing. Here we have the essence of what was, in its time, a scientific revolution. Psychology before Watson had largely been concerned with mental events, with introspective accounts of the furniture of the mind, and with attempts to rationalize these and reduce them to some form of scientific and rigorous lawfulness. Introspection was the main method, and many very able and highly sophisticated people tried to use it in their search for a scientific psychology. The fact that they failed, and failed abysmally, was not predictable on logical grounds. The attempt had to be made, but we should benefit from the failure, and realize that consciousness, and reports of conscious thoughts and feelings, do not make good fodder for scientific investigation. Of course it is possible that in time some great new figure will arise in psychology and teach us how to do this properly. This seems unlikely, but one can never be sure. Until he does, we must agree with J. B. Watson and his many followers that our primary datum is behavior, not consciousness, and that our laws must be laws about observable behavior, not about non-observable states of consciousness.

This does not imply (although some behaviorists write as if it did) that states of consciousness do not exist. As T. R. Miles puts it, "the case of the methodological behaviorist is rather that if there are such things as minds or mental events they cannot as a matter of methodology be regarded as proper objects for scientific study." Such a statement is subject to disproof and is hence a meaningful scientific statement. All you have to do, if you do not agree with the statement and wish to disprove it, is to put forward a method which would render mental states and events suitable for scientific study. Until and unless this is done, the behaviorists have a strong case, and many people feel that their revolution was a very timely one. As Sir Peter Medawar has pointed out, there is a great difference between saying: "The dog is barking," and "The dog is annoyed." Before the rise of behaviorism this vital distinction was only too often blurred. We are concerned with barking, and confess to not being able to say anything sensible about the putative state of mind revealed by the behavior of the dog.

To the behaviorist, the term "behavior" is much more extensive than it would be colloquially to the layman. It includes speaking and all measurable bodily reactions, however small and impossible to detect by the naked eye these might be. Thus changes in heart-beat would be included, or the subtle changes in the electrical conductivity of the skin which accompanies even slight alterations in emotion. Changes in the electric pattern of brain waves would count as behavior under this dispensation, and so would the secretion in the urine of catecholamines as a function of emotional experiences. Measures of the electrical changes taking place in the nerves leading to various muscles would constitute "behavior," just as much as the actual movement of these muscles. Most of the reactions studied by psychologists require highly specialized equipment in order to detect them at all, and their interpretation is a matter of considerable expertise. Telemetric methods, *i.e.* the attachment of recording devices to a person who can walk about unfettered because these devices broadcast changes in his behavior to a suitable receiving station, have greatly broadened the field of application of these methods.

"Verbal behavior" is a notion which makes many people uncomfortable. In what way, they ask, is this different from introspection? And if the latter is barred, why should the former be allowed? The answer is a rather simple one. If you say: "I have a headache," then there is no question about your having made this statement. It is in the public domain, and becomes material for scientific research. It cannot, however, be used directly as evidence that in actual fact you were suffering from a headache. That would be introspection, and hence suspect. After all, you might wish to mislead the investigator. Or you might claim to be suffering from a headache in order to escape from some duty. There is no question about your actual statement, but there is a lot of doubt about its meaning and veracity—so much so that special rules have to be framed in order to allow us to use verbal statements. It is one of the main criticisms of psychoanalysis that it uses no such carefully framed rules in dealing with verbal communications, and that it even goes beyond common usage in accepting and interpreting verbal statements as evidence of "unconscious" happenings.

How can we ever be sure that verbal statements can be properly used? Consider a very simple situation. We wish to construct a questionnaire to measure the personality dimension of emotionality or neuroticism. For this purpose we draw on our clinical insight, or on published work, or on our imagination, and write out a set of 100 questions like "I have frequent headhaches" which have to be answered *Yes* or *No* by the respondent. Suppose that one of your subjects says *"Yes."* Clearly you cannot use this as evidence of his having frequent headaches, for the reasons already given. But you can use it as evidence of his *complaining* of headaches; this after all is what he is doing at the moment. Now you can take a group of known and diagnosed neurotics, and compare them with a group of non-neurotic, perfectly normal people. Count the number of times that each group endorses the *"Yes"* answer to this question, and see if the percentages are in fact different. If they are very different, you can say, with complete confidence, that neurotics tend to complain more of headaches than do normals, and you can assign a person of whose status you are in ignorance, to the more probable group on the basis of his endorsement of this (and all the other items). Introspection does not enter into this process. You are dealing throughout with factual, behavioristic events.

Probably more important is another way in which we use verbal statements, namely in relation to sensory discrimination. Suppose you want to know whether bees can "see" colors. This is framed as a "mental" question. You seem to be asking about what goes on in the mind of the bee when it is exposed to a colored stimulus. But we can turn this into a behavioristic question: when presented with a problem which can only be solved by an organism having color vision, can the bee succeed or will it fail?

This is the form of the question chosen by the great
German biologist von Frisch. He presented sugar water in
little bowls which he always placed on blue-colored bits of
paper. In this way the bees would associate the color blue with
food. Later on he would present the same bees with a great
variety of bits of paper, some blue, the others all grey, ranging
in brightness from black to white. The bees unhesitatingly
settled on the blue bits of paper, demonstrating clearly that
they could discriminate the color from the grey bits of paper
having the same brightness. In a similar way a German
pediatrician in the last years of the nineteenth century solved
the problem of whether young babies could discriminate
colors—it used to be thought that they could not do so before
the age of four or thereabouts. He would offer the six-month-
old babies with whom he was working two milk bottles, one
wrapped up in green paper, the other in red paper, of similar
brightness. The green bottle was full of milk, the other was full
of water. The contents were completely hidden by the paper,
so that the babies had to learn (if they could!) to associate the
contents with the color. This they triumphantly did, very soon
grasping the green bottle, and rejecting the red. Thus the
behavior of the babies, and the bees, shows conclusively that
they possess the ability to discriminate color from grey, and
one color from another. It is, of course, possible to go on
beyond this point and determine the exact limitations of their
sensory equipment, *i.e.* how small a difference in shade or
color they can discriminate. There is a whole flourishing
literature on these topics, and discrimination learning is one
of the most important parts of modern psychology.

In principle we could do exactly the same with grown-up
human subjects. If you want to know whether your subject can
distinguish between red and green, you could sit him down in
front of an apparatus with two levers, made of opalescent
glass; inside each lever would be two light bulbs, one red and
one green. You could now work on the principle that each

lever would be illuminated in random order red or green, and that pressure of the green lever would be rewarded with a salted peanut which a properly wired mechanism would send on its way down a chute after the appropriate lever had been pressed. Assuming that your subject was hungry, and liked salted peanuts (both of which facts you could easily establish according to immaculate experimental paradigms), you would soon discover that he managed to learn very quickly to press the lever when illuminated by a green light, and not when it was illuminated by a red light. But, clearly, this would be a foolish way of doing things. You would go out of your way to set up a discriminant situation artificially when a much easier one is readily available—all you have to do is after all to ask your subject to call out the color of a piece of paper which you are showing him! If he can correctly discriminate red from green, then he can signify this by calling out the right color in response to being presented with a colored bit of paper. Given that he had no other cues (such as differential brightness of the bits of paper), his ability to respond verbally in the correct manner is sufficient evidence that he possessed the ability to discriminate colors.

This is the proper behavioristic use of verbal statements. There is no necessary implication in all this about mental events, or about your subject's inner life—his subjective experience of green may be totally different from yours, and indeed correspond to what you would call the mental experience of red. This is quite irrelevant, and there is no known way of solving the implied problem (if it is indeed a meaningful problem). All we are concerned with is his ability to discriminate. Given that, we can say that he is capable of color vision; the inverse does not necessarily follow. If he fails to discriminate, that may be due to actual incapacity, but it may be due to a misplaced sense of humor, or to actual malice. In such a simple situation there is no way of finding out. But if we take more complex situations in which we vary colors and also the differential brightness, or if we make measurements of just noticeable differences along some continuum, then it would be practically impossible to cheat successfully. There are well-known laws associated with these situations which the subject would be unlikely to know, and which would soon indicate that his judgments were made on an arbitrary basis, and did not resemble those of subjects with poor color vision, but honestly trying to do their best. Even an expert familiar with these laws could not cheat successfully for any length of time. The limitations on his sensory equipment would soon give him away.

Discrimination experiments still present some difficulties, but these are of a purely technical kind. Thus some people take more risks in their judgments, others are more careful. Present two different people having the same ability to discriminate with two stimuli differing only very slightly, and ask them if these stimuli are different. One may muster up enough courage to say yes, while the other requires more evidence before committing himself. This kind of problem can be overcome by using "forced choice" methods, *i.e.* by forcing each subject to commit himself each time. Or it can be done by allowing the subject to say how certain he is of his decision, and then going over his pattern of answers statistically to eliminate the influence of decision-making factors. By and large, the use of verbal judgments in the discrimination process is quite well understood, and presents no difficulties to the behaviorist. His use of verbal statements certainly does not carry with it the stigma of introspection in the traditional sense.

In a sense, one might say that almost all psychologists are now behaviorists in the methodological sense. The term ceases to have any discriminatory significance. All it means in fact is that psychologists apply the traditional scientific methods to their particular problems. There are still wide differences between them as to the theories they consider most useful, the problems they consider most important, and the specific methods they consider most appropriate. By thus restricting themselves to that which is observable and measurable psychologists have incurred a lot of criticism and hostility. It is often said that what they leave out is precisely that which most people would like to know about. This is possible, but it is also possible that the questions many people claim to be interested in have no scientific or meaningful answer. The fact that a question can be asked does not mean that it is in principle possible to answer it. However that may be, psychologists have asked certain questions, and discovered certain answers, using the behaviorist methodology. It is with the impact of these discoveries that we must now be concerned.

Before going on to this more substantive region, let me just briefly touch upon the third meaning of the term "behaviorist," *i.e.* the analytical. Mace defines it thus:

To the analytical behaviorist the existence of mind or consciousness defined as irreducibly distinct from matter and its behavior is not even conceivable in any positive terms. It enjoys, so to speak, the status of a prime number which is more than nineteen and less than twenty-three. Statements about mind or consciousness just turn out to be, on analysis, statements about the behavior of material things. Statements about "perceiving" turn out to be statements about "differential responses." Statements about "liking" and "desiring" turn out to be statements about "abient" and "adient" responses, and so on for every kind of "experience" or "psychical phenomenon."

This is in fact a peculiarly modern form of solving a pseudo-problem by submitting it to linguistic analysis. You do not change the facts, but you change your way of talking about the facts. This can be very useful, particularly when the old way of talking about the facts gives rise to inconsistencies and misunderstandings. It can also be very clumsy, and the circumlocutions needed to transform our essentially dualistic language into one appropriate to "analytical behaviorism" can make writing—and reading—even more of a trial than they usually are. For this reason I shall not attempt to do this in what I have to say about the impact of behaviorism. Philosophically minded readers can perform this office for themselves, if they so wish.

Out of all this, behaviorism emerges as something really quite colorless, and without any distinct doctrine. What it has to say is simply that psychology is a scientific discipline; that as such it has the right to pick the concepts which it finds most useful in carrying out its task; and that like other scientific disciplines it has only one request to make of metaphysics— get off my back! Behaviorism is not really a "school" of psychology, in the sense that its teaching has some specific content (as is the case with psychoanalysis, for instance, or the Gestalt school). Under its umbrella there are gathered extremely varied groups of psychologists with little in common other than an urgent desire to get on with the experimental work necessary to give a firm basis to the building up of a modern psychology worthy to be called "scientific." What is there in all this that causes people to wrinkle up their noses and give vent to their spleen?

One answer we may dismiss right from the beginning. It is always possible to find some behaviorist psychologists who, in an unguarded moment, say or write something silly or foolish. It is natural that exception should be taken to this, and no one can complain when such incautious attempts at philosophizing, or at politics, or at ethical writing, are slapped down severely. Watson himself, the founder of behaviorism, provides much material for critics. When he seems to deny the existence of consciousness, for instance, or when he makes impossible claims to be able to bring up any child to achieve anything in the world, provided he is given a free hand in the bringing up. But while such criticisms are salutary, they do not touch behaviorism as such. They concern particular utterances of particular people. Skinner, too, often talks outrageous nonsense (as in his *Walden Two*), and can be properly criticized for doing so. But what he says is his own opinion; it is not Holy Writ which binds other behaviorists. After all, we all do and say things which in our more sagacious moments we may regret. Our more controversial statements are sometimes made in order to make people think (in the manner of the paradoxes of ancient philosophy); it is not reasonable to judge a whole scientific discipline by such isolated outbursts. It is only on points of considerable unanimity that criticisms of a whole movement should be focused. To isolate single statements of individual writers, unrepresentative of the whole body of behaviorists, is a nice knock-down argument, as Humpty Dumpty said, but it is not serious argument.

Another answer is probably much closer to the root difficulty which most people have in taking behaviorism seriously, or even liking it. Sir Cyril Burt voiced this very common view when he complained that modern psychology, having first bargained away its soul and then gone out of its mind, seems now, as it faces an untimely end, to have lost all consciousness. In common parlance, which is intimately bound up with religious beliefs of the immediate past, human conduct is conceived of as purposive, as being mediated through a mind which thinks and governs our actions according to the rules of reason. It is also conceived of as being differentiated from the merely reflex activity of animals by some distinguishing mark which for want of a better term we may call "soul." (English writers, very unlike the French, sometimes tend to except dogs and horses from the universal law which denies soul to animals; female writers sometimes add cats to this privileged sect. The French are more logical in this, but then they have never been known as animal lovers.) Behaviorism, very much like the early materialism of La

Mettrie and Condillac, offends us by refusing to postulate such entities as mind, purpose, and soul. It seems to deny us what we prize most of all—our human heritage. Modern psychology, such is the complaint, reduces us all to Pavlovian dogs, slobbering over their food in conformity with buzzers rung by the experimenter. This is not a flattering picture, and we do not recognize ourselves in it. Surely a Mozart symphony, a da Vinci statue, a Rembrandt portrait, a Goethe lyric, a Shakespeare sonnet are qualitatively different from the products of the experimentalist's probings. Surely watching rats run mazes can tell us nothing about the specifically human problems on which our interest centers?*

These are not unreasonable objections, even though they

---

* In his book *The Ghost in the Machine,* Arthur Koestler has put the case with his customary clarity. "It is impossible to arrive at a diagnosis of man's predicament—and by implication at a therapy—by starting from a psychology which denies the existence of mind, and lives on specious analogies derived from bar-pressing activities of rats. The record of fifty years of ratomorphic psychology is comparable in its sterile pedantry to that of scholasticism in its period of decline, when it had fallen to counting angels on pin-heads—although this sounds a more attractive pastime than counting the number of bar-pressings in the box."

Note that Koestler has no doubt that the analogies *are* specious. No evidence is given, and the many experimental demonstrations that laws derived from rats-in-the-box can often be extrapolated to humans are passed over in contemptuous silence. And also note Koestler's predilection for counting non-existent angels as compared with the very real rats and their bar-presses; the anti-scientific spirit in human affairs could not wish for a more eloquent swan song!

Koestler and his many philosophical friends never seem to ask themselves what the alternative might be to behaviorism, or why those 19th-century psychologists who indulged in introspection and attempted to elucidate the laws of the "mind" failed so utterly. Psychologists are not blind. Show them a better, more successful method of working, and they will gladly join in. What seems so useless to them is the shrill, pseudo-philosophical condemnation of all that they are doing, without any attempt to put something better in its place. Many of the criticisms are justified, no doubt. What part of science is not subject to criticism? But in science criticism which does not suggest alternatives and improvements is empty and useless—particularly when it argues from philosophical and religious are emotional in essence. They resemble the complaints which arose when Copernicus banished the earth from its honorific position at the center of the universe and enthroned the sun there, or when Darwin dared to demonstrate our affinity through evolution, with flatworms, wart-hogs, and monkeys. These were all severe blows to our self-respect. We have survived the first two, and no doubt we will survive the third. What Copernicus and Darwin started, Pavlov has finished, and little thanks any of them received for their labors! There is, I am afraid, little anyone can say which will lessen the emotional reaction. Just as the Aristotelians refused to look through Galileo's telescope to see the four moons of Jupiter, so their modern counterparts refuse to look at the evidence demonstrating the important part which conditioning plays in determining human behavior. But there may be some rational objections mixed up with the emotional. (Just as in the case of the heliocentric theory there were many perfectly sound astronomical objections mixed up with the irrelevant emotional ones. The absence of stellar parallax, for instance, was a very difficult stumbling block for all those who accepted the heliocentric theory; the reply that this failure to observe parallax was due to the incredibly large distances involved was not considered very strong as there was no outside evidence for these distances, so that the whole thing seemed little better than a circular argument.) It may be useful to look at these rational objections, and to note that the behaviorist position can be phrased in two ways—one strong, the other weak.

THE STRONG POSITION would be that all human behavior is determined by general psychological laws; that these laws operate on an organism through the agencies of

premises, rather than from detailed experimental findings.

Has behaviorism actually failed? A fair-minded view of what it has achieved would not perhaps regard it as a wonder child, but it would also not consider it as a mental defective, which is the impression any reader of Koestler's book might receive.

heredity and environment; and that the function of psychology is to determine these laws in order to explain, predict, and control human conduct—just as through our knowledge of physical laws we explain, predict, and control the actions and movements of physical bodies. This view is probably held implicitly rather than explicitly by many psychologists. It is not illogical, but neither is it in itself a scientific view—it is a philosophical belief which is not at the moment subject to empirical proof, and in so far as empirical evidence is available it does not seem to favor this conception.

We are only just beginning to formulate far-ranging scientific laws in some of the physical sciences, while in others (such as cryogenics) we are still unable to proceed very far in this direction. But already we have found (as in the case of the Heisenberg uncertainty principle) that Determinism with a capital D is not an empirically supportable proposition. The discovery that in principle it is impossible to determine both the position and the velocity of an electron with complete accuracy, and that there is an irreducible quantum error involved which makes the determination of the one less accurate as we increase the accuracy of determination of the other, has made the kind of determinism popularized by Laplace untenable. If we believe that brain action is fundamentally responsible for conduct, then it follows that only the complete determination of brain action (down to the movement of every electron and every proton) can guarantee complete determination of conduct. The former being impossible on Heisenberg's principle, the latter also cannot reasonably be postulated. Hence as far as the scientific evidence goes, the strong form of behaviorism is not supported. It does not, of course, follow that the lack of support for complete determinism favors free will as an alternative. Physicists are by no means clear just what the implications of Heisenberg's principle are, but free will is not generally favored as an alternative. It is possible that the proper alternative is chance, which would not please those who favor the notion of free will on religious or other grounds. It is also possible that the movements and positions of electrons are in fact determined, but that for obvious reasons of observer interference we are barred from carrying out the necessary measurements to prove this point. It is even possible that this barrier is not absolute; many physicists think so at the moment, but others (including Einstein) did not and do not. There is little point in looking into the future; prophecy should be left to prophets. As of now the answer is that we do not know what the boundaries are to complete determinism. If this is so in physics, surely it would be unwise to claim more for psychology?

If we reject the strong position, we are on much safer grounds if we embrace the weak position. This simply says that our actions are determined in part (in large part, if you like) by heredity and environment, and that the function of psychology is to discover the laws according to which this determination takes place. We are not obliged to posit that every action is so caused. Our explanation may at most be partial. It is left to empirical observation to decide the degree to which deterministic explanation can be pushed. We do not set any limit; it is possible that we may end up by achieving complete success, in which case the strong position would coincide with the weak position. However, the strong position would then cease to be a philosophical belief, and be instead a scientifically proven doctrine. Such wonders are, of course, very much in the future. At the moment there is no suggestion even that we would ever be able to predict human actions with complete certainty, or explain them in detail in accordance with some set of general laws. Let us be modest; we have much to be modest about! But in that modesty there is also strength.

The weak position can be submitted to proof so overwhelming that no one familiar with the evidence can doubt the essential correctness of that position. Even simple common sense tells us that human beings are to some degree influenced by incentives, behave under certain circumstances according to prediction, and that their behavior can sometimes be controlled by the manipulation of suitable stimuli. Nothing more than this is needed to set up behaviorism in business. If there are some invariables in human conduct, then these can be searched out, their limitations determined, and their precise detail made subject to law. In this, psychology resembles physics in its modern, chastened mood. Both gladly leave metaphysics and arguments about free will and the like to philosophy, and instead of arguing about such sublime matters get on with the job of finding out just what they can do, how much they can predict, and to what extent they can control the variables which constitute their subject matter. If you wish to postulate a mind, or a soul, or even an unconscious, you are of course free to do so. All that the psychologist says is that these concepts do not enter into his formulae. And if you reply: "So much the worse for your formulae!" he would not be prepared to argue. The degree of his success in doing his job without recourse to such philosophical concepts will ultimately tell whether his choice was or was not a wise one. It does not seem that such a humble claim should call forth such vituperation; perhaps there is still a cloven hoof hidden under the trousers?

The cloven hoof is contained in the term: " . . . doing his job." What is the job of the psychologist? Surely it is to discover the facts relating to human behavior and conduct; to formulate theories on the basis of these facts; and, finally, to proclaim such laws as might seem justified in the light of his discoveries. These laws, theories, and discoveries could then with advantage be used and applied by an enlightened society in dealing with the multifarious problems which are thrown up in education, criminology, psychiatry, politics and social life generally. This may sound a tall order, but where problems are so very difficult and pressing as in these fields, surely even a little knowledge may be of advantage. Would we prefer to act in ignorance, or depend on hearsay, tradition, and past experience? Unfortunately the answer to this rhetorical question is almost certainly "Yes," and it is this sad truth which accounts for much of the opprobrium which is cast upon psychology. Psychological problems have always existed, and have been recognized since time immemorial. Specialists have arisen in order to deal with these problems. We have teachers, priests, doctors, politicians, managers, judges, prison officers and many others who have a stake in this matter. It cannot be assumed that they would welcome a newcomer who claims to attack with scientific precision problems which they themselves have dealt with in at best a common sense manner, and at worst in such a way as to make matters worse, rather than better. There are so many vested interests in the fields that psychology covers, and so many strong and at the same time vulnerable egos holding rigid opinions, that it would be a miracle if the voice of psychology were not drowned by the cries of dissent and pained surprise. And of course the people in question, who would have most to gain in terms of efficiency, and most to lose in terms of *amour propre*, are precisely those who hold all the positions of influence and power in education, in criminology, in psychiatry, and in all the other fields I have mentioned.

Let me illustrate the kind of situation that may arise when these two forces—the questing scientific spirit of psychology, and the dead hand of establishment authority—come up against each other. The event occurred shortly after I had obtained my first job ever—research psychologist in the wartime Mill Hill Emergency Hospital, which looked after mentally disturbed war casualties, mostly neurotic. In theory, these were given a diagnosis and then treatment was prescribed according to the particular "illness" that had been diagnosed—anxiety state, hysteria, schizophrenia, or what not. This medical model might or might not be suitable for

conduct disorders of the kind in question. What was obvious
was that this model requires that diagnosis should be
reasonably reliable—in other words, one psychiatrist's
diagnosis should agree with that of another, if both should
happen to see the same patient.

I had another reason for being concerned with this
problem. I was giving personality tests to patients variously
diagnosed, in the hope of discovering evidence for or against
the theory advanced by Jung that anxiety states and other
anxious patients were of an introverted personality type, while
hysterics were of an extroverted personality type. Clearly if the
diagnosis was unreliable, then no differences could be
expected to emerge on test results between two groups chosen
so as to represent anxiety states and hysterics. Now, as it
happened, patients were often transferred from one "house"
to another, with consequent change in doctor; hence many
patients were given two diagnoses by two different doctors.
These were not strictly independent, as the second doctor
knew the first doctor's diagnosis, and had his reports available
for study. It seemed interesting to me to find out just how
much agreement there was between the diagnoses given by
these different doctors. Accordingly, off I went to ask the
permission of the superintendent for carrying out this simple
piece of statistics.

He received me in a fatherly fashion, and listened
patiently to my plan. Then, to my surprise, he suggested that
there were so many more interesting things that could be
done, it would be a pity to waste my time in this fashion. After
all, did not everyone know that these psychiatrists had been
well trained, had medical degrees, and could therefore (almost
by definition) do no wrong? When I cheerfully suggested that
even such supermen might welcome definitive proof of the
reliability of their judgments he became more serious and
argued that it would be quite unbecoming for someone so
young, and in addition not medically qualified, to seem to

throw doubt on the accuracy of the work done by his elders and betters. And when I answered that I was not throwing doubt on anything or anybody, but just wanted to know with some precision how accurate these difficult and complex judgments could be, he told me in no uncertain terms that I was at liberty to collect these data, but I was also at liberty to look for another job. This argument seemed a winner, and I acknowledged its superior force by withdrawing from the unequal contest. I did, to be sure, collect my data but kept rather quiet about it.

The outcome was much as one might have expected. There was very little agreement between psychiatrists in their diagnoses, in spite of the contamination of the second judgment by knowledge of the first. This finding has been duplicated many times since. There is no doubt at all that diagnoses are highly unreliable, in the sense that they cannot be replicated by other psychiatrists. Within a given institution, or sometimes even within a given country, broad diagnostic categories can with some accuracy be distinguished, *e.g.* psychosis versus neurosis; but even this is not so when we take a broader view. A large international research unit working at the Maudsley has been taking closed-circuit television film of diagnostic interviews, and had the patients diagnosed by psychiatrists of good repute. It was found that chances of a given patient being diagnosed "schizophrenic" were five times as high if the psychiatrist was American as when he was British! This means, of course, that research results, outcomes of drug trials, and generalizations about the effects of therapy cannot transcend national boundaries. What is true of American schizophrenics is not necessarily true of British ones, and vice versa. It has also been shown that the relation between treatment and diagnosis is by no means close; psychiatrists seem to have their favorite treatments which they administer regardless of diagnosis, so that even if diagnosis were miraculously made very accurate, it would still not influence treatment very much. All these are important items of knowledge, and you might have thought that psychiatrists would be happy to have them, and be grateful to psychologists for pointing them out. But no such thing. Information of this kind is usually received in icy silence, and the usual comment is either that no one should pay any attention to this sort of thing, or else that in some mysterious manner the medical model, which regards neurotic behaviors as specifiable diseases, works in spite of the possible deficiencies of some of its parts.

Similar reactions are not infrequent in other fields. Educationalists are often given to bursts of enthusiasm for new methods, or new versions of old methods, and then there is a sudden change from one set to another. In Britain, for example, grammar schools and selection at 11+ are followed by comprehensive and no selection. No doubt in another twenty years we will be treated to a "new wave" of progressive opinion in favor of grammar schools (perhaps under some new name) and selection. These are fads, and it is important to recognize that they are not based on any factual evidence whatever. Just so did our mothers feed babies on schedule, while we feed babies on demand—it will be interesting to see whether our daughters will return to schedule feeding! There is not an ounce of evidence to suggest that one method is better than another. Indeed the probability is that whether a method is suitable in a given case depends on the personality of the baby (and possibly of his mother)—extroverted babies are likely to thrive on demand feeding, introverted ones on schedule feeding.*

I have discussed some of the evidence in the chapter on the mediocracy, and it will be remembered that some of the

---

* Psychoanalysts would probably invert this statement, and say that demand feeding is likely to produce extroverted babies, schedule feeding introverted ones. What a fascinating experiment this would make! Extrovert or introvert children on demand—or on schedule.

consequences of "going comprehensive" might be desirable for some types of children, some undesirable for other types of children. But such complexities are often lost on educationalists or politicians enthusiastic over the new system. Demands for research or proof are brushed aside, and the unsuspecting nation is committed to some new venture which might or might not work just a little better than what it replaces. And the most deadly venom is reserved for those who throw doubts on the new venture on the grounds that such proof is lacking. Political opposition is something politicians can understand, but a demand for scientific documentation, for experimental support, for *evidence*—that is clearly too much.

Judges and other people concerned with the administration of the law are often similarly inclined when it comes to discussions of ways and means of improving our dealings with criminals, and of substituting the notion of reclamation for that of punishment. In some way the idea has gained ground that judges (who sentence criminals) and wardens (who keep them under lock and key) are experts in criminology, and must know the answers to questions in this field. Yet nothing could be further from the truth. Judges by definition know nothing of the criminals they sentence. (They are not allowed to speak to them outside the confines of the courtroom, for obvious reasons; they do not know criminals' relatives, their friends, their circumstances, their temptations—and in most cases cannot even imagine these, coming from a quite different social class.) They know little of the effects of their sentence—does it discourage the particular criminals in question, does it make them vengeful, does it bring them in contact with more sophisticated criminals who can teach them to be better criminals and avoid arrest in future? There is no feedback in the typical courtroom situation. The judge's decision lacks any basis of information on the effects of previous decisions, and he is never brought up against the consequences of his decision. Add to all this that he is constantly flattered, and surrounded by lackeys who make sure that no criticism of any kind is made of his action, and it becomes clear why judges tend to have such a holier-than-thou conviction of certitude and rectitude which may impress the *canaille,* but has little scientific standing. And what applies to judges applies to most other legal appendages. Their knowledge is of the working of the legal system, not of the web of consequences which is set in motion by the court proceedings. Only strictly quantified follow-up studies of prisoners so convicted can give us the needed feedback, and these can only be undertaken by experts in the social sciences—not by legal experts or guardians.

It will be obvious by now what I am suggesting. There are traditional methods of dealing with human problems, and there are highly honored figures in each of these professions who pass as "experts" in these fields. Psychologists coming into contact with one or another field of human behavior will inevitably adopt a scientific attitude towards it, which means that they will question the value and adequacy of the methods in use, and the competence of the people employing and devising these methods. Such questioning, however well intentioned, and however obviously needed, will be regarded with considerable hostility by those posing as "experts." After all, to them it presents a direct threat to their position, renown and fiscal standing.

Hence there are very good reasons why psychology in general, and behaviorism in particular, is so heartily disliked. It calls the bluff on which so much of our daily life is based, and offends the establishment which is responsible for the introduction and the working of the methods exposed as unsatisfactory by the upstart scientists. Science, after all, is dynamite—the effects of the industrial revolution bid fair to be excelled by the effects of the psychological revolution, and Luddites can smell this kind of effect many miles off! There is thus nothing mysterious about the bad odor in which psychology is held. The very promise of "doing better," and substituting knowledge for ignorance, science for superstition, success for failure is an obvious threat to all those who have for so long, and in such a disastrous fashion, held on to the levers of power.

Yet to many people far removed from these "levers of power" the promise of the psychological century is far from reassuring. What the psychologist is really suggesting is simply that social action should be based on research. Before abandoning the grammar school and selection principle, he would say, do a large-scale experiment with comprehensives so that your action is based on knowledge. If you want to rehabilitate your criminals, he would say, set aside a whole large prison and use it for research purposes, with long-term follow-ups, proper comparisons with suitable control subjects in other types of prison, and with provision for the use of token economies or any other type of treatment that seems suitable on psychological grounds. If you want to cure neurotics, set up a special hospital in which large-scale control trials can be held of behavior therapy, aversion therapy, the use of token economies, implosion therapy, or whatever the psychological laboratory might suggest. In other words, before undertaking any large-scale social action, experiment until you know what you are doing; then you can go ahead with much more confidence, on the basis of certain knowledge of what the consequences would be.

This is a call for an *experimental* society. Before the scientist builds a bridge, or constructs a new ship, or designs a new factory, he carries out experiments to supplement his knowledge of what is involved; hence he is seldom mistaken in his belief that the bridge will stand, the ship will sail, and the new factory will not fall down. Why not try this same method in social life? Is it likely to prove worse than what we have at the moment? The wisdom of educationalists, doctors and judges has been with us for centuries, even millenia. Yet are our mental hospitals empty? Are our children better educated? Are we getting ready to pull down our prisons? If traditional wisdom is working so well, why is the number of mentally ill increasing so tremendously? Why is the crime rate rising every year in a truly terrifying fashion? Why is there so much trouble in schools, and why is there so much dissatisfaction with the way our children are taught, and the amount they learn? Clearly, if everything in the garden were lovely, there would be no need for scientific methods. The fact that everything is getting worse, and rapidly, suggests that perhaps a change in method may be useful and timely.

But, it is objected, people are not guinea pigs. You cannot seriously suggest that these experiments should be carried out on actual people, on children, criminals, neurotics, or what not? Psychologists may be tolerated as long as they stay in their laboratories. To suggest that we should carry out experiments in our social life, using actual people—no, that is just *too* much! Perhaps so, but remember that these experiments are being carried out all the time in any case. Old school systems are being abolished and new school systems are being introduced, changes are being made in the laws governing homosexuality and many other crimes, new methods of treatment are being introduced into hospitals. Nothing is standing still, and the lives of millions of people are constantly being affected by what sometimes politicians even call "experiments." New towns are being built, slum clearance is being carried out—these are all "experiments" of a kind. The changes are being made all right. What is lacking is the control group and the feedback. In other words, that which people object to ("being treated as guinea pigs") *is* taking place, but without any of the advantages which would accrue if the whole operation were run as a proper experiment. When in England all the grammar schools have been abolished, and all children are taught in comprehensives, we will be as ignorant as before about the precise effects of the change-over, because no one will have thought of the importance of documenting the changes in the educational consequences, or of arranging the whole thing in such a manner that proper scientific conclusions could be drawn from it. New towns will be built, but there will be no provision for research teams to be present from the beginning to study the precise consequences of this or that decision, to investigate the exact way in which the new population accommodates to the new surroundings, and the errors which inevitably will have been made by those planning the whole venture. Hence when another new town is being built, there will be no scientific knowledge to guide the builders and planners, and exactly the same mistakes will be made again. Where there is no feedback, there is no growth of knowledge. Where the whole venture has not been arranged properly from the beginning as an experiment, few conclusions can be drawn with any certainty.

PEOPLE NOT CONCERNED with such matters do not often have any real appreciation of how little facts and proof matter to most of those who are concerned with the guidance of affairs, whether political, educational, medical, or what not. Perhaps the sad but illuminating story of Dr. Ignaz Philipp Semmelweiss will give them some glimmer of an understanding of just what goes on when facts come up against the massive conservatism of establishment opinion. Semmelweiss was born in Budapest in 1818 and qualified as a doctor in 1844. He was appalled at the death rates among young mothers due to puerperal fever, itself mainly due to *Streptococcus Haemolyticus* invading the fresh cuts of the new mother, *ie.* the lacerations of the birth canal. When the bacteria reached the general circulation, septicaemia set in, usually followed by high temperature, delirium, and finally death. Death rates of 30 per cent were not uncommon, although this then mysterious disease seemed to run in cycles which were totally unpredictable. Infection was spread from woman to woman through the hands of students, midwives and doctors as they went from one infected patient to others not yet infected. Sterilization and even simple hand washing were unknown, as was of course the existence of such things as bacteria. It was Semmelweiss who first drew attention to the need for cleanliness. He objected to students going straight from autopsy room into delivery room, and had wash-basins placed between the two in which students were told to wash their hands. The students, in the sacred cause of academic freedom, objected, and would have nothing to do with all this washing. Semmelweiss, a small and excitable man, called them murderers. He was dismissed the day after. Did he have any facts on his side? Well, it was known that the mortality rate of women looked after by students was far higher than that of women looked after by midwives. Midwives, of course, never carried out autopsies, or came into contact with the dead.

Then came an unexpected event which seemed to prove Semmelweiss' rather nebulous speculations. His friend, the anatomist Jacob Kolletschkan died. He had received a small scratch during a dissection, and at the post-mortem all the symptoms of puerperal fever appeared in the dead man. Semmelweiss now put forward his theory in a more precise form: "Puerperal fever is a blood poisoning produced by the poison that forms in the corpse. . . . It is transmitted to the pregnant woman by the examining doctor." Semmelweiss was offered a post at a maternity clinic to test his theories. He replaced midwives by students (in order to make his experiments more scientific) and the death rate jumped from 9 per cent to 27 per cent; when students were made to wash their hands in chlorinated water before any examination, it fell to less than 1 per cent. Would this convince an uncommitted reader? It did not convince the medical profession. Many high-ranking obstetricians came to see, but did not stay to praise.

Semmelweiss simply could not get anyone to follow his practice. No wonder he became frantic and called his eminent colleagues "murderers"—to be dismissed again in 1849. He returned to Hungary, and successfully replicated his feat of lowering maternal fatalities to less than 1 per cent; even this did not convince the skeptics. At the Congress of Gynaecology in Paris in 1858, the President had this to say of Semmelweiss's theories:

It is possible that these are based on some useful principles, but the correct execution of them entails such difficulties that the highly problematical results do not warrant putting them into practice.

Semmelweiss died in 1865, at the young age of forty-seven. The cause of death, ironically enough, was septicaemia, caused by an infected wound received during his last post-mortem examination. As the poem says, and as he would have wished, we do *"when the forts of folly fall, find his body by the wall . . . "* The very day before his death Lister started his work of disinfecting wounds experimentally, and Pasteur was laying the foundations of modern bacteriology. Lister wrote his obituary when he said: "Without Semmelweiss my achievements would be nothing. To this great son of Hungary surgery owes most."

It is hardly necessary to comment on this story. These particular forts of folly have indeed finally fallen, but there are many others. The establishment (any establishment) will fight to the death for its right to defend them long after common sense and scientific proof have shown them to be imaginary. And none of these forts are defended so stubbornly as those housing the errors, the mistakes, and the follies of amateur psychology.

I MUST NOW TURN to another argument against behaviorism which is responsible for much of the antagonism which it encounters. This may be called the ethical or brainwashing argument. Essentially what is asserted is that behavioristic methods of treatment (the argument is usually broadened beyond psychiatric treatment, but it is most frequently employed in relation to methods such as aversion therapy) are inhuman and inhumane; that they treat human beings as objects, rather than as individuals; and that they introduce punishment and even torture into the healing situation. This cry of "Torture!" is of course highly emotional, so much so that one begins to wonder about the motivation behind its use. Nevertheless the argument must be taken seriously, even when it is taken to such extremes (*e.g.* by R.D. Laing) that all of orthodox psychiatry is put in the dock alongside behavior therapy.

Taken in its broadest form, the argument says that people are entitled to live their own lives, and to be safe from interference by busybodies like psychiatrists who are merely there as society's policemen. Their main function is to make everyone conform, and in the service of ensuring conformity they take the poor "mental patient," so called, and psychoanalyse him, give him electroshocks, perform leucotomies, give him drugs, or do aversion therapy. This is of course a caricature of what goes on, but it has some grim elements of warning in it. In the U.S.S.R. it seems now to be official doctrine that to be dissatisfied with the government is to be mad, and eminent intellectual critics, instead of being killed outright or shipped to labor camps, are now sent to mental hospitals where they are declared insane and subjected to putatively "curative" treatments. In much the same way, but not hitherto as outspokenly or as part of government policy, does the U.S.A. treat some extremist non-conformists; to be a "subversive" is often regarded as *ipso facto* evidence of mental disorder, and the suggestion is often made that such people should be medically treated. It is hardly necessary to point out the absurdity of such notions, or to protest against them. There cannot—or should not—be many people in a liberal democracy who would consider such methods as appropriate weapons against any political or social belief. But the danger is omnipresent, and Laing and his colleagues perform a useful service in drawing attention to it; this is a pit into which we must never fall.

But the notion that the people who are in treatment by psychiatrists in general, or by behavior therapists in particular, are in any remote sense of this kind is simply not tenable. Consider just some of the kinds of problems which are encountered by the busy therapist, and then ask yourself whether what he is faced with, and what he does, smacks of "torture" even in the most recondite sense.

Let me start with children who are behaving in a self-injurious fashion, *i.e.* they bang their heads against hard objects (often so hard that the retinas become detached); they tear or bite off pieces of flesh from their bodies; they may cut themselves dreadfully, or even kick themselves, or throw themselves off high places. Some kind-hearted people have thought that these children need love and affection. But it has been found that physical demonstrations of affection, and kindly, sympathetic and reassuring comments made to such children when engaged on self-destructive activities, make them even worse. However kind it sounds, such behavior simply does not work. As stated previously, it seems that whatever the origins of such self-injurious behavior, it is maintained in part by its social consequences, *i.e.* by the attention which it causes, the affection and sympathy which it produces, and the general concern evinced by all those around. Behavior therapists, working on this hypothesis, have shown that these very troublesome patterns of behavior can be eliminated in the space of a few hours by introducing social withdrawal whenever self-injurious behavior is manifested. The adults or children present simply withdraw without comment until the behavior ceases. When the particular type of behavior in question is too dangerous to be left unattended, a few mild electric shocks administered whenever the behavior in question begins, seem to abort it successfully. In one case, a schizophrenic boy had engaged in self-destructive behavior since he was two. When his physical restraints were removed he performed 3,000 responses including hitting himself during a 90-minute period! Four sessions, involving twelve electric shocks, almost completely eliminated this type of self-injury. Another girl had engaged in self-destructive behavior for over six years. Her head-beating was rapidly and permanently removed by the administration of a total of fifteen shocks. It should be noted that not only are these "symptoms" removed by the shock treatment and the social isolation attendant upon self-injury; general social functioning is also usually considerably improved. Children become more attentive and socially responsive, and their greater imitativeness enables them to acquire new and better patterns of adjustment. There is admittedly "torture" in all this administration of mild electric shocks (such as many students of psychology willingly suffer as subjects in experiments). But consider the alternatives.

Either the children are kept for months and years in restraints which make impossible any proper development, or the acquisition of much-needed social adjustments; or else they are left free, and allowed to literally blind themselves, or even kill themselves. These are not ethical problems to be discussed over the port at High Table. They are literally matters of life and death for the unfortunate children, and their even more unfortunate parents.

Imagine that you were the parent of a certain autistic three-year-old boy, whose social and verbal developments were grossly retarded, and who in addition exhibited violent tantrums which included head-banging, face-clapping, hair-pulling and face-scratching. After a trantrum, badly bruised and bleeding, he would refuse to sleep at night, forcing his parents to remain by his bedside. Sedatives, tranquillizers and physical restraints were tried without success. Finally, his refusal to wear eyeglasses (necessitated by the removal of cataractal lenses) endangered his eyesight.

What would you do? Refuse to let the psychologist treat him through behavior therapy, because you had ethical scruples or regarded such methods as "torture"? By a simple regime of social isolation whenever the boy misbehaved (no shocks!) he was completely cured in a few weeks. Even social isolation, of course, is "aversive" or "punitive" if you like, and the experiment was almost wrecked when some kind-hearted attendants spoke kindly to the boy when escorting him to his room and showered him with attention when taking him back! Many people confuse outwardly kind behavior (which may reinforce wrong and self-destructive conduct in the patient) with truly kind behavior, *i.e.* behavior leading to a cure for whatever ails the patient. Do-gooders often object to the latter because it may superficially seem unkind in the former sense. These are cases where we cannot let the heart overrule the head.

Take quite another type of case, already briefly mentioned in an earlier chapter. Suppose your son was addicted to heroin, and you were told that the most likely outcome was that he would be dead within five years. There are no known methods which would produce a cure with any degree of certainty. Would you agree to his receiving aversion therapy? He would be injected with the drug scoline, which after a short while paralyses his musculature for a minute or so, so that he could not breathe. This terrifying loss of the ability to breathe would be preceded about a second earlier by a self-administered injection of heroin, so that the injection becomes the conditioned stimulus, the paralysis the unconditioned stimulus. By the simple conditioning paradigm, after a few repetitions of this pairing of the injection and the paralysis, the former should now produce the fear and anxiety appropriate to the latter, and thus effectively prevent the patient from ever again injecting himself with heroin (or indeed anything else!). This seems to work very well. Investigations of ten or so patients in which random and unheralded urine analyses were carried out to detect whether they were still users of heroin cleared them in a follow-up study. All this, of course, needs confirmation and longer follow-up, but it is the most promising and the quickest method for treating these unfortunates which has yet been discovered. Is this torture? Would you advise your son against it—considering the alternatives? I have no doubt what my own answer would be. Mild ethical objections cannot compete with the urgency of saving a person's life.

HOW ABOUT sexual deviations which do not endanger a person's life, but might be said to be little but socially disapproved acts of no great importance—homosexuality, say, or transvestism, or fetishism? Here, admittedly, social pressure is important and may be the ultimate reason why a patient comes for treatment. The pressure may come from his wife; treatment may seem better to the patient than the breakup of his marriage. Or it may come from society in the broadest sense: seek treatment or go to prison! It is often difficult to unravel the strands of causation which lead the patient to the treatment room, but what is usually certain is that he has made a choice, given the various pressures and demands on him, which emphasizes the desirability of change. He had determined that he would be better off if he could slough off his homosexuality, or his cross-dressing habits, or his fetishisms. Many such patients are genuinely ashamed of these habits; there is not always overt pressure from society or its representatives. But whatever the reasons why a person comes for help, would it be ethical to refuse it, assuming that it were in our power to "cure" him?

A few years ago, before the methods of treatment for homosexuality had been sufficiently worked out to be routinely applicable, I gave a talk about behavior therapy at the Guildhall (as one of the Granada lectures). After it was over a famous Q.C., much respected in the legal world, came to see me and asked if I could suggest someone to him who could treat his homosexuality. He had been in psychoanalysis for several years, but without any benefit, and thought the methods I was suggesting might work. I had to decline; no one at the time was ready to use these methods. A few weeks later he committed suicide. It is easy for philosophers to say that homosexuals (and all the other sexual deviants) are being pressurized into treatment by society, and that it is unethical to treat them because they do not genuinely come "of their own free will" (whatever that may mean). Is it ethical to leave such a person to his troubles, and permit him to kill himself because he cannot get the help he needs?

I recognize, of course, that there are problems of an ethical nature attending all these treatments. What I cannot see, however, is that these problems are any different for behavior therapy than they are for other methods of treatment, or that we should assume without proof that the behavior therapist does what he finds works well because he is in fact a sadist who wants to hurt people and give them electric shocks, rather than because these are the only methods which at the moment can cure the patient who comes to him for help.

It is interesting that these discussions involve in nearly every case aversion therapy, rather than the removal of anxieties through desensitization, or retraining through modelling. Yet when all the cases treated by behavior therapy are considered, aversion therapy is used in hardly more than one out of a hundred. It is indeed difficult to see how removing a patient's phobias and anxieties, which have hag-ridden him for many years, can be put under the heading of "brain-washing." Nevertheless many philosophers and psychiatrists have tried to do so. I will spare the reader a refutation. There are statements which are so absurd in themselves that rational argument becomes impossible. If you feel that your common humanity is offended because someone who is driven to despair because of his vague fears and anxieties is offered a quick lasting cure by a process of desensitization, in which he is taught relaxation and imagines the sources of his terrors, then nothing I can say will have any effect. The only cure would be to go into a mental hospital and talk with a few patients.

I sometimes feel that the very success of behavior therapy is in fact the cause of the dislike of behaviorism. One can talk rather light-heartedly about psychoanalysis, in a literary sort of way, because whatever its attractions it clearly does not work. In other words, it does not constitute a danger. But suddenly society is confronted with a technology which is genuinely based on science, and which does work. Obviously this produces all sorts of defense reactions, of self-interested refusals to deal with the newcomer, and of hostile murmurings. There is an obvious swing against science. The savior of the nineteenth century has become the Frankenstein monster of the twentieth. This reaction is, of course, unreasonable. Science has given us power, but the objection is not against the power itself, but against the use which we make of it. It is pointless to blame the scientists for doing what we want, *i.e.* giving us the knowledge and the technology which can produce cars and television and planes and atomic bombs. The fault clearly lies in ourselves who do not know what to do with this Pandora's box. The confrontation between socially responsible science and socially irresponsible politicians is wonderfully portrayed in the story of how the decision was made (by politicians, against the earnest advice of scientists) to drop the first atomic bombs on Japan. In fact, the history of how politicians and military people took over the entire project and pushed it to its absurd and fatal conclusion should be made compulsory reading. However this may be, there is little doubt that this general concern about the benevolence of science has affected people's judgment of psychology. In a way, the more scientific and successful it is, the greater are their doubts about it. The objections will, of course, not always be rational ones, but they will still be heartfelt and it is this "backlash" phenomenon which accounts for much of the unpopularity of behaviorism.

The "inhumanity" of behavioristic methods is one of the stock-in-trade objections made, and we have already seen how thin this argument is when seen against the beneficial effects of behavior therapy. A more recent example is of some interest, because it involves government intervention. We have seen in a previous chapter how the introduction of a "token economy" into a chronic mental hospital ward can work seeming wonders in rehabilitating the in-patients. Yet these methods were banned in several states in the U.S.A. as inflicting cruelty on the inmates. How so?

The answer was that these inmates had a legal right to food, television viewing, and all the other entertainments which in the token economy they had to earn through their own exertions. It was considered cruel to deprive them of all these things, even in the interests of treatment. Thus we have the cloud-cuckoo-land doctrine that patients are better off ill, incapable, and incompetent than they are when capable of rational behavior, self-supporting, and able to live ordinary lives in the outside world! All our lives are built up on the rule of social contingencies. We receive what we earn—by work, by good behavior, by kindness. Patients are thrust into an environment which abrogates these rules. They are attended to when they behave badly, they receive kindness when they are obstreperous, they are talked to when they are irrational. No wonder that often in this topsy-turvy world they get worse, not better. There is much evidence, as we saw in the chapter on behaviorist technology, that much of their "madness" is in fact hospital-produced. Now the kindly state, in its wisdom, ordains that a regime which makes patients madder shall continue, and that a regime which cures them and makes them able to take part in a world where contingencies govern behavior shall be outlawed—all in the name of kindness!

This interesting reaction to behavioristic success is likely to set a pattern. Much the same sort of objection is being heard in relation to criminals. We have no hesitation in keeping them locked up under conditions which ensure that they should learn none of the skills which alone could make them useful citizens when they have finished their sentences. We make certain that they should accumulate as much hatred of the laws and rules of society as possible in the time they spend in prison. And we take care that they should learn from fellow prisoners how to do better next time. But suggest methods such as the token economy which would at least make a beginning in teaching them the rules of social contingencies which they never learned outside prison, and immediately the defenders of prisoners' rights rise up in wrath! Talk about rehabilitation is fine, but the moment the actuality comes into view, and threatens really to work, there are all sorts of reasons and excuses why such methods must not be used. Truly, Semmelweiss was not the last of the innovators to beat his head against a brick wall. Modern establishments have learned nothing from his persecutors.

There is, thus, an anti-scientific reaction, and arguments about the ethics and the "inhumanity" of behavioristic methods are really beside the point. What is at issue is the extension of science to human behavior. I am sure that the general feeling that there is too much science, and that we should declare a moratorium on further advances, is mistaken. It is an emotional, not a rational reaction to our problems. A good case could be made out for the notion that as the last century was that of physics, this century is that of biology, and the next (if there be one) is that of psychology. We have answered many of the practical questions we have to ask of physics; we are in process of answering many of the practical questions we have to ask of biology. For the future our most important questions are bound to be psychological.

We have conquered nature; now we have to conquer ourselves or go under. We have tried religion and failed; we have tried politics and failed; we cannot afford many more failures. If only we could divert some of the countless millions which we still pour into physical and chemical research into biology and psychology instead; the theoretical and practical rewards would be immense. We know enough to say with confidence that it is possible to rehabilitate criminals, to cure neurotics, to improve educational practices beyond recognition. We know enough to say with confidence that the deleterious effects of films and television programs can be recognized and measured, and counteracted, given the will to do so. We know how to persuade people to do those things which will prolong their lives, make them healthier and happier, and prove more satisfactory in the long run. We have made a beginning, and we know enough about these things to feel sure that properly directed research could in a relatively short time, and at relatively little expense, improve the quality of life and reduce mental misery in a very substantial manner.

All that stands in our way is the bugbear of science. We are afraid of trusting to reason, and prefer to rely on emotion— that old emotion which has led us astray for so many centuries, and is still bidding fair to lead us to self-extermination. Mankind has achieved what it has achieved through the use of reason. In some countries it has gone far to overcome ignorance, disease, hunger, poverty and superstition through science, which is simply organized reason. We cannot go back, much as the idea of doing so may appeal to the ignorant; we cannot stand still, for fear of being left behind. We must go forward, and our only guide is reason. Without this, we shall without question share the fate of the dinosaurs. Science is the tool and the creation of human reason; now is the time to introduce it into human affairs as well, and base our conduct on scientific fact. This is the text of the behaviorist's sermon. As Watson put it, "psychology as the behaviorist views it is a purely objective experimental branch of natural science. Its theoretical goal is the prediction and control of behavior." If we do not learn to control our behavior, before we use our knowledge of physics to blow up our planet, we are not likely to learn anything else very much. The psychologist is trying to help—don't shoot the behaviorist, he is doing his best!

Further Reading

AYLLON, T., and AZRIN, N., *The Token Economy*, New York: Appleton-Century-Crofts, 1968

BARRY, J. V., *Alexander Maconochie*, Melbourne: Oxford University Press, 1958

CENTERS, R., *The Psychology of Social Classes*, Princeton University Press, 1949

DAVIS, N. P., *Lawrence and Oppenheimer*, New York: Simon & Shuster, 1968

EYSENCK, H. J., *The Biological Basis of Personality*, Springfield: C. C. Thomas, 1967

—*Crime and Personality*, Boston: Houghton Mifflin, 1964

—*Dimensions of Personality*, Routledge & Kegan Paul, 1957

—*Fact and Fiction in Psychology*, Baltimore: Penguin Books, 1969

—*The IQ Argument*, New York: The Library Press, 1971

—*Psychology of Politics*, New York: Praeger, 1955

FLOUD, J., and HALSEY, A. H., "Intelligence tests, social class and selection for secondary schools", *British Journal of Sociology*, 1957, 8, 33-9

FORD, C S., and BEACH, F. A., *Patterns of Sexual Behaviour*, New York: Harper, 1951

FURNEAUX, W. D., *The Chosen Few*, London: Oxford University Press, 1961

GRIFFIN, A., "Selected and non-selected secondary schools: their relative effects on ability, attainment and attitudes", *Research in Education*, 1969, I, 9-20

HYDE, H. M., *A History of Pornography*, New York: Farrar, Straus & Giroux, 1965

JENSEN, A. R., *Environment, Heredity and Intelligence*, Harvard University Reprint Series No. 2, 1969

KOESTLER, A., *The Ghost in the Machine*, New York: Macmillan, 1968

KRONHAUSEN, E., and KRONHAUSEN, P., *Walter: the English Casanova*, New York: Ballantine Books, 1967

MASTERS, W. H., and JOHNSON, V. E., *Human Sexual Inadequacy*, Boston: Little, Brown, 1970

MORGENSTERN, A. (Ed.), *Grouping in the Elementary School*, New York: Pitman Publishing Corp., 1966

NOTT, K., *A Soul in the Quad*, Routledge & Kegan Paul, 1969

PEYREFITTE, R., *The Prince's Person*, New York: Farrar, Straus & Giroux, 1965

RACHMAN, S., and TEASDALE, J., *Aversion Therapy and Behaviour Disorders*, Coral Gables, Fla.: University of Miami Press, 1969

SCHOFIELD, M., *The Sexual Behaviour of Young People*, Penguin Books, 1968

SKINNER, B. F., *Walden Two*, New York: Macmillan 1948, 1962, 1966

"WALTER", *My Secret Life*, New York: Grove Press, 1966

WISEMAN, S., *Education and Environment*, Manchester University Press, 1964

YATES, A. (Ed.), *Grouping in Education*, New York: John Wiley & Sons, 1966

YOUNG, M., *The Rise of the Meritocracy*, New York: Random House, 1959

Author Index

Subject Index